T0358322

Regulators of Last Resort

How do public whistleblowers prevail despite employers' attempts to silence them? Whistleblowing is essential for raising awareness of extreme wrongdoing within organizations. Yet, despite changing laws designed to offer more protection, workers exposed for making public disclosures frequently find themselves the targets of extreme retaliation. Featuring high-profile cases from Amazon, Facebook and Theranos, Kate Kenny reveals the critical – and often unseen – role that skilled allies play in supporting whistleblowers when official channels fail. Novel and sophisticated means of silencing require new strategies for whistleblowing – and supportive partners are key. In this new era of whistleblowing, oppressive lawfare is used against truth-telling workers, and official channels can be weaponized. Yet powerful employers can still make mistakes. *Regulators of Last Resort* shows how aggressive reprisals can yield surprising advantages for dissenters. Working in partnership with advocates, public whistleblowers can find strategies to survive, persist and bring their disclosures to light.

KATE KENNY is Professor of Business and Society at the J. E. Cairnes School of Business and Economics, University of Galway. She holds a PhD from the University of Cambridge, where she was also a postdoctoral and research fellow, and has held a network fellowship at Harvard University's JE Safra Center for Ethics. Kate has published four books on whistleblowing in organizations, and numerous journal articles. Her research has been featured in the *Financial Times*, the *Guardian*, *The Atlantic* and the *Irish Times*. *Whistleblowing: Toward a New Theory* (Harvard University Press, 2019) was awarded Book of the Month at Cornell University's Catherwood Library.

Regulators of Last Resort

Whistleblowers, the Limits of the Law
and the Power of Partnerships

KATE KENNY
University of Galway

CAMBRIDGE
UNIVERSITY PRESS

CAMBRIDGE
UNIVERSITY PRESS

Shaftesbury Road, Cambridge CB2 8EA, United Kingdom

One Liberty Plaza, 20th Floor, New York, NY 10006, USA

477 Williamstown Road, Port Melbourne, VIC 3207, Australia

314–321, 3rd Floor, Plot 3, Splendor Forum, Jasola District Centre, New Delhi – 110025, India

103 Penang Road, #05–06/07, Visioncrest Commercial, Singapore 238467

Cambridge University Press is part of Cambridge University Press & Assessment, a department of the University of Cambridge.

We share the University's mission to contribute to society through the pursuit of education, learning and research at the highest international levels of excellence.

www.cambridge.org
Information on this title: www.cambridge.org/9781009425636

DOI: 10.1017/9781009425629

© Kate Kenny 2024

This publication is in copyright. Subject to statutory exception and to the provisions of relevant collective licensing agreements, no reproduction of any part may take place without the written permission of Cambridge University Press & Assessment.

When citing this work, please include a reference to the DOI 10.1017/9781009425629

First published 2024

A catalogue record for this publication is available from the British Library.

Library of Congress Cataloging-in-Publication Data
Names: Kenny, Kate (Kate Marguerite), author.
Title: Regulators of last resort : whistleblowers, the limits of the law and the power of partnerships / Kate Kenny, National University of Ireland, Galway.
Description: Cambridge, United Kingdom ; New York, NY : Cambridge University Press, 2024. | Includes bibliographical references and index.
Identifiers: LCCN 2024019530 | ISBN 9781009425636 (hardback) | ISBN 9781009425612 (paperback) | ISBN 9781009425629 (ebook)
Subjects: LCSH: Whistle blowing. | Whistle blowers. | Business ethics.
Classification: LCC HD60 .K4821 2024 | DDC 174/.4–dc23/eng/20240605
LC record available at https://lccn.loc.gov/2024019530

ISBN 978-1-009-42563-6 Hardback
ISBN 978-1-009-42561-2 Paperback

Additional resources for this publication at https://www.cambridge.org/gb/univer sitypress/subjects/management/business-ethics/regulators-last-resort-whistleblow ers-limits-law-and-power-partnerships

Cambridge University Press & Assessment has no responsibility for the persistence or accuracy of URLs for external or third-party internet websites referred to in this publication and does not guarantee that any content on such websites is, or will remain, accurate or appropriate.

Dedication
To Ada, Seán and Shane

Contents

Acknowledgements

Thanks to friends and experts who took the time to read, discuss and share their thoughts: Brian Martin, Dana Gold, Lauren Kierans, Mahaut Fanchini. Thanks also Meghan Van Portfliet, Mary Inman, John Blenkinsopp, Anna Myers, David Lewis, Iain Munro, Jenny McCudden and John Devitt. This project began as an unsuccessful grant proposal in 2019, and I am pleased with the direction it took. Huge thanks to Stephen Gaffney, a research assistant in the early stages, and to my colleagues at University of Galway and hosts at Grenoble Ecole De Management where the book was finished while on sabbatical in 2023. I am grateful to editor Valerie Appleby at Cambridge University Press and her team there. Shane Quill as always is my primary reader and discussant, thank you for your patience! Most of all, with thanks to the whistleblowers who continue to speak up, and the many people behind the scenes who help them to do it.

Prologue

Why Public Whistleblowers?

We continue to learn about serious wrongdoings on the part of organizations. We discover that corporations are making money at our expense. Or state institutions are corrupt. We discover that these organizations' practices impact our privacy rights, our health, our children's safety and our democracies. The information does not always come from the sources we expect: the investigative journalists, regulators or law enforcement officials. Whistleblowers bring these stories to light in many cases: ordinary workers come forward with information, often risking a lot in doing so. In the years to come, there will be more overreaches by organizations wielding unchecked power. There will be more whistleblowers.

Whistleblowing is having a moment. 'Now is the time to embrace whistleblowers', declared the *Financial Times* in response to the rise of fraud and corruption during the height of the COVID-19 pandemic. 'Unlawful activities and abuse of law may occur in any organization, whether private or public, big or small', warned the European Commission in 2018, 'and if they are not addressed, it can result in serious harm to the public interest.' Workers, the statement went on, are 'often the first to know about such occurrences and are, therefore, in a privileged position to inform those who can address the problem'. Whistleblowers, it seems, represent one of the last bastions of safety against our descent into exploitation by tech-fuelled obfuscation on the part of powerful institutions. When organizations are determined to conceal what they are really up to, only workers can show us what is actually going on. The Organisation for Economic Co-operation and Development (OECD) and the United Nations' Principles for Responsible Investment call for employers and governments to heed whistleblowers. Politicians pronounce whistleblowing a crucial mechanism for safeguarding our democratic institutions, consumer rights and safety at a time when organizational secrecy is on the rise.

Today, the loud calls are being heeded. These sentiments led to the most comprehensive set of whistleblowing laws ever seen across the globe: the EU Whistleblowing Directive of 2019.[1] This focus on whistleblowing is shared by various US agencies. While weaker than its European counterpart, the federal Whistleblower Protection Act remains, on paper at least, 'committed to protecting current and former Federal employees and applicants for employment from interference and retaliation when making protected disclosures'. From Albania to Zambia, every year sees new countries join the list of nations claiming dedicated whistleblower protections.

A flurry of expert activity has resulted from this upsurge in protection for whistleblowers. Those looking for a webinar on whistleblower protection will not have to look too far. I count about two per week.

This is my area. A professor at a business school, I research whistleblowing. By this stage of my engagement with the subject, I have examined most of the angles: why people do it, what happens to them, why retaliation may be an outcome and, if it is, whether the whistleblower can find work again. With colleagues I have studied how much money whistleblowing costs, the perspectives of managers who receive disclosures from whistleblowers and how employers can stop whistleblowing from getting serious before everyone suffers. After writing two books on this topic, publishing peer-reviewed articles and giving speeches on panels, webinars and at conferences, I remain frustrated. Something is missing.

Amid all the recent activity, there is something that cannot be ignored: a narrowness of focus – people seem concerned only with improving the official channels for whistleblowing. The basic idea is that we can best protect whistleblowers by creating smoother pathways for them to disclose their information. These pathways make up the official channels: the speak-up system, the outside regulator's hotline or the government department's disclosure procedure. Workers should know where to go when they speak up: which speak-up manager or hotline number to call. They should be provided with the latest high-tech solution, ensuring confidentiality and secure case management. And if these routes seem dangerous because the other end of the hotline sits on the desk of a manager who knows all about the fraud, then the worker should know which independent, external recipient will take their information, protect their identity and make sure they are safe. The worker should know which outside regulator to call, which ombudsperson to email. Through all of this, the law provides a safety net, a comforting backdrop. If the whistleblower's pathway to disclosure ends up being less than smooth – if they get push back, harassment, demotion, threat of dismissal or any other kind of retaliation for having spoken up – then they have a right under law to claim a remedy for the reprisals.

Smooth pathways through official channels, it seems, represent the solution whistleblowers require. And if there is no pathway – if the employer has not bothered putting whistleblowing systems in place – then the fault lies with management.[2] They are mandated under law and, as such, they have failed in their obligations. The basic idea we all seem to be working with is that, done right, the official channels will enable effective whistleblowing disclosures and act as shields for those making them.

This set-up has been described as *institutionalized whistleblowing.* Institutionalized whistleblowing is about keeping it all within the system. Of course, the pathways can be rocky: retaliation is not uncommon and speak-up arrangements can be flawed, but the overall sentiment is that whistleblowing works best when a worker makes a disclosure using internal reporting mechanisms. Thus, work continues: perfecting the channels, improving legal protections, incentivizing people to speak up, designing clearer processes and more impressive technology.

I am part of this world. With colleagues, I interviewed speak-up recipients and wrote a book giving managers ideas about what it is like to operate those channels, so they can make better ones. We shared our findings as widely as we could, helping organizations design systems. I write opinion pieces demanding that this legal loophole is closed, or that legislation is strengthened. I spoke in Parliament trying to convince politicians to close these loopholes and strengthen these provisions, backing my appeals by citing all the research. Invited to submit submissions to governments when they propose new laws, I put time aside and off I go. I do the work, with my colleagues, of shoring up institutions. The work is niche, but these changes are important. Yet, still, there is something we continue to ignore.

Every few weeks, I receive an email from another whistleblower caught in a difficult situation. The law has failed them. The speak-up system was used against them. The employer is simply ignoring things that they are supposed to be doing. The official channels are not working: they are not even acknowledged by managers, never mind followed. With all my research, the whistleblowers ask, what do I advise that they should do now? Beyond pointing to useful 'how to whistleblow' guides provided by support groups and giving the number of a legal advice helpline, I don't know what to tell these people. At this point in my career, to be honest, I am unsure as to what to tell myself, hence, this book.

Of course, the official answer is that we need better laws and more speak-up arrangements. Year after year, however, I see how many employers intent on silencing whistleblowers simply achieve their aims through their increased clout, legal power and money, disregarding even the strongest laws. The point is not that no employer can tolerate workers speaking up. Many do and some actively encourage it. This is all to the good. But sometimes, this doesn't happen. Sometimes employers can become entrenched, defensive and determined to maintain silence.

When official channels fail, and they do fail, workers are left exposed, vulnerable and tempted to abandon their disclosures of serious wrongdoing. For this group, it is not a question of merely opting out. If you have been named in public as a whistleblower and are now without work, chances are high that you will find yourself blacklisted in your sector. For this group, the situation has simply gone too far to allow them to turn back.

This category of whistleblower does not get much attention in the research, despite a small number of high-profile cases appearing in films, books and newspaper articles. To start the conversation, it is helpful for us to use the term 'public whistleblower', which we can define as someone reporting deep-seated, systemic problems, named publicly and subject to reprisals by their employer. This book begins with the principle that the public whistleblower is distinct and requires attention.

Public whistleblowers need to find others who are located outside the organization and, often, outside the official channels: to listen to them, to offer support and to help them act. Ideally, these others will have influence. They will know how to use it. Partners come in many forms: lawyers, journalists, activists and politicians. Working with knowledgeable and experienced partners is often the only realistic way of countering an employer bent on retaliating. And yet we know very little about this side of whistleblowing. Compared with the thousands of expert hours and millions of euros spent on perfecting the official channels, the effort spent on this aspect of worker disclosures is negligible. People, I am sure, are aware that supporters help. But there is nothing formal, nothing explicit – few details of how, why and with whom this all-important whistleblower support emerges. Academic research is likewise sparse.[3]

This was on my mind as I watched scenarios play out over the last few years – the Facebook insider, the healthcare workers speaking up while fighting COVID-19, the Amazon warehouse whistleblowers and the college graduates who helped to bring down Theranos. I saw how all were forced to go outside the official channels. And it was clear to me that, despite the differences between these cases, there are patterns. When a public whistleblower's claim is taken up by helpful others, things get easier. The whistleblower gains a platform, courtesy of these others. They get some credibility. Their voice is amplified. More than this, people speaking up can get a sense of psychological relief, of stress partially alleviated, of feeling that they are not the only ones seeing this terrible thing and not the only ones interested in speaking up about it.

This support is powerful in terms of helping a whistleblower. But it is also rare. Most public whistleblowers have a difficult time getting journalists to take an interest in their case.[4] Whistleblowers who do not receive help often end up at the mercy of a counter-narrative designed by their former employer using their influence with the media and opinion-shapers – a narrative that plays down the wrongdoing and casts doubt on the whistleblower's character and their credibility. For the whistleblower experiencing reprisals, the stakes get higher when they speak publicly. Stress builds and money worries accumulate with each legal bill that arrives. And we must not forget that, despite whistleblowing having a moment, despite the *Financial Times*' calls to 'embrace' this group, meaningful help can be hard to come by. Certainly, it is fashionable today to support whistleblowers, but this support is often light touch – a post on social media celebrating their bravery, a thumbs up to the news of an important disclosure. But practical help involving actual work on the part of the helper? This is more elusive. A sense of ambivalence still persists around public whistleblowers. Even would-be supporters, well-meaning activists and journalists can find themselves unsure whether to support this lone figure, especially when established employers publicly call them liars. For a whistleblower, gaining the kind of support they need is fraught and unpredictable. And there are nuances: those who do help often have some kind of shared agenda with the whistleblower, maybe the thing they are disclosing provides evidence for a story, a political campaign or a protest. The alliance can be short-lived, lasting as long as it is useful to the supporter, with the well-being of the whistleblower an afterthought. The result is that heroic efforts to speak truth to power often result in nothing at all, perhaps just a few lines in a local newspaper or a socials post that evaporates into the ether after a few shares.

How does a whistleblower forced outside the official channels come to be involved with real, effective supporters? How do whistleblowers make the meaningful connections often needed? Getting help is very difficult in practice, but getting help is transformative both for surviving the experience and for effectively disclosing information to a public that needs to know. And yet these facts are overlooked again and again. Silence persists in research by business ethics and legal scholars, in media commentary on whistleblowing, in popular books and by politicians claiming to be whistleblower champions.[5] Why?

Perhaps it is not comfortable to acknowledge that the institutional routes can fail: to think about different ways forward. We like to think that the current system will eventually work; it merely requires some tweaking. Many consultants, lawyers and academics have invested lots of time and money in this task of tweaking. They don't want to hear that they were too focused on just a small part of a bigger problem. More than this, what does it actually mean to talk about organizing disruption to the system – outside the official channels? To examine patterns, to develop strategies that cannot be 'institutionalized' because they are, by their nature, always outside the institution? To ask questions that might lead to something like a blueprint to dismantle the ordered status quo? Surely, therein lies chaos. Perhaps we shouldn't be surprised that this kind of work is not the activity of choice for experts.

I began my efforts to ask these questions in 2014, publishing an opinion piece in *The Atlantic*. Conscious of the format, I used my best opening. 'Think whistleblowing is a matter of telling the truth?' it began. 'Think again!' I was reflecting on all I had learned from studying truth-tellers in financial services, speaking up about what was going wrong prior to the financial crisis of 2008. It really did seem like 'success' was arbitrary.[6] The odds were stacked against banking whistleblowers, and those that prevailed, it seemed to me, only did so through fortuitous circumstances. I went on to declare that '"successful" whistleblowing, in which the protagonist actually manages to make themselves heard in the media and get the support of the public, is a matter of luck'. The point was bolstered with 700 words worth of examples from my financial sector whistleblowing cases. The piece insisted that successful whistleblowers are not the ones with the most shocking truths, but rather those whose 'stories match up with what the media are excited about, what the public are angry about, or what the politicians can use for political capital at that particular time. Rather depressingly, therefore', I concluded, 'the truth is a matter of trends. Whistleblowing remains something of a lottery ... people's lives – and their disclosures – are left up to chance.'

Shortly after, I received a long and somewhat irate email from Dana Gold, whom I knew from our time together at Harvard's J. E. Safra Center for Ethics. A lawyer and an activist, Dana worked at a leading non-profit whistleblower protection and advocacy organization in Washington DC: Government Accountability Project. I had got it wrong, she wrote. It is not luck, it is strategy. Her team knew all about this. Since supporting Daniel Ellsberg and other Nixon administration whistleblowers in the 1970s, they continue to use this strategy to successfully work with whistleblowers. 'Here are all the cases I can tell you about', she went on. I read her email, blushing quietly at my desk.

I feared I had embarrassed myself. And perhaps I had. But, to my knowledge, this strategy she spoke of is not widely known.[7] And it is even less widely used. My exchange with Dana remained with me since then, as emails that make one blush often do. Her points raised ideas of disruption patterns, the organizing tactics that might support these, and the work needed to draw them out and make them explicit. They evoked strategies beyond official channels: strategizing for dissent.

Public whistleblowing may feel unpredictable but that does not mean we don't rely on it. Still etched on people's memories across the world are the public whistleblowers working in healthcare who told us about dangers to life posed by substandard protection equipment during the outbreak of the COVID-19 pandemic. During this time, the UK charity Protect, for instance, estimated that, according to people ringing their helpline, for every five whistleblowing disclosures related to the virus, and raised internally, two were completely ignored by employers. Many whistleblowers persisted and were punished. Meanwhile, workplaces continued to be sites of widespread COVID-19 transmission. Subject to retaliation, the whistleblowers who went public were given few legal protections. This is because they were in too much of a rush to wait for slow official channels to work, a prerequisite of many whistleblower protection laws. But, as we saw then, we needed to know what they were saying: immediately. Public disclosure was the only, albeit desperate, choice for these health workers. Ignoring this side of whistleblowing is dangerous for us all. The chapters in this book do the opposite. Public whistleblowers are the focus.

Inspired by the work of activist-lawyers and others who work behind the scenes, this book examines the organizing practices and alliances they form. Grounded in scholarly research and academic insight,[8] it examines the experiences of workers who find themselves outside the official channels: outside the organization, and sometimes outside the law. It follows their journeys to secure support from whatever sources make themselves available: legal avenues, caring colleagues, other whistleblowers, knowledgeable journalists and helpful advocacy groups. The book takes a deep dive into the sorts of connections that seem to work, or at least to help, and explains why. It also looks at the reasons why they sometimes don't work, or work only a little, because, if one learns anything from studying this area, it is that it is ambiguous and complex, and that something that seems like a resolution today can look very different tomorrow. The aim is to paint a picture that is somewhat richer than the anaemic sketch we currently have.

In attempting to answer the questions set, this book does some things, and it does not do other things. It is not a roadmap for whistleblowers to follow; it contains no simple formula for success or survival. Many – perhaps all – whistleblowers do not win in the traditional sense, because the journey can be gruelling. But the experiences of partial victories, and of forming alliances and connections, of revealing critical and hidden information so new investigations can be started and demands for more can be sparked, can lead to a reframing of what winning might mean. These experiences must be explored and interrogated so we might learn how people navigated them in the past. Specifically, we will ask how partnerships emerge through which whistleblowers speak truth to power in tandem with others, how these relationships are organized and the challenges and opportunities they offer.

It appears we cannot ignore this aspect of speaking up. In the face of serious and systemic wrongdoing, most workers simply decide to stay silent.[9] Of course they do. Why risk it? Silence is a feature of institutions and organizations today, and it is likely to remain so in the future. Democracy, flawed as it is, is challenged by rising authoritarianism in many countries, while the accountability of public figures and institutions often seems to be waning. With the increasingly opaque goings-on inside organizations, we depend ever more on genuine whistleblowers. We need new ways to help them succeed. A better understanding of the dynamics involved in whistleblowing, and how its challenges can be overcome, is a good place to start.

Before we move on, it is important to clarify what we mean by prevailing: what we understand as whistleblowing 'success'. This is difficult to specify because public whistleblowing is so complex. Success could arguably encompass some or all of the following: acknowledgement of wrongdoing by the employer; the ending of the wrongdoing; some kind of reparation for suffering caused by retaliation; success in a court case[10] – or indeed mere survival on the part of the public whistleblower and their family who have been subject to a devastating campaign of attack. Achieving any one of these goals by no means ensures the others are attained, and all are rare in themselves. Discussing his observations of the aftermath of whistleblowing, social science professor Brian Martin does not mince words when it comes to whistleblowers: 'the prominent, lionized beacons of hope are the rare exception, and even most of them pay a horrible price with lifelong scars'.[11]

A more holistic definition of success is therefore required. The widely accepted definition of whistleblowing as the 'disclosure of illegal, immoral, or illegitimate practices under the control of (one's) employers to persons or organizations that may be able to effect action' is useful here.[12] A version of 'success' we can work with is to see it as ensuring one's disclosure reaches – that is, is understood and acknowledged by – another who may be able to effect action. A successful public whistleblowing disclosure, for our purposes, is one in which the speaker is failed by institutional channels yet succeeds in reaching an audience that can do something about the wrongdoing. The hope, of course, is that action will be taken. But reaching the audience is the essential first step. And a 'genuine' whistleblowing disclosure is, following international legal and research best practice, defined here as one in which the worker disclosing holds a reasonable belief that these wrongful practices are indeed occurring.[13]

Introducing the Book

This book moves through the different aspects of a whistleblowing journey that, taken together, forms the beginning of what might be understood as the organizing practices of public whistleblowing. We begin with the official channels, the first stop for most workers speaking up. While these can sometimes work well, they can in some cases prove impotent in helping a disclosure reach its audience. More than this, we see how these channels can be actively used against a whistleblower who has not yet gone public but is realizing just how unwanted their disclosure is. After this, we examine the legal landscape of whistleblower protections, offering promises that can sometimes prove useful, but can also be undermined by powerful employers with deep pockets intent on exploiting loopholes in the law. The experiences of the high-profile whistleblowers from Theranos, Silicon Valley's blood-testing start-up whose founders were convicted of fraud, offer valuable illustrations in Chapter 2. By the time we reach Chapter 3, we will have seen how the popularized solutions to whistleblowers' woes – the official channels and the laws – can be not only weak but also dangerous. When formal shields prove useless, whistleblowers can turn to other workers in the same situation. Groups form, providing essential support and solidarity. As the experience of Amazon warehouse whistleblowers during the COVID-19 pandemic demonstrates in Chapter 3, whistleblower groups are as complex as they are valuable.

In many cases, whistleblowers find themselves in the public eye, bringing a whole new set of problems. Addressing this, we start to look for other ways forward. Chapter 4's focus is the media: those journalists and reporters who represent a vital means by which a public whistleblower gains support. But dealing with the media is fraught with uncertainty, as Facebook whistleblower Frances Haugen's journey shows. By now a surprising element is emerging: how whistleblowers make use of the mistakes made by anxious, defensive employers, and the unintended consequences of their retaliations. These can be turned around to backfire on the would-be attackers, helping a public whistleblower secure support even when up against a well-known employer with deep pockets.

Next, Chapter 5 introduces the whistleblower advocates – the small group of organizations that bring whistleblowers together with interested stakeholders: journalists, other whistleblowers, activists, sympathetic lawyers, oversight bodies, lawmakers and many others, all the while doing their best to keep the whistleblower safe from harm and minimize stress as much as possible. But these campaigns come with challenges, leaving the landscape uncertain for people who disclose. The powerful story of whistleblower nurse Dawn Wooten raising concerns on behalf of female immigrant detainees housed at a US Immigration and

Customs Enforcement (ICE) facility offers insights into the difficulties experienced by those who speak up without financial means, but also how national attention to the problem can be secured with partners.

Chapter 6 brings it all together, drawing together the learnings emerging from patterns. A new way of looking at the organizing practices of public whistleblowers and their allies is introduced: collective bricolage. Collective bricolage is how whistleblowers and partners work together outside the official channels to generate new and creative ways of disrupting the status quo and disclose serious wrongdoing. Collective bricolage can involve capitalizing on limited and sometimes surprising resources and opportunities, including the unintended consequences of reprisals and the mistakes of a retaliating employer. Developing this concept, Chapter 6 examines the partnerships that bring whistleblower disclosures to light: the personal relationships and connections that seem to provide a force for collective action, where more distant ties, including those enabled by social media, fail. It shows the darker side of whistleblower partnerships: the difficulties and obstacles inevitably characterizing such stressful, precarious endeavours. This chapter teases out the nuances of collective bricolage: how the experiences of well-resourced whistleblowers with powerful allies differ drastically from the experiences of 'ordinary' workers speaking up, and also how the discrepancies contain valuable lessons.

Throughout, this book draws on academic research and theory, but this is moved to the background; instead, relevant ideas and concepts are referenced throughout the text and a full literature review, methodology and analytic discussion is offered in Appendix 1.

Last Resort Public Whistleblowing

It is critical to understand that public whistleblowing is a small part of the overall landscape of worker disclosures. The vast majority of workers first try to speak up inside their organization.[14] Becoming a public whistleblower changes the game completely. It happens when people feel they have no other option but to go outside: to the media, activists or politicians for example. The whistleblower must find an outside audience that will listen, assist and act. Some are willing to be named, because they understand that disclosures are usually more credible when there is a face, a professional title and a personal story accompanying them. Others, terrified of reprisal, request they remain anonymous, but their names are revealed anyway, by colleagues, by court testimony that becomes unsealed, through leaks or other methods.

Regardless of how people arrive at public whistleblowing, here is the problem: right now, there is little help available about what to do and how to survive. If a well-planned discrediting campaign is doing what it is supposed to be doing, one's colleagues and perhaps even friends and family might be ambivalent at best, sometimes even hostile. There is no strategy for gaining support, no outline, no plan for how to communicate the issue beyond the individual whistleblower's immediate situation to a wider public.

To present public whistleblowing and strategy together feels somewhat incongruous. We associate the first term with the uncommon, the erratic and the uncontrollable. And strategy evokes ideas of schemes, tactics and being *organized*. Yet perhaps to not think of these things together is to ignore what is actually happening and what is needed. This is not my big idea. As we will see, some people have worked like this for years, supporting whistleblowers. But the research emanating from these efforts is scant. The likely reason is that most advocacy groups are trying their best to raise the money to keep the legal helpline going, to host information awareness events, to support their clients and to challenge ongoing abuses by formidable institutions albeit from a position of less power and fewer resources. Undertaking the kind of research-based strategizing required is a luxury not many have.

These aspects barely get a mention when we hear about whistleblowers in the news, or even when academics and policymakers turn their attention to the hot topic of how to help them.[15] This is somewhat bizarre. To ignore the webs of connections and relations that support the survival of whistleblowers is to leave people truly in the lurch. Public whistleblowers have often come too far to turn back. It is not simply a case of giving up because things are not working out, going back to one's life before it all started. Named in public, while the option to give up might be compelling, it is often not available. To try to make sense of this messy, confusing situation is critical.

To accept this project as worthwhile, we need to accept some uncomfortable ideas. The first is that things can sometimes be very wrong indeed. For many of us, this is difficult to fathom. We have a deep-seated desire to believe that justice can be obtained, and that there is a system or structure out there that will eventually work. Our modern way of thinking about society assumes a kind of continual upward progress; we are getting better and smarter, and the truth will someday come out. As many public whistleblowers find out first-hand, however, this is often simply not the case.[16] Employers are mostly fine and good but sometimes they are not. Sometimes they respond with aggression to truth-tellers threatening the control they believe they have. And sometimes they win – even where serious wrongdoing and apparently self-evident disasters are at stake. Facts and truth are not always enough; sometimes they speak for themselves, and a groundswell of support and attention wells up behind them. And sometimes facts and truths are quashed and silenced. You do not need to be a crazy conspiracy theorist to hold both these competing ideas and be at peace with their co-existence. It is important, however, to look at them coldly, accept our need for happy resolutions and acknowledge that they don't always happen. In writing this book, I found these grey areas in which struggles occur to be where small glimmers of what might be called hope can be found. So, it is here that the book is located.

Second, we may not reach an ending. This book may disappoint if we look for an either/or result; either the whistleblowers prevail and the problem is dismantled for good or employers have all the power and will quash every sign of dissent. It is likely that it will be both: it is a dance, a cycle. A scandal breaks, reprisals ensue, resistance is organized and attempted, and on it goes. Meanwhile, we see waves of legislation and regulation that then recede in the face of political opposition, until the next crisis and a new wave of legislation and regulation. What we do know is that we will always have whistle-blowers and the world is generally better off for what they disclose. While we must work to create better laws and stronger systems, we will always have whistleblower reprisal. And perhaps we cannot rely solely on institutions to counter this. It will always be thus.

At the same time, there are, and always will be, gaps and fissures emerging: opportunities for solidarity, survival and the ability to reach new audiences. What is new is the work we do to formalize these opportunities, to listen to those with years in the field. To examine the scene presenting itself to us and put shape on it, to think about the kinds of scaffolding that might be constructed around this messy and chaotic situation. If we don't do this, we continue on the current path assuming that efforts to perfect legislation and official channels are enough. This won't help. Where to start? It is useful to begin with the core of the issue: a whistleblowing disclosure and the official channels.

Notes

1. IBA (2021).
2. Throughout this book, 'employer' refers to the organization at which the whistleblower worked.
3. See Appendix 1 for an extensive literature review along with the academic background and contribution of this study.
4. Jones (2013).
5. With some notable exceptions in academic scholarship and practitioner literature, thoroughly examined in Appendix 1.
6. Paul Moore, one of the most well-known UK whistleblowers of the time, had a friend at the BBC who helped publicize his information, even while his former bank HBOS was waging a smear campaign. Martin Woods, the Wachovia whistleblower whose disclosures led to the largest ever money-laundering fine levied against a bank at the time, happened to find work at Reuters despite a blacklisting campaign, while Rudolf Elmer at Swiss Bank Julius Baer found support at Wikileaks. Other examples are discussed in *Whistleblowing: Toward a New Theory* (Kenny, 2019).
7. One exception I know of is Brian Martin's work, see e.g. Martin (2012, 2013), Martin & Rifkin (2004).
8. See Appendix 1 for the academic background and contribution of this study.
9. The two main reasons workers give for remaining silent are: fear of retaliation and fear of futility (that speaking out won't make a difference).
10. See Near & Miceli (1995) for discussion. Note that they define effective whistleblowing as that leading to the cessation of wrongdoing. Vandekerckhove et al. (2014, p. 306) define successful whistleblowing as a disclosure that results in 'managerial responsiveness to the primary concerns about alleged wrongdoing aired by the whistleblower about wrongdoing; and managerial ability or willingness to refrain from, or protect the whistleblower against, retaliation or reprisals for having aired those concerns'. Both definitions set a high bar for a single whistleblower, and each implies a degree of responsibility for, and control over, outcomes that not many whistleblowers have in reality. Hence the definition chosen here.
11. Martin (1999, p. 19). (Note: Updated version = Martin (2013).)
12. Miceli et al. (2008, p. 6)
13. This includes wrongful practices that have occurred or are likely to occur, following best practice legislation, cf. Miceli & Near (1985), EC Council Directive (2019).
14. Kierans (2023).
15. See Appendix 1, including notable exceptions to this.
16. Martin (2013, p. 48).

1 | *When Official Channels Fail Whistleblowers*

Official Channels and Their Problems

Seamus went on national TV to talk about how his electricity company ESB was leaking hazardous oil into Dublin city's water supply. The cables had been laid in the 1950s, by hand. They needed replacing and this wasn't happening. About 50,000 litres of fluid containing mineral oil seeped out each year, into the water supply, into the canal where people canoe and where kids swim in summer. Seamus talked about other things too: a propane gas explosion in a housing estate in 2015, a fireball into the air high above the pavement, a near miss for the workers. As it turned out, the training the workers had received and the safety equipment they were using were all out of date. Like the cables, the training and the equipment had not been updated. There were other things to talk about: a menu of persistent problems at the electricity company. Seamus had recently been promoted to Technical Development Manager, which meant these were his problems now.

Seamus had not rushed to the TV company. He had first told his managers about his concerns, and waited. Two years later, it looked like nothing was being done. But these were his workers. The oil seeping into the Dublin water supply was on his watch. He had to speak up. Again, he followed the process. He used the formal channels and approached more senior people in the firm. Finally, he made ten separate disclosures in January 2019 to the then Minister for the Environment, Richard Burton. He listed ten separate problems.

I had read about the case. But hearing him speak was different – the carefully chosen words, his care to back up every statement with a statistic. The calm, detailed account of how his company, the national energy provider, had worked so hard to shut him up. Watching, I could feel the familiar overwhelm that comes with hearing the stories of many – most – genuine whistleblowers who go public. It's this initial sense that it all sounds too crazy. It's too unlikely. If that actually happened, surely something would have been done about it.

The TV programme turned to Seamus's personal life.[1] His wife was sitting in their kitchen, pictures of the children beside her. He was twenty-five years with the company, his first job out of college. They were explaining their situation, the dilemma they were in. They had secured all the things a whistleblower needs for protection. They had a good lawyer. More than this, Seamus's disclosures had been proven correct. Before the prime-time TV show highlighting the leaks and the explosions was aired, the Environmental Protection Agency had stepped in. They publicly stated that he was right. Some of the cable circuits were rated 9 out of 10 for environmental risk. Leaks had not been repaired, sometimes for two years. And Seamus had already given evidence in Parliament; the Committee on Communications, Climate Action and Environment had invited him into government buildings. At that meeting, the company had begun by denying his statements but had since changed its position. Now, its spokesmen told us it was addressing all the issues.

I was confused. Surely, in that case, all was in order? He had the lawyer, the Minister, the NGO and the TV people: all busy investigating what he had said, proving him correct and supporting his position. Seamus's disclosures seemed to be doing quite well. But Seamus was not. It seems that things had gone wrong when, during those two years of waiting for answers within the firm, he had contacted a government minister in May 2018, something he had never done before. That had seemed to get things moving, but in a somewhat unexpected direction. Within a month of sending that letter, Seamus was served with a written caution and a disciplinary complaint. The reason was failing to use the correct internal procedures for his disclosure and raising issues in an inappropriate way. He was told to take part in mediation. He was offered a termination agreement and given three days to decide. By the end of the month, he was off sick with the stress.

But hang on, hadn't he won? He had blown the whistle and been proven right. Outside authorities were lining up to support him, from the Environmental Protection Agency to national TV and the broadsheet newspapers. The national press covered his story, but still the company seemed to be doing everything it could to make his life difficult. 'ESB whistleblower got "nothing but stress" by speaking out', announced the *Irish Times* in the days leading to the Committee hearing, as part of its coverage of the case. Watching that evening, it all felt familiar. My God, I thought. This again.

Official Channels and Helpful Whistleblowers

Whistleblowing, at its most basic, is where a member of an organization discloses something wrong. It is the act of speaking up about things that are 'illegal, immoral or illegitimate' occurring at your workplace, according to the most popular definition. You bring the illegal, immoral or illegitimate thing to a person or persons who can do something about it, often your own line manager. And that's it. You've blown the whistle. About one in every five workers says they have, in the past, had 'good reason to believe that wrongdoing was taking place' in their workplace.[2] Of those, two-thirds alerted someone who could try to stop it. So, on a rough count, about one in ten workers has engaged in some kind of whistleblowing in their lifetime.

Over the past twenty years, it has slowly dawned on people in charge of organizations that they should pay attention to these whistleblowing workers. Almost every major disaster – from Chernobyl and the Challenger Space Shuttle to recent financial crises and the outbreak of COVID-19 – involved workers trying to speak up about the impending catastrophe, while being ignored or actively silenced. For each of these disasters, the inevitable public inquiry came to the same conclusion: management didn't listen to the whistleblowers, but they should have. Every post-disaster inquiry report has the same clear instruction to corporate executives: to support whistleblowers in the future.

The idea that we need better ways of hearing these disclosures has gripped lawmakers, managers and shareholders. Today, supporting and encouraging whistleblowers is big business. We now know that half of all counts of fraud – costing trillions each year – are disclosed by insiders coming forward: not by law enforcement or auditors, but by ordinary workers. The United Nations' *Principles for Responsible Investment* has a new recommendation for investors seeking well-run and reliable companies: look out for strong whistleblowing systems. Executives talk about the BP share price still not having recovered from the Gulf oil calamity, which involved dissenting workers who were ignored and silenced. A phrase I increasingly hear at industry events is that the whistleblower is, in fact, 'a forward indicator of risk'.

More and more, whistleblowers are framed as valuable employees: a source of insight. Warren Buffett praises whistleblowers as early warnings that a disaster might be impending – a valuable governance tool. As far back as 2005, he was speaking with pride of the 4,000 calls Berkshire Hathaway's speak-up hotline gets every year, only noting his regret that he hadn't realized this sooner: 'Berkshire would be more valuable today if I had put in a whistleblower line decades ago. . . . You've got to act promptly, and I don't know any better system than hotlines and anonymous letters.' 'Most of them are frivolous', he cautioned. 'The guy next to me has bad breath, or something like that. But there are a few serious ones.'

Bad breath or not, whistleblowers are, right now, high on the agenda. New laws have been introduced; new organizational systems have been designed. All of these aim at making sure that workers can alert bosses safely and effectively, without being punished for it. The new laws tell employers about their obligations to workers speaking up. Given the whistleblower's new status as an undeniable asset, attempts to shut them up should be discouraged. Retaliating against whistleblowers is just dysfunctional behaviour. It causes suffering to the whistleblower, yes, but it also leaves the wrongdoing undetected, putting the employer at risk. Retaliation can also prevent other employees from speaking up, fear being a major reason for people staying silent.[3] Retaliation can damage reputations, increase fines and hurt profits.[4]

And this, more or less, is where we are now, in the world of whistleblowing. The focus of experts, policymakers, consultants and academics is firmly targeted on twin goals: developing legal protections against retaliation, and effective channels for disclosure. The collective aim is a decent one: to create strong safeguards that protect workers who speak up. The market for these safeguards, or shields, is exploding; the value of the global whistleblowing software industry was estimated at $80 billion in 2019 and is projected to reach $150 billion by 2027. All this technology has been developed in the name of protecting the company and the worker from the vagaries of whistleblower retaliation. I have spent years with colleagues researching these shield-building efforts, sometimes taking part in them. There is only one problem: the shields don't always work.

Official Channels and Uncomfortable Truths

A few years ago, I had the privilege of researching what it is like to be the person in the organization who operates the whistleblowing channel. Colleagues and I interviewed people working in different sectors: a multinational bank, an engineering company and a public healthcare organization.[5] It was the job of these people to receive whistleblowing disclosures, whether through telephone hotlines, internal websites or simply old-fashioned discussions. We wanted to find out what makes this job easier, what the obstacles are and what helps the system work.

Here is what I learned. First of all, people don't like the term 'whistleblowing channels'. Whistleblowing, as a word, brings up all kinds of negative associations. In the new spirit of positivity around the whole business, it seems that we now talk about 'speak-up systems'. Speak-up systems, when run well, can be great. They offer a smooth process for the person using them. The better ones are operated by empathetic staff, who make sure they have the well-being of the whistleblower at heart, checking in with them in the weeks and months after disclosure to make sure they are okay and are not being retaliated against by bosses or colleagues. The better systems have processes for keeping the worker's name and details as confidential as possible.[6] They have triage processes to check if wrongdoing might be occurring, and methods for escalating concerns into investigations when disclosures seem serious. The collection, storage and analysis of data lies at the heart of these systems. Hence, regular reports are part of the work process. For instance, 'this month we received two disclosures: one in marketing, one in accounts. We are investigating.' Data can help spot patterns. 'This department or that yields lots of complaints. Why? Let's find out.' Speak-up systems enable reports of serious disclosures to be brought to the attention of senior management and members of the board.[7]

So, these, in short, are some of the 'best practices'. These are what we wrote about in our book *The Whistleblowing Guide*, and what we reported to our funders, and these are what we summarized in the headlines of our three-page 'Recommendations Aimed at Managers', widely circulated after our launch. When I am asked to help employers assess whether their speak-up systems are adequate or not, to speak at industry events, or on panels, these best practices are where I begin. Good systems are also properly resourced. They need to be so, because it is stressful working on the speak-up desk. It's not all toxic oil and propane firebombs, but they do appear. You are dealing with people who have thought long and hard about whether to come forward. A lot is at stake. You are sometimes the bearer of very bad news to your senior managers. There needs to be enough staff, sufficient training and a lot of positive signalling from the CEO that the speak-up desk should be taken seriously.

But these resources do not always come with the role. The challenges for speak-up staff can be significant.[8] Many employers don't bother with the training part, or they don't gather or analyse the data for patterns. Often, our interviewees told us, working on the speak-up desk is only a small part of their job; they might work in human resources (HR) mainly in charge of recruitment. Or they are compliance staff. And this important and potentially stressful speak-up role is meant to be a side responsibility. Most employers, it appears, are very far from 'best practice' when it comes to their speak-up systems. So, there was plenty of material to fill our book, plenty to be discussed on the panels and in the events after we launched it. The importance of these best practices, we insisted, cannot be taken for granted.

Almost all these problems are fixable. But there is one thing that, when I bring it up, always leads to uncomfortable silence. Because it is not at all clear whether it can be fixed or whether indeed we should even be talking about it. Most people, I feel, know about it. I tend to bring it up anyway, respectfully, to see what people say. The uncomfortable thing is this: only certain kinds of disclosures work this way. Only certain kinds of disclosures pass smoothly through the well-designed speak-up system, gradually morphing from disclosure to investigation to resolution. These are the kinds of disclosures that the people on the board want to hear about, or at least don't mind hearing about. They are the kinds of disclosure that can be sorted out without too much fanfare. Maybe a process needs to be adjusted, maybe a product needs recalling, maybe even some people get sanctioned or fired for isolated incidents. Case closed. The employer goes back to business as usual. A scandal is prevented; a disaster is stopped before it spirals out of control. The workers' minds are placed at ease; this remains an ethical company. Look at our corporate social responsibility policy – we are still for the public good. Congratulations all around for implementing the speak-up system.

Speak-up systems are designed for dealing with lower- and mid-level wrongdoings: fixable wrongdoings, practices that do not involve senior management, or, if they do, hopefully only one or two senior managers, who can be fired without too much damage. Speak-up systems deal with wrongdoings that, if revealed, do not threaten the whole organization, wrongdoings that do not point the finger at all those colleagues who knew about it but said nothing.

What happens, though, when the wrongdoing is systemic: part of the day-to-day running of the business? What happens when the entire business model is based on a fundamental assumption that turns out to be a little shady? Or widespread ambivalence about health and safety of both workers and the public? What if the problems are simply too expensive to fix? Perhaps there has been a recession, and the public company has been underfunded for years. Perhaps senior management is stuck in a chain of cost-cutting mandates over which it has no control.

When we think of the speak-up operator here, it is difficult to envy their role. How does one even begin to consider bringing a 'wrongdoing' to senior management, when the wrongdoing is inseparable from the employer organization itself? Imagine this kind of 'speak-up' event, listed as bullet point number one in the monthly report to the board of directors. Imagine the CEO encountering their own name as part of the problem. What happens in such disclosures?

When I mention this at events, seeking ideas, I find it is normally skirted around, or passed off, or remains one of those questions that are left hanging in the Q&A session as the clock runs down. I asked speak-up staff about this directly during those research interviews. The response was usually a nod and a grimace, but nothing is said out loud. Nothing is written down or recorded on the interview tape. We tend to focus on what we can actually do, people told me. I raised this question at the end of some consultancy work I had been asked for, during the part at the end when we go through my draft report before it gets signed off. I met with the senior manager clients, to iron out the final glitches. The policy was strong, I told them; a lot of work went into it. But just one thing: 'What happens when the wrongdoing goes so deep as to involve the senior team?' 'We look after that side of it, in-house', came the reassurance. 'No need to include it in your report. You can delete that section.'

Ideally, of course, what happens when the wrongdoing goes so deep as to involve the senior team is that the disclosure gets escalated to an external party: an industry regulator, for example, or a government minister with oversight on the sector in question. This can often prove effective in addressing the problem. But equally often, regulators will return a disclosure to the place from whence it came for examination and fact-finding. It goes back to the employer. The rationale for this is that regulators are busy, and organizations have the facts needed to probe the claims. And often, a regulator does not have the requisite powers to do anything about the wrongdoing. With the disclosure returned to the employer, an internal investigation ensues – often under the influence of those named; outcomes are recommended, and little is actually done. In cases of systemic wrongdoing, the problems with this approach are clear. Of course, there are many instances in which regulators will independently investigate, because the issue has become too big to ignore. Here, though, sanctions are not always meaningful – they are not enforced, or, when they are, they represent small fines levied with little impact on the perpetrator.[9] The regulator route is part of the official channel.

Some academics point out how official channels are unlikely to yield radical challenges. They call the kind of whistleblowing that is considered acceptable, which makes its way through the speak-up channels, 'institutionalized critique'.[10] Institutionalized critique is criticism that complies with the rules and doesn't violate accepted norms too much. It allows us to get on with business as usual: to tell the board and the shareholders that we have had some whistleblowing complaints, we have dealt with them and that we are all the better for it.

But what happens to that other kind of information, that unlucky disclosure that nobody wants? Well, nothing, so far as I can gather. It disappears into the ether. New, more acceptable, disclosures come in; new data, new reports and new investigations take over. We move on. As for the worker who brought it up in the first place, managers hope that they too will move on: read the situation for what it is, understand that nobody really wants to hear and go back to work. One of the top reasons workers cite for not escalating whistleblowing complaints is a sense of futility: a belief that nothing will be done. Watching the official channels in action can stoke this belief. Of course, there is always the chance that the worker won't give up. And that is what happens with people like Seamus.

The Persistent Whistleblower and the Anxious Organization

Official whistleblowing channels give the impression that they can deal with disclosures of wrongdoing. They appear comprehensive, often buttressed by a thirty-page policy explaining the expansive and intricate journey awaiting a worker's disclosure. But sometimes they cannot deal; sometimes the disclosure is impossible to accept.

And sometimes, regardless, a worker keeps going. They get back in touch with the speak-up desk. What about the disclosure? You said it would be triaged, investigated, reported? My careful research, the diligent explanations, the clearly written reports – where are they now? What about my staff? Seamus was asking, will they go out in their vans tomorrow morning to drill holes near dangerous cables? What about the mineral oil, the canal, the water supply? What about the things I have been telling you about for years? Some workers, seeing that their efforts to use the official channels are thwarted, intuit that their claims are less than welcome, but keep going regardless. They keep talking. The situation escalates.

Seamus's electricity company had a policy for whistleblowers, just one example of the millions of speak-up arrangements that have made their way into organizations in the past few years. I checked the policy; it was on the company website. It stated that, in accordance with Ireland's Protected Disclosures Act 2014, ESB's procedures are designed 'to foster an environment in which workers can feel safe in raising concerns regarding potential wrongdoings that have come to their attention in the workplace'. For Seamus, however, this advertised blanket of safety seemed to be missing.

After speaking up, he had not been listened to. Once he escalated, Seamus was moved to a role he had worked on ten years previously. He described this as humiliating. As the dispute with his firm intensified, he was asked to enter mediation talks, which led to an offer of a termination agreement. Seamus was then asked to sign the agreement in three days, barely enough time to return home and speak to his family about it, let alone get any meaningful professional advice from lawyers or financial experts. His firm, he recalled, had shared his disclosures with other organizations in the industry. Finding new work would not be easy. He went on sick leave. Seamus seemed to be stuck in an endless bureaucratic process of mediation, and he was paying lawyer fees for the privilege.

The real trouble started with the first legal letter. Of course, Seamus had done nothing wrong from a legal perspective. Quite the contrary. The company, nevertheless, let him know that they had appointed an external legal expert to advise on his case. So, he felt he had to do likewise. 'We had to get forty-seven grand pulled together', he told the TV interviewer. 'The legal situation seemed to get ramped up', his wife Hilary reflected on that time. 'And we felt huge pressure merely to match the ESB's correspondence. Detailed correspondence. With a lot of legal jargon.' She recalls her husband standing on the steps of the government buildings. He was about to give evidence to the committee. He would have to relay the breaches of safety to life and health to a room of experienced politicians and people representing his employer. But instead of reading his notes, Seamus was on the phone trying to secure the loan he would need to pay his lawyers. This forty-seven grand, it seemed, was only the start of it. 'I am still out on my own', he later told the interviewer, '[e]ngaged in a legal process that is costing us an absolute fortune.' 'It is having a toll on us now', Hilary added. 'We are an ordinary family; we cannot mobilize financial resources that easily. It is constantly living with fear, that is the life of a whistleblower. It's still a frightening, lonely role, and it's very, very uncertain.'

Watching this unfold, as someone who has written books about whistleblowing and was supposed to be an expert, I winced. Perhaps it was that we live in neighbouring counties, which means something in rural Ireland. Perhaps it was that I had trained as an engineer too. But it all felt so wrong. This professional who had served his company and his staff so well now felt compelled to appear on national television, to tell people how speaking up had 'taken a far bigger toll' than he ever anticipated, to explain how his mental health had suffered and his family was bearing the brunt. All this exposure is just to protect himself and his loved ones. I would not have found that easy.

Why all the reprisal? Seamus was just raising concerns, like the policy said. He was meant to feel safe along the way: the policy was supposed to make sure of this. What had gone wrong? It seems like it wasn't simply the amount of concern-raising Seamus was doing that landed him in this mess. It was to whom he was raising those concerns. It was the fact that he had gone to politicians, to the Environmental Protection Agency, to journalists. He had gone outside the organization.

Organizational Anxiety and Public Disclosures

At this point, when it comes to the speak-up systems, we have strayed off the map. Best practices do not cover this. We are now entering a new space within the organization, where more opaque things are going on. It is helpful to look at the deeper level at which they occur.

We are all familiar with the typical whistleblower scenario. We have watched the films. A solitary individual stands up against a soulless company or institution, which protects its own interests with alarming, even lethal, force. In this scenario, caricatures abound: the noble truth-teller versus the evil manager, to name two. Such stereotypes, however, are of little use in the real world. Corporations are made up of individuals who, by and large, are not villains. Managers go to work, return home, phone their mothers, try to save for a holiday; most of them do not enjoy retaliating against whistleblowers. So, why does this retaliation happen?

Organizations are useful to society and reassuring to those of us employed by them. They help us work together by providing structure and clarity. They assign specific roles so that each of us knows what we are meant to be doing. They also have chains of command: hierarchies with senior positions to which we aspire, so that we will continue to work hard. These features are designed to deal with one of the biggest challenges encountered by any organization, that of scale. Large numbers of employees and a multitude of functions need to be managed, and this is difficult. Look at ESB group, Seamus's company. According to the website, 8,000 staff work there. Clear structures and hierarchies help coordinate activity at this scale.

Unfortunately, hierarchies and structures are not merely benign organizational features that facilitate the flow and execution of work; they can also be a major source of anxiety for employees. Consider the issue of delegation, for instance. One of the main purposes of a hierarchy is the allocation of responsibility so that tasks get done efficiently. Yet the complexity of any large organization means that most of us do not have control over the steps preceding, or following, the task we are expected to perform. Decisions made higher up the chain are passed down to us. As Robert Jackall argues in his classic text *Moral Mazes*, this ensures that those in power remain insulated from any blame that might result, because they do not have detailed knowledge of how their decrees are carried out.[11] For the worker receiving instructions, despite having had no say in their formulation and little control over the final results, they become responsible for their execution and answerable for the outcome. Whether or not we agree with the original decisions, and whether or not the tasks are doable, we are expected to implement them: to represent and defend them to the outside world.

The result? Anxiety. Working in large organizations, we are made responsible for things we have little say over.[12] Adding to this anxiety is the fundamental uncertainty of organizational life. In any complex organization, even a small one, the multiple variables, people and events we encounter make the internal environment frequently unpredictable and the external one even more so.[13] Neither people nor outside events can be easily controlled. In the obscuring fog of large bureaucracies, chaos sometimes prevails.

Standing before the assembled members at the parliamentary Communications Committee, energy whistleblower Seamus described the responses he had received from management in the months after he disclosed his concerns about risky practices and exploding gas mains: 'I received six different instructions from senior management as to how to progress the propane gas issue. And despite my best endeavours, I received no commitment on resources, senior management buy-in or finance in this time.' This statement appears to suggest that, while there was plenty of activity, little of it was meaningful and that, overall, there was confusion about how to proceed. This is perhaps not surprising, given that ESB's 8,000 staff are spread across eight separate functions, each run by a different executive, with the company as a whole under the oversight of the CEO and his deputy. Organizations can be messy. Systems and processes go awry, and this appears to be reflected in Seamus's company's response to him.

When the fantasy of control comes up against unpredictable reality, the result may indeed be chaos and crisis. This is inevitable. But, in organizations, this messiness cannot be admitted. Organizations like to maintain an illusion of order at all times. Charts, rules, plans and strategies are all artefacts working to support the fantasy that everything is under control, that we – the organization and its staff – are in charge.[14] We are managing. In organizations both the inherent volatilities – and the anxiety they bring – must be downplayed. Most workers know this and act accordingly.

Situations like Seamus's threaten this unspoken arrangement. They reveal the lack of control underlying organizational practices. The question is, when things go wrong, what does this mean for the employee or manager who is supposed to be in charge? Once again: anxiety. Unrealistic expectations of control can make managers defensive in the face of failure, particularly if the company ethos is not one that tolerates the reporting of errors. In such cases, the combination of defensiveness and the need to cover our backs may cause us to look for something or someone to blame. It is tempting to seek out a scapegoat. In their eloquent analysis of these phenomena, sociologists Steve Fineman and Yannis Gabriel talk about how organizational hierarchies quickly become 'highways along which blame travels' in crisis situations.[15] This is exacerbated, they argue, by our need to identify with something bigger than ourselves, which can be satisfied by our sense of belonging to an organization. As traditional sources of belonging, such as tight communities or organized religion, decline, business organizations can fill the gap they leave. Large organizations offer strong cultures that enhance a sense of kinship, of being part of a greater whole. In this context, when we find ourselves facing potential blame for mistakes, we may be deeply shaken. As Yannis Gabriel argues, workers in a large bureaucratic organization can 'feel threat of annihilation out of proportion to the actual blame placed on them. Strong feelings of rage, anxiety and fear generated by such events are evidence of regression to an earlier, more vulnerable age', an age when we sought places and things that would keep us safe.[16] The significant efforts spent on generating powerful and binding corporate cultures, which have been a focus of CEOs since the 1980s, intensify workers' sense of belonging to the organization. They also intensify our resulting distress when we feel our place in the corporate 'family' is at risk, such as when we make a mistake.

This all might sound like extreme, dysfunctional behaviour. Not so. It is a feature of large organizations. The dynamics described above are not the result of shoddy or even nefarious management but rather are part of the nature of any organization operating at scale, and denying how badly wrong things can sometimes go. The troubling reality is that, although rarely discussed, 'blaming, victimisation and scapegoating are not only major ingredients of the emotional life of organisations, but derive from the nature of bureaucracy itself, rather than from maladministration'.[17] The reality of organizations is that no one is fully in control, but we are all encouraged to pretend that we are. Management is a difficult, demanding job, often requiring that decisions are made in uncertain, high-pressure conditions. While some managers learn to understand the effect of these pressures on themselves and their colleagues, and to accept the darker sides of organizational life, others do not. From his study of manager ethics in a US corporate bureaucracy, Jackall tells us that, in these kinds of organizations, survival is dependent on managing one's image, avoiding blame and ingratiating oneself with powerful leaders. 'Morality' becomes a cost–benefit analysis applied to each situation. The capacity to exercise individual judgement in the face of serious wrongdoing is greatly reduced in such settings, while dissent is extremely difficult.[18]

We can try to imagine what it is like to be a member of a senior management team feeling itself backed into a corner because one person is speaking up. Who is going to tell the CEO? How will this look on my CV if this all goes pear-shaped and I'm back on the job market? If we are in the private sector, how can we give up our underlying business model now, and let down all those shareholders? The situation must seem unbearable.

Redrawing the Boundaries

Whistleblower disclosures, especially those that escape the controlled pathways of the official channels, are disturbing. They unsettle the delicate balance of fantasy, reality and the manager's psychic capacities to keep anxiety at bay. Disturbing this precarious balance is dangerous. For the senior manager in such a situation, according to C. Fred Alford in his book *Whistleblowers: Broken Lives and Organizational Power*, '[t]he most terrifying thought is that representatives of the outside are on the inside, traitors in our midst'. Whistleblowers trigger an organization's deepest fear: 'that someone inside represents the interests of outside, that the organization cannot control its own boundaries, that it does not even know them'.[19]

With anxiety levels skyrocketing, it is tempting to seek a return to the one thing that holds the organization together: the comforting sense of control. Restoring control now centres on restoring the boundaries between the inside of the organization and the world outside. Particularly for the organization in which serious wrongdoing goes on unremarked, these boundaries are critical. Boundaries provide a buffer, a protection from scrutiny. On this view, the whistleblower is more than an inconvenience, they become 'an insidious disease, a boundary violator', breaking the rules by bringing the outside in.[20] The work of restoring control becomes about redrawing boundaries to exclude this disease.

Various moves are required in this redrawing exercise; it is not straightforward. Let us not forget that many whistleblowers are middle or senior level. They are often loyal employees whose work evaluations – those end-of-year assessments of performance – have been unfailingly solid. In his twenty-five years with the company, after moving from his role as an electronic engineer into health and safety, Seamus had recently been promoted to Technical Development Manager and praised for his achievements.

When it seems to us outsiders that a whistleblower's disclosure has thrown their organization into a state of confusion, paranoia and panic, it may well be that a delicate balance has been tipped. The defences keeping anxiety at bay have been damaged. When we scratch our heads over apparently irrational, over-the-top, personalized attacks on whistleblowers, perhaps we are merely witnessing the urgent and often erratic work of redrawing boundaries to restore that all-important sense of control. This is what fuels the intensity of reprisals against public whistleblowers: their very existence ignites the underlying anxiety that organizational control is nothing but a fantasy.

The whistleblower who ignores the messages to keep quiet is unpredictable and, ultimately, impossible to contain. They represent a transgression of the essence of organization itself. This is why moral behaviour – behaviour that means you sometimes have to act alone and break with the crowd – is often simply incompatible with organizational life.[21] Breaking with the crowd happens rarely, because pressures to conform are so strong. But when it comes down to it, when the niceties of employee-friendly policies, dispute resolution processes and official channels are stripped away, a fundamental conflict is revealed. The employing organization needs to neutralize what Bauman calls 'the disruptive and deregulating impact of moral behaviour'.[22] If the behaviour cannot be neutralized, it must be eliminated. The research is clear: workers who report deep-seated, systemic problems in public are particularly vulnerable to retaliation.[23]

For the employer interested in eliminating the boundary-violating worker speaking up, its options are increasingly limited by law. It can be difficult to fire a whistleblower: employment tribunal judges tend not to like it. An easier route is to make them want to leave of their own accord, through initiatives that stop short of dismissal. We see moves like the reassigning of tasks, which basically involves giving someone more menial work to do, for example when Seamus was suddenly moved to a role he had worked on ten years previously, with all the embarrassment this brings. Colleagues grow suspicious: perhaps the demotion is warranted? Other whistleblowers are placed under scrutiny: their arrival time at work is carefully monitored with discipline warnings for being a few minutes late, as just one example. Especially if the disclosure is systemic, threatening the long-term survival of their employers, co-workers can often be relied on to step in and help to isolate a discloser, making life unbearable. Mental health issues can naturally arise, and sometimes the worker needs to go on sick leave, which employers can then use to cast doubt on their credibility. In some instances, whistleblowers are asked to undertake psychiatric evaluation by an employer's medical team, ostensibly for their own good.[24] These measures can indeed help, but in some cases the same evaluations are used to discredit the whistleblower. Once some of these things are arranged, a worker might think of leaving of their own accord. If they do decide to leave, other employers might hear about the whistleblowing, or be told to avoid this worker, as they become blacklisted.[25] The problem for the whistleblower is that it is often difficult to tie any of these activities directly to one's whistleblowing. It is difficult to prove whistleblower retaliation – even if it is outlawed – in court.[26]

All of this – the exclusions, demotions, threats, financial pressures and legal prosecutions – amounts to acts of aggression against the whistleblower.[27] But they are not really acknowledged as such because, by now, something has changed in how the whistleblower is perceived within the organization. Because they have been constructed as a dangerous threat, this persecution is seen as legitimate. In situations such as this, a person's identity – how they are seen by themselves and others – can radically shift. People who are considered to have gone too far in transgressing a fundamental norm within the group can end up abject, less-than-human, and hence they become legitimate targets of aggression. Organizations are places in which structures of power and strong cultural norms come together to result in painful, harmful acts of exclusion for specific groups of people who dissent.[28] It would seem that whistleblowers can find themselves in this situation. No longer 'one of us', they have become targets.

When Seamus took his disclosures outside – to journalists, non-governmental organizations and the government committee – the employer responded by denying what he said. A spokesperson told the committee that the oil was biodegradable: there was no hazard here. This was swiftly contradicted – in public – by the Environmental Protection Agency, which had been busy investigating. The mixture, it turned out, was indeed hazardous, certainly not biodegradable, and the company had done nothing about it despite knowing this for years. The newspapers picked up the initial findings: 'ESB failed to report hazardous cable leaks on 48 occasions', read just one of the headlines in the *Irish Times*. It must have seemed to management like control was slipping away at a frightening pace. Meanwhile, Seamus and his family were dealing with the impact of the anxious and aggressive response.

Official Channel as a Tool for Reprisal

It is clear that we have now moved away from the figure of the whistleblower put forward by the billion-dollar software industry designing official channels, the figure praised by Warren Buffett, applauded by investor groups and celebrated by politicians as a human governance tool. We have left behind the CEO's favourite 'forward risk indicator', the useful whistleblower at the centre of the recent excitement around whistleblowing protection laws and systems. That whistleblower appears in every policy document, article and webinar PowerPoint deck in the same way. They are, fundamentally, helpful to the employer. They are among the four out of every five whistleblowers who say they spoke up about serious wrongdoing and nothing bad happened as a result, because their disclosure did not pose an intractable problem.[29]

We are not talking about that sort of whistleblower anymore. We are talking about another version, a version not so fortunate: the discloser who reads the situation, gets the sense that their information is not welcome, acknowledges the start of reprisals and keeps talking anyway. These people are not deemed helpful for the employer; they have become threats and targets. Seamus was one such whistleblower, and there are many others like him.

The life of a whistleblower takes on a new dimension once they become a target. Their project to stop the wrongdoing is now split into two tasks: stopping the wrongdoing and defending themselves against reprisals while trying to gather proof they are even happening. Both are big projects. They take the kind of time, money and resilience that not many people have.[30] Most whistleblowers I encounter do not start off by thinking of themselves as whistleblowers at all, of any kind. They get called whistleblowers by observers, placed in this category by a journalist, an advocate or a lawyer, because of the reprisals they are experiencing. It is not as though they planned for this to happen. Many whistleblowers end up in this situation after speaking up on behalf of others. We often think of whistleblowers as workers, but they are often also managers of staff, people whose job description would surely include things like protecting their charges from electric shocks and fireballs as Seamus was trying his best to do. Many whistleblowers are simply doing their job to the letter.

It is these whistleblowers that we hear about in the news: people whose names have become attached to an act of disclosure. 'Wherever possible, avoid adopting the identity of a whistleblower', advises Tom Devine, because he has seen what happens when you do.[31] The public whistleblower, the focus of this book, is one who has been given this identity and named as such in the media. Implicitly blamed for so much more than the wrongdoing their disclosure reveals, the focus of so much anxiety, public whistleblowers can find themselves in even more trouble. Seamus had gone from a manager following process to becoming a public whistleblower. This, it seems, was because he took his role seriously.

Weaponizing the Channels

The trouble with the public whistleblower is that they now have an audience. The question for the employer becomes: how can we make them a problem for everyone else, so that people stop listening to what they say? Casting doubt on a whistleblower's credibility is the main order of business when an organization is redrawing its boundaries to exclude them. Doubts over credibility take the edge off a disclosure. They create clouds of scepticism, and hosts of reasons not to believe. This is not easy. The whistleblower is often eminently credible owing to their role, their length of service, their expertise. There are lots of ways, however, to chip away at that credibility.

Official channels come into play here. This can take one by surprise. The very shields that were put in place to assist the discloser can be turned against them. The disclosure process becomes a means to query their credibility. That written caution issued to Seamus was followed by a formal disciplinary complaint, based on his 'inappropriate way' of raising issues, and his failure to use the internal procedures as he should.

The outcome of this application of the official channels' rules was to demonstrate that Seamus was at fault. And, specifically, that the employer was not. By stating that an investigation was underway, Seamus's employer could claim it was following the recommendations set out in Ireland's whistleblowing law at the time, the Protected Disclosures Act 2014. The ESB spokesman was asked by the *Irish Times* about why his firm ignored the ten protected disclosures raised by Seamus; the process was dragging on with no conclusion in sight. 'We are satisfied [that the company] has complied at all times with the *Protected Disclosures Act* 2014' came the assurance. Indeed, they had. 'At all times' being an ominous turn of phrase. The firm could continue to comply with the Protected Disclosures Act at all times, and, so long as disclosures were languishing 'under investigation' somewhere in the labyrinth of the official channel, the employer might keep on reporting its satisfaction with itself.

Official channels reframe information about wrongdoing by carefully dividing it up into different categories according to policy. Complex issues are split into narrow technical points, each to be considered separately. The whistleblower's claim for redress for harmful retaliation is just one of these points. In this act of division, the overall picture of what is happening becomes impossible to see clearly. A story of widespread, high-level, authorized wrongdoing and attempted cover-up – so urgent and shocking on first hearing – has now been magically transformed into ten separate little issues. Seamus's treatment as a whistleblower was number ten in his list of ten protected disclosures. The retaliation 'issue' is typically sent off to HR to investigate, and human resources is a profession well known for automatically placing the worker at the centre of situations occurring. In whistleblowing cases, HR staff tend to view concerns raised by workers as 'personal issues': problems with the worker themselves, particularly if that worker did not follow the formal process to the letter. The same spokesman elected to speak to the *Irish Times* responded to a query about why Seamus himself appeared to have been targeted and punished for speaking up. 'ESB Networks cannot comment in detail on a HR issue' was the regretful response. He went on, however, that the company has 'sought at all times to meet our responsibilities to all of our employees and to ensure that they are all treated with respect and dignity in the workplace'. Another policy complied with; another box ticked. The wilfully disingenuous manner in which some employers can cling to the following of procedures, such as official channels, as justification for ignoring the bigger picture, suggests these procedures are working as another form of social defence. They shield those in charge from the anxiety of the current situation. In cases like this, social defences can work to sustain existing power structures: helping 'the powerful avoid learning, forcing less powerful others to carry what those in power cannot bear to know or feel'.[32] When I teach students about organizations and ethics, I tell them about situations like this. The bureaucratic organizational form seems benign from the outside, but in practice can be very dangerous indeed.

Of course, if Seamus was experiencing retaliation, he could always turn to the anti-retaliation laws – that second shield that we in the whistleblowing research community spend so much time discussing. In many cases, whistleblower protection is available, or at least much more readily available, when the official channels are used first during the process of disclosure. These laws, however, can be vague on just how long a whistleblower has to wait for an answer from the official channel.[33] Left hanging, and waiting, the wrongdoing continues. Escalating a disclosure out of frustration from the blatant lack of action, because you have been told how the propane gas explosion was going to be prevented in six different ways by six different people, for example, represents a bypassing of the official channels. In many countries, claims for redress for whistleblower retaliation evaporate with this choice, precisely because the whistleblower did not wait and thus the formal process was not followed. Employers can fully comply with the law, leaning on the official channels they have in place, and whether or not they were used 'in an appropriate way'.

It is not surprising that four out of five whistleblower retaliation legal claims are shot down in court, a figure that bears out across many countries.[34] The employer tends to hold the balance of power. The whistleblower has their word, and sometimes a record of strong evaluations showing that they had been considered a valuable employee for years right up until their disclosure. But that is it. The employer has in its corner all the files, all the records, all the witnesses and email archives, its large-organization legitimacy and its own interpretation of its policies. All they have to claim is that there was some other reason for the apparent reprisal. The burden of proof is a tough bar. 'I wasn't brave', Seamus responded to the interviewer who had told him he was. 'I was terrified for what I was putting my family through. And all I need to do is make one wrong step.'

This is the alchemy performed by speak-up systems. They can transmute a serious breach of principle and policy into 'an act of private disobedience and psychological disturbance on the part of the whistleblower', to quote C. Fred Alford.[35] In his book *Official Channels*, Brian Martin agrees: this is how we get 'organizational deafness organized through procedures'.[36]

In the bureaucratic world of charts, rules and procedures, offences against policy are taken very seriously. We have the strange scenario of a damaged fantasy of control repaired by deploying alternative mechanisms that uphold the same fantasy.[37] The speak-up system had become a process for reinforcing the decisions the organization was making, and countering statements it didn't like. It had become a process for performatively, and painfully, creating problems out of the source of these statements, the whistleblower, with the organization enjoying final authority over what can and cannot be said.[38] This aspect of the official channel makes it ideal for an organization bent on defending itself against the 'outsider on the inside': the public whistleblower. They can now be presented to onlookers as a problem for us all, a rulebreaker.

This dynamic can be seen across the different kinds of official channels ostensibly designed to deal with speaking up and assist in the meting out of fairness and justice in a structured manner. Courts, grievance committees, complaint procedures and regulatory and oversight authorities all rely on the bureaucratic splitting of big issues into lots of little ones. It is not always a problem when this happens: '[o]fficial channels work fine in many circumstances, and most of the people on appeal committees and working in agencies are concerned and hard-working', Brian Martin tells us on his blog. Concern and hard work, however, are weak assistants for these people when faced with whistleblowing that is deemed unacceptable: 'when a person with less power tries to challenge one with more power, or challenge the entire system, it is usually a hopeless cause'. This is, Martin continues, what he tells whistleblowers when they come to him, asking about whether they should use the speak-up system. '[Y]ou might be very lucky and find justice in official channels, but don't count on it. Indeed', he cautions, 'you should assume they won't provide the justice you're looking for.'[39] These are serious warnings.

So, for public whistleblowers, it seems that an opaque mesh of bureaucratic cul-de-sacs awaits. This wasn't, for Seamus and his wife, a role they were able to opt out of. Their names were in the papers. The scenario was growing increasingly bizarre. The things that were supposed to help were not really helping. 'You get sucked into a process', Seamus described. 'It's an anxious time. ... The EPA [Environmental Protection Agency] vindicating my claims: on one level, it has brought a level of reassurance. But we are still caught in this situation where it is going to be very difficult to extricate ourselves.' The laws and the systems have little to say on extrication from the tangled bureaucratic web in which the public whistleblower now finds themselves and their family.

Fifteen minutes on social media platforms frequented by whistleblowers is sufficient to get a sense of the pain of those who are likewise caught. Social media threads are filled with visceral frustration. These are people who acted rationally and reported actual wrongdoing with facts to hand. They are people who got lost, tossed out or even crushed by a convoluted, bureaucratic process in which facts did not appear, in the end, to carry much weight. Logic was presented as the guiding principle at every turn in the formal process, but it felt throughout as though power and influence were in fact the driving forces. Many whistleblowers in such situations continue to meet up in groups, or online, where experiences of being caught in bureaucratic traps like this can be shared. These are unique and valuable spaces because it can be hard to convince others, who have not been through it, just how deep-seated the injustice of a maze constructed by formal processes can be.

Each year I get emails from people in this situation. I help where I can, pointing to this research study, that helpline, a new book. But many people are simply stuck in this morass of unwanted whistleblowing. This is why, with colleagues, I started writing up these whistleblowers' stories and putting them out as they are, recording whistleblowers who have been in this situation talking about it, and putting the recordings online, alongside the academic research that helps understand such situations.[40] There might be something in these stories that helps because simple answers do not. Each person's situation is so complex to navigate, filled with processes and pathways, and channels, that often lead nowhere. We do what we can. Mainly, however, I feel guilty because I work in this area, and I have had little of use to say about this.

Towards Protection for the Unwanted Whistleblower

By the time I watched Seamus's appearance on TV, I was clear: the official channels were not helping people in his situation. But I had no answers. It was difficult to find the words to articulate it clearly; on some level I knew that we can push all we want for better whistleblower protections and we can work to improve institutions so that employees can disclose safely. But when an employer finds itself backed against a wall, on the defensive, with no options but to hit back, all those protections can come crashing down. If an employer decides to really dig its heels in, even the finest laws can be unpicked, shredded and rendered useless. The most thoughtfully designed whistleblowing systems can be ignored and, worse, they can be used against the people who report through them. These things happen, I was beginning to realize. It was time to face this fact and look for something else.

Right now, stories of what happens to persistent, public whistleblowers carry little weight in the official debates about whistleblowing and how to support it. At some point over the past twenty years, it appears that people with expertise in the field of whistleblowing decided something. They decided to channel their energies to work within the system. Experts appear too busy polishing policies and perfecting laws to listen to evidence clearly showing them failing outright. Most people working in this world, fighting for change through the official routes, the laws, the systems, do not seem to spend much time thinking about the other side: the unwanted whistleblowers and the weaponization of official channels against them.

To be fair, most workers who disclose do so without reprisal. Plus, it is much easier to argue for change in law and policy, in an era when economic discourse is especially valued, when you can talk about cost-saving whistleblowers, human governance tools and risk indicators. And the vast army of consulting firms and IT providers selling their services keep this narrative top of the agenda through events, articles and polished communications strategies. This story is a happy one, or at least it has a happy ending: allowing us to ignore all that talk of anxiety and illusions of control. That talk is difficult because there is something of the impossible about the unwanted whistleblower: caught in a system, with no protection and disappearing disclosures. And there is something disturbing about when they go public.

Yet, the knowledge that these things happen haunts the space in which we work. It forms its backdrop, even if we don't speak about it. I don't know if other academics and practitioners feel this way. What I do know is that it needs exploring. Even if there is no answer, this absence needs to be encircled, interrogated and teased out for any insights that might emerge as useful or familiar – even, or perhaps especially, those that seem incoherent and paradoxical. It may be possible that within this work there is something that would help these lost disclosures escape the fate of disappearing into a hopeless bureaucratic ether. There might be the outline of an idea, the bones of a plan. Right now, there is nothing, or very little. We have to ask, though, where is the real protection for the unwanted whistleblower and how can we make it so the problems they raise are addressed? What might this look like? Where should we go next?

Any expert worth their salt will tell you the same thing, if you ask them what to do about making a whistleblowing disclosure: you need a good lawyer. Yes, the law is flawed and full of holes, lawyers are expensive and the language is arcane. But without it, disclosers are wide open for reprisal. And we already know this journey is not going to be straightforward. So, let us begin with the lawyers.

Notes

1. *RTÉ Investigates* (2020).
2. Transparency International Ireland (2017).
3. In fact, retaliation for speaking up happens less than we often assume – research shows approximately one in five whistleblowers can expect reprisal (IBA, 2021, Transparency International Ireland, 2017). The key point to note is that harsh retaliation can be a disaster for the person and their family.
4. Stubben & Welch (2020).
5. Led by Wim Vandekerckhove of the University of Greenwich, the project resulted in *The Whistleblowing Guide: Speak-Up Arrangements, Challenges and Best Practices* (Kenny et al., 2019c).
6. The better systems also circle back with the whistleblower about the status of the investigation, letting the worker know that the concern is being taken seriously. As we argued, this can build trust in the speak-up

systems signalling to other workers that it is safe to use (Kenny et al., 2019c).

7. Legislation, including the 2019 EU Whistleblowing Directive, enshrines aspects of best practice in law, including obliging organizations to make annual reports. See Appendix 2.

8. Kenny et al. (2019c), Kenny et al. (2020), Van Portfliet et al. (2022).

9. A classic tale told in whistleblowing circles centres on Jes Staley CEO at Barclays. He ignored the rules about whistleblowing confidentiality and tried to uncover a whistleblower's identity on three occasions. He was sanctioned for whistleblower reprisal and ordered to pay a fine representing a small fraction of his salary and bonus package. Fines for individuals and for employers can be budgeted in as a small cost of doing business. Meanwhile, the risk of investigation and sanction is usually low, given regulators' limited resources and in some cases revolving-door recruitment practices.

10. Vandekerckhove & Langenberg (2012, p. 43). The authors detail how institutionalized critique is the kind that does not 'disrupt existing limits, conventions, norms'. See also Martin (2020), du Plessis (2020) and Monk et al. (2015). The question for scholars is whether institutionalized critique can be considered critique in the first place because criticism that really makes a difference is, by its very nature, radically disruptive.

11. Jackall (2010).

12. See Jackall's (2010) study of morality among corporate managers in the US. He describes how uncertainty and fear are distinguishing features of the corporate bureaucratic form. Jackall focuses on the US but his work has relevance for studying large organizations more generally.

13. Gabriel (1999). Jackall (2010, p. 14) provides a detailed analysis of the omnipresence of turmoil and crisis in large bureaucratic corporations, and what this means for ethical behaviour.

14. These structural aspects, according to a psychosocial perspective, represent social defences. These are 'collective arrangements – such as an organizational structure, a work method, or a prevalent discourse – created or used by an organization's members as a protection against disturbing affect derived from external threats, internal conflicts, or the nature of their work' (Petriglieri & Petriglieri, 2010, p. 47). In organizations, workers can cling to such defensive structures in times of crisis. See also Jaques (1995), Schwartz (1991).

15. Fineman & Gabriel (1996, p. 119).

16. Gabriel (1999, p. 227).

17. Gabriel (1999, p. 226).

18. Jackall (2010).

19. Alford (2001, p. 129).
20. Alford (2001, p. 99). See also Warren (2007), who shows how, when a scandal hits an organization, the response can involve shifting the stigma of the wrongdoing onto the whistleblower.
21. Philosopher Hannah Arendt's analysis of the organization of the Holocaust is a classic example. Bauman (1989) and especially Jackall (2010) provide insightful analysis of why the bureaucratic mindset causes people to bracket the moralities they hold outside of the work environment.
22. Bauman (1989, p. 215).
23. Retaliation and reprisals get worse when a whistleblower discloses things that go to the heart of how an organization operates, that relate to the organization's very reason for being – its entire business model, for example, or a core product on which all its value depends (Mesmer-Magnus & Viswesvaran, 2005). The same is true when the wrongdoing is likely to elicit a serious reaction from the public that might be harmful (Near & Jensen, 1983).
24. Kenny et al. (2019a), Lennane (2012).
25. Blacklisting occurs in approximately one-third of the cases in which a whistleblower leaves their role because of disclosing (Kenny & Fotaki, 2019).
26. It is for this reason that, prior to the 2019 EU Whistleblowing Directive being implemented, activists pushed to shift the burden of proof in whistleblower retaliation cases from the whistleblower to the organization, whose representatives must now prove a given detriment was *not* because a worker was whistleblowing.
27. Kenny (2018), Kenny et al. (2019c).
28. See Tyler (2019) for an extensive discussion, and Kenny (2018) describing this issue in the context of whistleblowing.
29. Transparency International Ireland (2017, p. 36). For background, definitions of 'whistleblower' differ in the academic literature. For some, the term refers only to those who receive retaliation (Alford, 2001). Others consider it to encompass all workers who speak up (Near & Miceli, 1995). The latter interpretation is used here.
30. See Uys (2016) for a study of the importance of resilience on the part of whistleblowers coping with reprisal.
31. Devine & Maassarani (2011, p. 49). See also Tom Mueller's *Crisis of Conscience* (2019), which is clear on the point: for many public whistleblowers he studied, the best outcome was to try to return to a state of being relatively unknown: to stop being identified as a whistleblower.

32. Petriglieri & Petriglieri (2020, p. 424); see also Petriglieri & Stein (2012), Casey (1999), Ekman (2013).

33. In the EU Whistleblowing Directive, for example, a set of conditions must be met before public (e.g. media) disclosures can be deemed protected against reprisal. These include that (1) the person first reported internally and externally or directly externally, but no appropriate measures were taken within the set time frame, or (2) the person has reasonable grounds to believe that the breach may constitute an imminent or manifest danger to the public interest, or the person has reasonable grounds to believe that, in the case of external reporting, there is a risk of retaliation, or a low prospect of the breach being addressed, for instance because the authority might be in collusion with the perpetrator (EC Council Directive, 2019).

34. IBA (2021); for a detailed analysis of why whistleblower legislation can be flawed in practice, and recommendations for change, see Kierans (2023).

35. Alford (2001, p. 32).

36. Professor Brian Martin's book *Official Channels* (2020) offers first-hand experiences of the limits of these channels. See also Alford (2001, p. 32), Vandekerckhove & Langenberg (2012, p. 40).

37. An organization's claims for plausible deniability could potentially be strengthened if the specified channels were not used by the discloser, or were used incorrectly. See Devine & Maassarani (2011, p. 49).

38. Weiskopf & Tobias-Miersch (2016). To counter this threat of ongoing obfuscation, legal professionals have argued in court that failure to investigate a whistleblowing claim is itself an act of retaliation; see, for example, Ireland's *Conway* v. *Department of Agriculture* [2020] IEHC 665, Hyland J.

39. For advice on using official channels, see Martin (1999, p. 46). (Note: Updated version = Martin (2013).)

40. We do this on www.whistleblowingimpact.org.

2 | *Lawfare Tactics and Legal Advice at Theranos*

Losing Control and Turning to Law

Erika walked up to the stand at the Robert F. Peckham courthouse in San Jose, California. She was the second witness called to give evidence against Elizabeth Holmes in one of the US's most important white-collar crime cases.[1] Erika told her story to Judge Edward Davila, twelve jurists and a room of people gripped by every detail of this unfolding scene. She described her initial excitement joining Theranos at the age of twenty-two. She spoke about how things had gone wrong. Erika detailed the responses she received from her boss when, as a new graduate hire, she had raised genuine concerns. She described how private investigators followed her in the summer of 2015. Her words were backed up by private investigator invoices Theranos's team turned over in discovery.[2] The *New York Times* called her testimony, alongside that of other whistleblowers, pivotal in the decision to convict Elizabeth Holmes. What made these accounts so powerful, they said, was the picture they painted of a company where well-intended attempts to question things were so aggressively suppressed. The whistleblowers were proof that a culture of secrecy and conformity was enforced from early on, with serious consequences for those who spoke up.

But the *New York Times* commentary and the thousands of pages of newsprint produced after this verdict missed one important aspect. Erika's account told a bigger story. It reflected the fact that even reasonably well-crafted laws, designed to be shields protecting workers who speak up, simply crumble when faced with a well-resourced employer bent on protecting its boundaries. Erika's account spoke to the new reality that works in the service of employers like this, every day. It told of how good law is no match for well-funded lawfare.

Rapid Growth and Shambolic Systems

I had first seen Erika Cheung on stage at one of those industry conferences for women entrepreneurs. She was accompanied by her lawyer Mary Inman, whom I knew from whistleblowing events. Erika's talk that day was just one of many she was giving at forums across the world, as the whistleblower whose testimony helped convict the founder of Theranos. She seemed so young.

When Erika signed up with Theranos, she had just graduated. It was, she later told her alumni magazine, '[m]y first big girl job'. And what a job to get. At the recruiting fair on campus, the Theranos stand had the longest line. The application process included interviews with various managers, including one woman Erika had followed closely for a long time. She had read everything she could about Elizabeth Holmes, CEO of Theranos. Like Erika, Elizabeth was a rare female in the science world. She too had overcome challenges: Erika grew up in a one-room trailer and graduated from Berkeley with honours. Elizabeth was a college dropout who founded a flourishing company. When Elizabeth was Erika's age, she had already raised $6 million in investment and her company had been valued at $30 million. This company was going to change healthcare for good.

Erika had seen the pictures of Theranos's sleek, black machine, about the size of a small printer, with curved edges and a muted blue screen. The company's mission was simple and outrageous. They wanted this blood-testing machine in every pharmacy in the US to begin with; later there would be one in every home in the country. Using just a drop of blood taken from a finger, transferred to a tiny vial, the little black laboratory-in-a-box would give patients a cheap, immediate picture of the state of their health. It would give answers to the medical worries of so many. This promised a path-breaking move towards affordable and accessible healthcare in a country badly in need of both.

Erika finally made it through the recruitment hurdles to a role in quality control in October 2013, signing a non-disclosure agreement (NDA) as part of the paperwork. By then, the company was abuzz; $45 million had been raised from investors, including Rupert Murdoch, Henry Kissinger and Oracle's Larry Ellison. With her piercing blue eyes and youthful appearance, Elizabeth was set to grace the covers of *Forbes* magazine, *Fortune* and *Bloomberg Business*, dressed in the ever-present black turtleneck that was her homage to her hero Steve Jobs. At her side in the photographs were the curved lines of the black machine – the miracle device. Erika was entranced by the success of the company but also by the person who founded it. When we spoke, she told me how Elizabeth was, to her, a woman whose background as a dropout didn't matter, as she followed her vision regardless. 'It wasn't just that she was a female leader; she was an underdog, a bit quirky and weird. ... And she was a scientist.' Working in her lab, Elizabeth's vision would now be Erika's too: 'it was a job I could see myself working at for ten years. I thought I was really lucky.'[3]

Within a few weeks, Erika was beginning to question her luck. Those machines were not doing what the company said they could do. Erika worked in the same department as Tyler Shultz. Both were scheduled on the night shift team. They got chatting.[4] Tyler was also concerned with what he was seeing. The little black boxes were far from ready.

There was this mechanical arm that had a pipette on the end that would go and suck up different reagents. Oftentimes, it either wouldn't pick up the right tips, and then they'll usually fall off sometime during the test ... into the bottom of the machine and it would get in the gears. This wire, I think it was just like a clothes hanger.

This gear-grinding, shambolic system was a long way from the game-changing invention being sold to investors: '[t]he doors wouldn't close. So, you'd have to tape it shut to see if taping it shut changed the result'.[5]

In a biotech lab, these kinds of issues are normally picked up by quality control. This was Erika's job. She worked on testing the machines, checking whether they were passing the regulations. They repeatedly failed. But when results emerged that did not fit the required conclusion, she and her colleagues were simply asked to ignore the unruly data. 'So, essentially how it got resolved is: they took out data points. And they said, "Oh, well, this is like: the best two out of six".'[6] Erika documented the results and the errors so that others could see the lack of progress: 'I would put up error reporting sheets by the machines. And they would be taken down. Like, people didn't want to actually know the number of times that we were having issues. And it was probably because they were starting to realize: we were having them so frequently.' Basic scientific integrity was bypassed in order to give a good news story. This was not how quality control should be done, and Erika was painfully aware.

According to Erika and Tyler, many other employees also knew about the machines' frequent failures. 'A lot of people would pretty much joke about how awful they were', Tyler recalled. 'I went out with some of my housemates, and I saw some of the product managers there. One of them … hitting on one of my friends, was saying that … [laughs], he was clean, STD-free. But I mean, we were making jokes about how we didn't actually know because he was tested with a Theranos device.'[7] The machines were a joke to Tyler and his colleagues. But by now they were also being used to test the blood of real patients as Theranos expanded its reach. A new partnership with Walgreens had recently been announced with fanfare. Formal approval to carry out certain blood tests had been secured. Theranos machines would soon be within the reach of every home in America through its chain of pharmacies.

Speaking Up at Theranos

Erika describes raising these concerns to Elizabeth's second-in-command, Sunny Balwani, who supervised lab operations. He had asked her how she was getting along in Theranos, '[a]nd I said "I really enjoy working for this company, but there are a lot of problems. We're having a lot of issues with our quality controls".' She recalled his reaction: '[a]nd then he just sort of lost it at that point. And he was like "Well, what makes you think that we have problems? What was your training in statistics? I'm tired of people coming in here and starting fires where there are no fires and problems".' Erika was taken aback. She kept going with her work, but it made no difference, the results were the same. 'It failed. And it kept failing. I kept running it over and over and over. And how it was handled [by Sunny] totally blew me away.'[8]

Sunny's aggressive response reflected the general atmosphere at Theranos when it came to questioning practices and speaking up about concerns. People were strongly encouraged not to. There was strict physical separation between the different parts of the company. Walking between sections meant using fingerprint scanners and identity cards, while sharing information with colleagues in other functions was subject to strict rules. People were prevented from talking and mixing; this meant that few had a full picture of what was really going on. And those who did, Erika's colleagues in the lab, were often recent graduates like her, lacking experience in the practices they were being asked to carry out. As emerged in the subsequent trials, many people responsible for selling the idea to investors and for marketing the magic black machine to partners were not aware of what Erika and her colleagues were facing each day: clanging machines and data errors.[9]

I asked Erika about the support she got from her supervisors, when she was raising concerns. 'There was a lot of resistance at that level', she told me. 'Like, "oh well, I cannot deal with this right now. . . . This isn't in my purview . . . you should go talk to this person over there. . . . A kind of run-around.' Dissent and questioning were discouraged at Theranos. 'It was just sort of instilled in us in our onboarding', Erika recalled. 'Like, "we need to keep certain things secret; you're not allowed to talk to your friends and family about what's going on here". They would barricade certain portions of the lab so you couldn't see.'[10]

This culture of secrecy went hand-in-hand with a sense of fear. According to Erika, '[p]eople were very scared of upsetting Elizabeth Holmes and upsetting Sunny Balwani', '[they] were blatantly saying that they were scared of losing their jobs'. She described how people would work 'insane hours' to ensure they were safe. And when things went wrong, the result was a frenzy of accusations, where 'everyone was looking to point to someone to blame'. Sunny's initial response to Erika's concerns about quality control failures was just one example of this.[11] 'People aren't trying to understand what is actually going wrong, but people are just getting upset about what is going wrong', she continued.

The anxiety and fear were palpable, from Theranos worker accounts like Erika's. Theranos was an organization that had scaled rapidly. It had 800 staff at its height.[12] Sunny and Elizabeth were managing all this and they were doing so under a media spotlight.

And people had started asking questions. John P. A. Ioannidis, a professor of medicine, health research and policy and statistics at Stanford University, was poking around to find out why such powerful medical breakthroughs were not being shared or peer-reviewed with other scientific experts.[13] *Wall Street Journal* reporter John Carreyrou had begun to look a little deeper, seeking out employees who would talk to him about the reality behind the Theranos success. And against all this, senior Theranos executives were persisting with their promise that the future dream was almost upon us: 'access to your own blood data with a finger prick of blood'.

Erika's colleague Tyler was vocally questioning what was happening, raising the issues with executives. The response was a rebuke from Sunny. He asked Tyler to apologize for his rudeness.[14] Next, Tyler's emails were reviewed, revealing a link to Erika. Sunny confronted her directly, she recalls. 'The reception that I got was basically: "You need to sit down and keep your mouth shut and you don't know what you're talking about, and you need to do the job that I hired you for, which is process patient samples".'[15] But Erika kept asking questions. She sought help from her lab director and medical director to carry out studies that would double-check what she was seeing. She consulted with statistician colleagues to see whether the data were in error. And yet the problems persisted. With Tyler, Erika's concerns were raised to the board. She recalled to me how she simply wanted to stop these mistakes happening while the machines were processing patient samples; 'I wasn't striving for the stars!' she reflects, discussing how explosive these attempts to speak up would eventually become. 'I was just like: "you are telling me to do the thing. It's not doing the thing. What do I do?"'

If 'regular' organizations are hotbeds of anxiety and a constant battle for control against chaos,[16] Theranos was veritably pulsating with a sense of dread. The tech was not working. Carefully designed silos to keep control over potential knowledge leaks were cracking. A healthy organization is one that allows workers to speak up, to question and to challenge. Not so at Theranos. Concerns were sidelined. The senior team had other worries. The boundary between inside and outside was fraying rapidly. And it was the potential of workers to speak up: to scientists, to journalists, to regulators, that posed the biggest threat. Without insiders, people like Carreyrou would have no story; he later reflected on how, without whistleblowers' testimonies, he could not publish.

The anxious highways along which blame travels in search of scapegoats, that we saw at ESB in the wake of its scandal, had come to life. The chain of command was the path along which responsibility was pushed down to those at the coal face: the lab technicians felt the full force of the simmering fear of senior executives. And when they challenged, their protestations were met with anger out of all proportion. The 'rage, anxiety and fear' produced by a visceral loss of control was let loose, resulting in a twenty-two-year-old graduate being told to sit down and shut up.[17]

A strong sense of loyalty keeps workers quiet about wrongdoing: and Theranos had plenty of this, but it would only last so long against the reality of what people were witnessing in the labs. One of the most powerful silencing dynamics, when the appeal of fitting in and a sense of loyalty begins to wane, is a dread fear of reprisal.[18] Fear needed to be deployed, and here the law offered an ideal tool.

Scarecrow Lawyers and Policing the Boundary

'The threat of litigation was always in the air when you worked at Theranos', Carreyrou later reflected. 'And employees knew it was not an empty threat because Elizabeth had sued former employees in the early years of the company. They also knew that starting in 2011, the outside counsel for Theranos was David Boies.'[19] David Boies had personal responsibility for overseeing the legal side of secrecy. Famous across the US, Boies had represented Michael Moore and Al Gore, and litigated in the US government versus Microsoft case. He had helped defend big tobacco firms and represented Harvey Weinstein. 'For Theranos employees, he was a scarecrow', recalled Carreyrou. 'They thought that if they expressed their misgivings, either internally or after they left, to a regulator or a reporter, that it would be David Boies and his law firm that would be coming after them.'[20]

Fear of litigation was fostered at Theranos through actual legal contracts, including non-disclosure agreements (NDAs). An NDA is a contract aimed to deter workers from sharing sensitive company information with others. There is no standard format. The exact wording tends to be defined by the employer. Non-disclosure agreements cover whatever information the employer deems to be 'confidential' or 'proprietary'. This can include things like financial forecasts and performance data. Non-disclosure agreements can even be written as non-disparaging agreements, outlawing disclosures that might be deemed 'embarrassing' for the employer. Ironically, the actual text contained in an NDA is, in itself, part of what is deemed confidential. The text of these agreements is not generally available for scrutiny, although some have emerged when people break their NDAs, or as part of evidence in court.[21]

An important part of the NDA is the level of detail provided about what happens if you violate it. Non-disclosure agreements can include severe wording. Some deliberately undermine workers' rights under law to speak up in the public interest whenever they encounter wrong-doing. Some agreements require workers to let the employer know when they disclose to outside parties. They threaten disciplinary pro-cedures or dismissal if they do so without asking the legal department first. Other somewhat bizarre features include clauses that make the worker liable for the employer's legal costs. If the employer feels they must enforce the NDA and pursue the worker because they have blown the whistle, the worker pays the lawyers.

Common in the tech sector, NDAs are now increasingly seen else-where. They come in many shapes and sizes. I first encountered them as part of settlement agreements, a frequent conclusion to whistleblower disputes.[22] Once a whistleblower and their employer agree to settle, the whistleblower typically signs an NDA contract promising not to speak about the wrongdoing and the amount of money they received.[23] Some well-known whistleblowers I contacted for interview explained that they couldn't speak to me about specific things, restricted by their NDAs.

Theranos made full use of NDAs; Erika had to sign one before she even interviewed for the job, despite having not yet seen anything to disclose. These kinds of NDAs are, in essence, a promise to not speak up about things in the future: a kind of pre-emptive commitment to silence about whatever is to come: 'I don't know what I will see but I promise not to say anything.'

For Erika and colleagues, the NDAs were an important part of the overall culture of silence. Theranos's senior managers and their legal team did not have to do a whole lot to actively maintain this oppressive ethos, besides putting contracts in front of people. They let it be known that some workers had been sued for breaching theirs, and thus by implication, others might be sued. Stories circulated around the offices and labs: the one about the sales executive and legal counsel who were fired for pointing out unrealistic revenue projections to members of the board, and the one about the scientist dismissed for asking why lab practices contravened protocol. These stories helped shape the scene for any Theranos worker thinking about whether or not to speak up.[24] We saw the 'scarecrow' figure of David Boies, and his team, looming large over the company. A benign, inactive policeman who simply needs to be there – to be visible – in order to achieve the desired silencing effects. Potential leaks had apparently been controlled, through very little active effort on the part of the firm. On this view, engaging one of the most expensive legal firms in the US must have seemed like money well spent.

After Sunny confronted Erika for speaking with Tyler, she felt she had had enough. Calling her father, she cried down the phone. She was making good money. She was working in a top firm. Everyone else seemed to believe in the vision but she couldn't understand why this was, when the reality was so different.

Seven months after signing up, she quit Theranos. She was finished with the firm. Or so she thought. Erika and Tyler, aged twenty-three and twenty-two, respectively, were about to find out what can happen when the law morphs from a background threat of litigation into one of the aggressive methods of boundary policing: active lawfare.

SLAPPs and Silencing Laws

Lawfare is a practice with a long history and some new tactics. Lawfare – for our purposes – is the idea that law can be used as a weapon in whistleblower disputes. Problem whistleblowers are often targets. The general premise is simple: law is very complicated and has lots of loopholes that can be used to one's advantage. If, that is, one has the means to hire a specialist law firm that knows where the loopholes are, what is required to use them effectively and, especially, how to put pressure on a defendant. Specialist firms' services are not cheap. Lawfare tends to favour the party with the deepest pockets. In whistleblowing cases involving a challenge between an individual worker and an organization, one can imagine which side tends to hold the advantage. Lawfare and its tactics are, more or less, available for purchase. In addition to this, with its opaque language, its expensive-looking letterheads and all those courtroom wigs, law is a terrifying and foreign entity to many people. Legal threats spark fear in the uninitiated and a chilling vista for those without the experience or the means to defend themselves. The threat of falling foul of the law – of being criminalized – is a devastating form of reprisal that alters a whistleblower's very sense of self, and damages their reputation, sometimes irreparably.

But where did whistleblower lawfare come from? Laws defend the rights of people. They also defend the rights of companies. And increasingly, over the years, the laws defending the rights of companies to protect their information have become more sophisticated. The basic idea is that knowledge is property, and a company has a right to its property. Nowadays, however, knowledge is increasingly leaky. Thanks to the new technology, it can be shared quickly and discreetly. Even worse, knowledge often lives inside the heads of workers inside an organization: workers who tweet, post and email; and workers who get annoyed and ultimately leave, taking the knowledge with them. Protecting this 'in-the-head' knowledge from being disclosed is the primary aim of anti-whistleblowing lawfare.

Trade secret laws, contracts specifying NDAs and other methods set out the rules for workers. They specify what can and cannot be shared. They specify the terms for violation too, detailing what will happen if a worker discloses secret and confidential information. Legal institutions tend to take their role in this game seriously; there is a long precedent of courts deferring to companies and upholding their rights to protect the knowledge-property when disputes emerge.[25]

This is all part of the anxious clamour to defend boundary breaches, on the part of the defensive organization. When carefully cultivated cultures of silence are ruptured, the ensuing panic can lead defensive employers to cleave to the legal resources on offer. Imagine the scene in the executive meeting room. Whistleblowers are speaking up, the threat of outside exposure looms. 'Where do we stand? Call the lawyer.'

Erika's case and the Theranos story offer a primer to some of the more popular lawfare strategies available to today's defensively minded employer and its legal team. As outside scrutiny ramped up, the passive background threats of legal action via NDAs and famous law firms on retainer were no longer enough. It was time to get active. In a California parking lot one evening, Erika would encounter the lawfare solution in its most effective form.

A Threatening Letter

Some months after quitting Theranos, Erika was working in a biotech company, trying to move on. Elizabeth continued to appear on magazine covers and was raising more money from fresh investors. New firms were agreeing to partner up with Theranos and help bring its technology to even more patients. Those machines were still being used to test patient samples.

The hype was growing; the company's value had shot up: a \$9 billion estimation was published in *Forbes* magazine. Reporter

John Carreyrou approached Erika directly. He needed insiders to verify the story he was planning for the *Wall Street Journal*. She researched his background, saw that he was a healthcare fraud journalist and agreed to help him. 'At that point, I was desperate to get it out', she recalls. 'I was like, "this was one more door you can take to make this happen.... And he is going to keep you anonymous. Just get the truth out; this is one opportunity".' But she was afraid. Erika had already signed an NDA upon joining; another followed after her resignation, alongside a backpack search and a warning not to post about Theranos on social media.[26] Erika insisted her name be kept out of the stories John would write. Even though she had left the firm, she 'was really concerned about staying anonymous. Because we had signed these non-disclosure agreements and confidentiality agreements and Theranos made it very, very clear that if we violated them, they would come after us.'[27] Erika began calling former colleagues with whom she was still friendly. She did not tell them she was in touch with a journalist. Rather, she recalls, her aim was to sense-check what she had seen, and to find out if the machines were still being used; 'I just wanted to get their thoughts on it ... to get their perspective.' She had hoped, she reflects, to get more people to come forward, 'because I felt my case was so weak'. But people were afraid. Some friends tried to deter from her helping the reporter. But by now, she told me, her mind was set: 'My goal was to stop them processing patient samples. I was very one-track-mind on that.' The *Wall Street Journal* story went ahead.

It was evening time in the Biotech lab, and Erika's colleagues seemed nervous. There was a car in the parking lot with a man inside; he had been there all day. As she tells it: 'It scared my own co-workers.'[28]

I didn't even realize they were sitting outside of my workplace, but my co-workers had come up to me because I was working late. And they said, '[w]e are not letting you get out of this building alone. There has been this man that has been sitting in the parking lot all day and he is freaking us out'. So, they escorted me out.[29]

As she walked with colleagues out of the office and to her car, the man approached. He handed her a letter. Erika was confused: 'The letter was addressed to an address no one knew I was living at. It was a temporary home. So, it freaked me out, like: are they following me? How did they figure out where I lived? Because even my own mother had not known this address.' Erika had disclosed trade secrets, the letter read. She must submit to an 'interview' immediately.[30] The letter was signed David Boies.

Erika had spoken to John Carreyrou in confidence, but it seems Theranos had traced something in the article back to her. They knew. Whistleblower protection law might have ended up as something of a support for Erika. But back then, standing in the Palo Alto car park, she wasn't thinking that way. She was not even thinking of herself as a whistleblower: the phrase had not occurred to her yet. All she knew was that she was in her early twenties, with very little money in the bank and a threatening letter from the US's most famous litigator in her hand.

As a researcher, I struggle with this part of the story. But these kinds of incidents do occur. I remember the first time I began to hear about the extreme responses of employers, or, rather, I remember trying not to hear. I would be interviewing a whistleblower for a book or an article I was researching; all would be going well. Then they would tell me something that would make me pause, ask the question again, double-check that what I had heard was correct. Being followed by detectives gathering information to be used in a counter-campaign designed to smear a whistleblower, or receiving serious threats against oneself or one's family: it is like people are describing another world. But, while extreme retaliation for speaking up is relatively rare, it does happen.

The fact that ordinary people working in organizations can, when backed against a wall, become aggressive is not easy to take. David Morgan is a psychoanalyst who works with whistleblowers, often on a pro-bono basis for clients who have lost their livelihoods. He describes how he initially shared my disbelief. 'At first, when they talked about how paranoid they were, and how many people were after them, I saw them very much like ordinary patients and treated them accordingly', he says. 'But after two or three months, I became paranoid myself: I realised what they were talking about was real, not just a mental health issue – their lives were under threat.'[31] Mostly, employers do not react in extreme ways when a whistleblower comes forward. Sometimes, however, they do. On reflection, I struggle because both these things are true, and I was looking for a simpler answer.

But I still find it hard to hear these things. I feel a part of me resisting, wishing people wouldn't say them, because they are too much. These are the things that happen in films, when Russell Crowe's car catches fire after a chase by investigators paid for by Big Tobacco in *The Insider*, when Keira Knightley's husband gets deported in *Official Secrets*, because she has raised concerns about US interference in United Nations support for the war in Iraq. Russell and Keira, however, are playing Jeffrey Wigand and Katharine Gun, and these things did happen to those whistleblowers. My interviewees are not on screen but in front of me, speaking into my tape recorder about organizations I know. It is not easy to digest. For new graduate Erika it must have seemed farcical to be threatened by a top US litigator. But here it was. The law plays a central role in forceful whistleblower reprisal.[32]

Persistent Whistleblowers Attracting Lawfare

Lawfare is not cheap. It is only to be used in the most drastic of cases. And public whistleblowing, as we saw earlier, can represent an emergency for the defensive firm. From the perspective of senior Theranos people, Erika Cheung was questioning the very integrity of the famous black machine: that symbol of the company, the centre point of everything it did. She was besmirching the device that had inspired an ad campaign personally overseen by the director of the award-winning movie *The Thin Blue Line*: the man behind Apple's adverts. Erika's accounts of falsified test results and failing processes evoked visions of the chaotic inside of that mysterious black machine: the misfiring tips dripping patient blood into smoking gears, the flailing wire arm, the doors taped shut. The issues she raised went to the core of what Theranos does. They indicated that the CEO was involved or at least aware: that senior management knew about it for years and said nothing to investors, customers and partners. One can only imagine how weak the 'normal' organizational response when serious failures are publicized must have seemed. Press releases and scientific reports to defend the company would just not cut it. Even if they were to admit something wrong, the standard approach of apology, backtrack, let one person go because they messed up was unlikely to work with an accusation of this depth.

No senior executive, I imagine, wants to threaten and pursue a young, idealistic worker who is speaking up in the public interest: it is not a good look. It comes across as bullying, as defensive. If the organization is well known it will also make a great news story. Think of the heartfelt 'insider' interview: the recent graduate with her life ahead of her, persecuted by the big corporation. Think of the quote from the incensed customer who has had a false cancer diagnosis, the suffering patient who took the wrong drugs as a result, the outraged politician, all lining up to denounce the extreme reprisals against the honest young whistleblower. Public support for whistleblowers has arguably never been higher, bolstered by recent scandals that highlight how much we depend on them. Who would aggressively pursue someone like this? Only an employer backed into a corner, for whom the whistleblower has now become a serious problem. And lawfare presents a solution that looks legitimate.

New Tactics: SLAPPing Whistleblowers

It has always been the case that money talks when it comes to legal matters. Lately, however, things have been changing. In response to the new, tech-enabled leakiness of knowledge-property and the plethora of recent laws protecting whistleblowers, lawfare is evolving. The SLAPP suit is probably one of its most striking manifestations, and it is most effective.

Short for 'strategic lawsuit against public participation', a SLAPP is a lawsuit aimed at preventing people from talking about things the litigant does not want them talking about, whether these are journalists criticizing firms acting against the public interest or employees speaking out. The genius of the SLAPP is that its power lies in the threat of being sued. Nothing actually has to happen, beyond the dispatch of threatening letters and the proclamation of other intimidating noises. In order to file a SLAPP suit, you don't actually need to believe your case has a chance of winning in court. You just need to have the funds to cover the lawyers who will be sending those letters and doing the threatening on your behalf. And you need to be able to pay them for as long as it takes to have the desired effect of silencing your critic. So, it's a game of money and time. You win when you have drained the resources and the resilience of the other side, and they either quit or settle. In whistleblowing cases, SLAPPs are usually based on the protection of knowledge-property through invoking and enforcing tools such as NDAs and trade secret contracts.[33]

It was Erika's colleague Tyler Shultz who first spoke to John Carreyrou in 2015. He was frustrated that his concerns were being ignored. 'John had a lot of information and the right track record, so I felt like giving him more information would go towards correcting a lot of the problems that I saw while I was there, which would ultimately save some patients from getting incorrect medical results', he recalled. 'I guess I felt like John would actually ask the right questions.'[34] Senior executives, however, became aware that Tyler was talking to a journalist. His grandfather and board member of Theranos, George Shultz, was asked to intervene. As Tyler tells it:

My dad was on the phone with my grandfather. And then got off the phone and he asked me, 'Have you been speaking with a *Wall Street Journal* reporter?' And I said 'Yes.' And he said 'They know. You're totally fucked.' And he was more angry with me than I'd ever seen him in my life. He said, 'They know you did it. You know how aggressive they are, why would you do this? They're going to ruin your life,' basically.

Tyler phoned his grandfather.

And he said, 'Well, Theranos knows that you've been speaking to a *Wall Street Journal* reporter.' And I said, 'I don't know why they would think that.' And he said, 'Well, in any case, there's a one-page confidentiality agreement and if you sign it, it will make everything go away, so how about you meet with the Theranos lawyers tomorrow morning and you sign this agreement?'[35]

The financial threat was clear, even for a family of significant means.[36] As with Erika's letter in the car park, the threat was based on a single issue: stealing knowledge-property, via the breach of NDAs and the disclosing of trade secrets.

The notion that knowledge is commercially valuable and should be protected as a trade secret dates back to the industrial revolution. Companies have a right to protect their 'know-how': it is deemed part of an organization's assets.[37] The term 'trade secret' refers to quite specific kinds of intellectual property. At least, this used to be the case. Over the years the definition has expanded and now includes things ranging from commercial data and information on customers and suppliers to business plans, market research and even sales strategies.[38] The disclosure of trade secrets in the private sector is often punishable by law. In legal disputes, courts tend to look for evidence that the secret is something that gives a competitive advantage; they want to see proof that its disclosure to competitors would be a problem for the firm. Courts also want to see that these things are actual secrets: that is, their value is related to the fact that they are ordinarily hidden. All that said, secrecy laws increasingly include carve-outs that allow for disclosure of information if the public interest is at stake. The idea is that, if information about serious wrongdoing needs to come out, NDAs and trade secrets contracts should not be allowed to stop a worker speaking up. In reality, using these carve-outs in defence cases is rarely straightforward, often resulting in messy laws that cause confusion among lawyers and judges, not to mention ordinary workers trying to avail of their protections. But it was, overall, likely that the Theranos whistleblowers would stand a good chance of prevailing.[39]

SLAPP suits, like the ones threatened against Theranos workers, have been widely criticized for being a cynical use of the law of the land: an abuse of the legal system and a threat to democracy, and a threat that is growing exponentially. The cynicism of the practice is evident in the numbers alone: three out of every four of the cases that are heard in court are defeated – and many don't even make it there.[40] And the SLAPP suit is not just reserved for whistleblowing workers – it can be launched against anyone disclosing information that threatens a powerful party. These lawsuits are used to silence activists and journalists too.

SLAPPing Journalists

Theranos's legal team was not going to sit around, once they learned about Tyler and Erika's new friend at the *Wall Street Journal*. John Carreyrou was in his office at the newspaper one afternoon in June 2015, finalizing his first Theranos article, when a team of lawyers headed by David Boies came into the building. According to John, they stayed for over five hours. At the meeting, he recalls, 'their demeanour was very aggressive. They proceeded to tell us that I had misappropriated Theranos trade secrets and that I needed to destroy them or return them immediately . . . We made clear that that wasn't going to happen. We tried to keep things cordial, even though they were pretty aggressive.'[41]

Despite the aggressive stance, the Theranos lawyers refused to answer the most basic questions John had sent in advance, questions such as 'how many tests do you use proprietary Theranos technologies for, and are the tests reliable?'. Trade secrets made an appearance once again, this time in the lawyers' evasive responses. 'When I started asking those questions, they would not answer, invoking trade secrets.

And so, we kind of went around in circles for hours.' But John was encouraged by this, 'it was frustrating but . . . the stonewalling was also a sign that I was on the right track. And so, I came out of that five-hour meeting feeling like we were onto something big. And I was just going to redouble my efforts.' Before leaving the office, the legal team doubled down on the threats:

> David Boies lets us know during the meeting that we are going to be receiving a letter pretty soon, making explicit Theranos' legal stance. Sure enough we get that letter a couple of days later. It again reiterates that I have essentially stolen Theranos trade secrets and that I need to destroy them or return them. A 23-page-long letter comes a few days after that. . . . And at the end of that letter the threat is very explicit: that Theranos is going to sue if we proceed with the story.[42]

What more effective way to defend the boundary of an anxious employer than through a lengthy and costly legal action? With his editorial team and executives at the *Wall Street Journal* behind him, John was able to move forward and publish the story regardless. He had the financial support to fight the financial threats. John Carreyrou had the *Wall Street Journal*. Tyler Shultz had his family's wealth, should it be needed. What has an ordinary worker speaking out got?[43]

Signing Away Speech Rights

Of course, legal tools protecting knowledge are entirely appropriate in many cases and are even an essential part of doing business. But when they are used to stop workers from speaking out about serious wrongdoing, it does appear that we have a problem. The problem is currently getting worse. In the case of trade secrets, for example, definitions increasingly extend to cover new aspects of business practice. Such moves enable trade secrets laws to be misused for the purpose of enforcing inappropriate levels of secrecy, including around public-interest matters. The broader the category of document that can be labelled secret, the fewer the kinds of disclosures that can be deemed immune from prosecution.

And there is a larger issue to consider here. When a whistleblower is portrayed in public as having disclosed trade secrets, support is often harder to come by. People generally empathize with workers who feel compelled to speak up when they see wrongdoing. But there is also some sympathy with the company that needs secrets to be kept so that they can get on with business. And this affects how whistleblowers tagged as 'secret-revealers' are perceived.[44]

The response to all of this has been whistleblower advocates lobbying for changes to secrecy contracts to include stronger carve-outs for public-interest disclosures. Meanwhile, secrecy tools like these remain a critical aspect of many SLAPP suits being launched against workers like Erika and Tyler.

Fighting Back: Whistleblower versus Lawfare

With David Boies's letter in her hand, Erika had to figure out what to do. Here she was, with an aggressive, litigious company worth $9 billion, apparently intent on pursuing her, with one of the US's most famous attorneys on its side. What were her options? Erika needed support. Aware that her bank balance would barely cover six months' rent, let alone a legal battle, Erika began asking around. She was struggling to find the help she needed. 'I had no cash in the bank for lawyers at this point. So, there was a lot of calling of friends, badgering anyone who was in law school, who was a lawyer, who had a parent who was a lawyer. Trying to get all the free advice I could possibly get.' Finally, she found someone who could help, a healthcare fraud lawyer willing to give her twenty minutes of his time. Conscious she was now under observation by her former employers, she called him on a burner phone. The conversation helped allay the fears she was having.

Luckily . . . the one strange thing about this case was the fact that I was 22. . . . [I]f they did actually sue me, it would go into the public record. And how were they going to explain why they were suing a recent graduate who was 22, 23? Hence, why I just played the . . . just keep silent until you absolutely have to lawyer up and go to court.[45]

Advised by someone with knowledge of the law, Erika's first move was to gamble on Theranos's fear of a public scandal. She betted the firm would not follow through on its threats.

A Friend's Legal Advice

While the chances were low, Erika remained, potentially, wide open for litigation. She was being followed and threatened. Despite having tried her best to stay anonymous, Theranos executives and lawyers had traced the disclosure of information back to her. And Erika was simply not able to pay for formal legal representation to even begin considering how to make her way through the complexity of it all. Erika's newfound friend-of-friend with legal training understood the situation. 'It was that call', she told me later; 'he said, "You can whistleblow".' He could see the vulnerabilities of the case. He understood the risks involved. Her best chance for decent protection, he told her, was to formally notify Theranos's oversight bodies. But she needed to do it right. Erika would have to contact the correct regulating agency. She would have to focus on the firm's 'regulatory non-compliance', showing clearly that their practices violated the rules for proficiency testing. If she did this, and specifically if she showed legal violations, it would be very unlikely Theranos could enforce its NDA.

It was, Erika recalled, surprisingly simple to do, once she knew the correct steps. In September 2015, she got to work on her email to the Centers for Medicare and Medicaid Services. 'I've been nervous to send or even write this letter', she began. 'Theranos takes confidentiality and secrecy to an extreme level that has always made me scared to say anything.' Erika went on to carefully detail all her concerns about unethical, sloppy and – crucially – illegal laboratory protocols that had been used for Theranos's blood diagnostic technology.[46]

Finally, it seemed as though she had got everything right. She followed the rules and reported to the correct regulating agency. She knew how to frame her disclosure: it now showed clearly how the practices at Theranos violated testing regulations. Because she was now reporting legal violations, if the case came to court, it would be very unlikely Theranos could pursue her for speaking up. As a whistleblower in the US, she now had legal rights to protection from retaliation. But it was less clear that, if the information she gave the regulator could be shown to contain trade secrets, she would not face prosecution. While California had strong whistleblower protection laws on paper, they were tricky to navigate and weak in practice, with complicated carve-outs for secrecy clauses that left even professional lawyers flummoxed. The California Defend Trade Secrets Act had not yet been updated to today's standard.

Having never intended to go public, Erika was subpoenaed some months later to appear in a lawsuit filed by a hedge fund claiming Theranos defrauded them. The deposition was unsealed, which meant her name was out in public. 'I started to get emails from friends saying, "Hey, I saw you in the *SF Chronicle*, I saw you in Bloomberg." And I'm freaking out.' Being a public whistleblower, and an unwilling one at that, 'was a bit of a scary reality'.[47]

Erika was in a precarious situation. And she was up against an employer that did not like to let things slide. Her circumstances – as an ordinary worker doing the right thing – show up all the problems and complexities of whistleblowing protection law in practice.

When Erika was still working, she had 'reported internally', that is, she raised her concerns to her managers, including Sunny Balwani. This kind of whistleblowing is protected under law in many places. While, overall, US state whistleblower law is described as 'murky, piecemeal and disorganized', in California, where Erika was, whistleblower rights were considered to be relatively robust.[48] Employers were not allowed to have any policies in place that prohibited workers from making reports about information they believe to show legal violations. They had to protect those workers who speak up; punishing whistleblowers was prohibited.[49] Employers trying to get in the way of workers exercising their rights to speak up were liable for a fine of $5,000, or imprisonment for up to a year. Workers whose rights were impeded could take their claim to an administrative workplace dispute forum – designed on paper to be more informal than the courts: more accessible, quicker, less intimidating for a worker in dispute with their employer. The statistics are not good for whistleblowers in these settings. The chances of a worker winning were about one in every ten in the US at the time.[50] Nonetheless, on paper at least, whistleblower protection law offered a second, potential, defence for Erika, should she have needed it. But there were two problems.

First, the law is so complicated as to be effectively useless without advance legal assistance. Let's consider Erika's protections, back while she was working at Theranos. Whistleblower protection laws like the one governing her situation include tests to prove whether one qualifies as a 'protected discloser'. These tests are tightly prescribed and need careful interpretation.[51] California's anti-retaliation statute only protects workers reporting internally if they reasonably believe the activity they report is unlawful at the time they are raising concerns.[52] When Erika spoke up to Sunny and other managers, she was reporting many worrying things: unethical behaviour towards patients, for example, and dangerous testing practices for the blood machine.[53] But did she, at that time, report them as lawbreaking? It seems as though she didn't think about them in terms of the law – she thought about them in terms of the problems they were causing patients, employees and Theranos itself. It is therefore unlikely she would have been protected by the relevant law governing whistleblowers in the State, and she would have certainly been excluded from Federal and FCA provisions. She would have had no recourse to legally challenge Sunny's aggressive responses, or any negative behaviour coming her way for speaking up. So, as it turned out, even if Erika had been able to hire a lawyer after the fact, it is not likely that she would have been protected against retaliation for those early disclosures. And it is hardly realistic to expect a worker like her to consult a lawyer *before* even raising concerns in the lab to the boss.

Second, if Erika had tried to go it alone as a whistleblower, without a lawyer, she would have needed to know about her rights. The law in California at the time required employers to clearly post notices informing workers they would be protected if they spoke up about wrongdoing. And the law goes into plenty of detail about how exactly these notices should look. Companies were supposed to 'prominently display in lettering larger than size 14 point type a list of employees' rights and responsibilities under the whistleblower laws, including the telephone number of the whistleblower hotline'.[54] But many employers don't do this, or at least don't do it in a manner that is easily noticed by workers.[55] It is not clear exactly where at Theranos this size-fourteen-point-type advice was displayed, but in any case it appears Erika, Tyler and many other whistleblowers either were not aware of their rights or felt they had little bearing on their situations.

What about when Erika went outside the firm, disclosing to a media outlet? By speaking with the *Wall Street Journal*'s John Carreyrou, she was potentially liable for breaching her NDA. She might also be liable for exposing trade secrets, especially if it could be shown that the details she had given the journalist about the blood-testing technology – details she needed to give to back up her story – amounted to revealing private sources of competitive advantage. There may have been immunity from prosecution for disclosing trade secrets in whistleblowing cases, but it was not straightforward.[56]

In practice, where secrecy contracts are present, whistleblower protection claims are messy and the question of how to apply the law is often left up to the judge in each case. The provisions available are complex. Precedents are few, and there is a long history of courts presumptively enforcing contracts in favour of commercial interests. We must remember that these are laws designed to ensure businesses run smoothly. The underlying principle of this kind of law, as the contract lawyers tell us, is 'to provide predictability in the market economy and lower the transaction costs of business'.[57] And whistleblowing gets in the way of this desired predictability and cost-lowering. These cases do not result in jury trials: the worker and the employer appear before a judge only. The judge in these settings has a lot of power; because the law is so complex, the subjective judgement of the person in charge carries a lot of weight. Whistleblower lawyers sometimes talk of supportive, helpful judges who advise workers about their rights, in some cases explaining how to navigate the complicated legal aid process so they can pay for their own lawyer. But often judges are seen to favour the employer, perhaps because of bias, because of common backgrounds, college or familiarity through having encountered each other before in commercial court. But also because of poor training in whistleblower cases, where acute sensitivity is required, and a capacity to understand that a self-representing litigant is less likely to be well versed in complex legal terms.[58] Picture young Erika facing a judge with the US's most well-known attorney the only other person in the room. So, Erika's whistleblower rights were hardly bullet-proof. Under the law at the time, disclosures to the media were not automatically protected where trade secrets were involved and there were contractual obligations around non-disclosure.[59]

Messy Legal Protections

In the end, Erika had found a relatively secure, although still risky path to addressing the wrongdoing she had been so determined to stop. On paper, Erika is, more or less, a 'protected whistleblower'. But her story shows just how messy, ad-hoc and dangerous her journey was and still is. As a worker speaking out, she was left very vulnerable. She had reported in three different ways: to bosses, to a *WSJ* reporter and finally she went to the regulator. Mostly, the laws protecting her as a whistleblower did very little to help her. Erika and other whistleblowers at Theranos ended up in a mishmash of failed and partial attempts to stop what was happening, which went on for years. If there were processes for reporting, it appears they were completely unaware of them. If there were protections available, they didn't know. When we met, I asked Erika about her whistleblower status and what this had given her. 'I did not know I had any protections', she insisted. When she reported, she did not hear back from the regulator, nor was she told of the outcome. She was still being followed and threatened at the time, she reminded me, and there was little protection from this: 'I was in the dark. About everything.' Believing it was up to her to protect herself, she relocated overseas. 'I just said, "That was terrifying. I don't know what world we live in." And for me, protection was: I just moved out of the country.' Erika had some money saved and had always wanted to spend time in Asia. So, she went.

Reflecting on Erika's journey, it seems that the messy reality of being a worker speaking out, with all the different aspects that do not fit the model of perfect whistleblowing, makes for a dangerous scene. The law is not set up to deal with the complications of real life.

Whistleblowing advocates and experts know a lot about this mess. Other whistleblowers encounter similar complexities.[60] This is why the first message to potential whistleblowers is always the same: 'seek legal advice before speaking out'. This is why legal clinics and free advice lines are often the first whistleblower supports to be set up when a country decides to take whistleblowing protections seriously. But as is now clear, even this simple message is not as simple as it seems. There is often no 'before' when it comes to speaking out. The reality involves a lot of smaller enquiries, a lot of questioning emails, a lot of little 'speak-outs' during a time when one is simply asking questions. The idea of being a whistleblower is far from people's minds at this early stage. Usually, it is only after the retaliation has occurred, and more than once, that someone realizes they seem to have got themselves in trouble because of their disclosures. And often the word 'whistle-blower' is first heard from a lawyer or an advice helpline; people do not normally set out to 'become' whistleblowers. Recall that it was only after her second set of disclosure attempts – and the threatening letter in the car park – that Erika realized she might need protection. By then she had already violated secrecy contracts, and disclosed in ways that left her exposed.

'Legal advice', despite its importance, is no panacea. Just securing a lawyer does not necessarily mean you are home safe. Bad advice is a common problem for whistleblowers. Erika was lucky: her pro-bono legal adviser understood the situation and knew the law. Others at Theranos were not so lucky. Tyler Shultz did what many whistle-blowers do: he went to an attorney known to his family, who sent him to a specialist firm with expertise in business disputes. Soon he had racked up over $400,000 in legal fees yet remained 'completely unaware' that there were whistleblowing protection provisions available to him. Another anonymous whistleblower, given the pseudonym 'Alan Beam', had tried to get help from a boutique law firm but was rejected. He ended up paying a retainer to a lawyer who turned up in an internet search. This person had expertise in personal injury and medical malpractice law, but not in whistleblowing. Her advice? 'Alan' should go along with Theranos's lawyers' demands and delete evidence of wrongdoing by the firm from his computer. Alan ended up in a difficult situation. And beyond this, the reality is many people would struggle to pay a lawyer – even a useless one.

The fact remains: employers' intent on silencing whistleblowers will pay for ways to get around the law. While new laws and high-profile exposures do stand to change cultures, we will always have the kind of scene we are dealing with here: entrenched employers that create targets out of workers who try to disclose publicly. For sure, there are gradations; some laws are stronger than others, and harder to get around, as recent innovations in the EU and the US, among other countries, demonstrate.[61] Often the law does work. And the reality is that most employers are well meaning, have employees' interests at heart and do their best. That said, for those not in this camp, the opportunities to engage in lawfare are on the rise. Researchers and policymakers working hard to debate and design robust new legislation tend not to want to think much about how – in a pinch – powerful employers can simply ignore their responsibilities. What is the point of ever better laws when we don't seem to care at all about whether and how they are enforced, and the flaws in their implementation?

Lawfare Tactics: Stress and Fear

Whether lawfare is based on NDA or trade secrets violations, the available strategies are both nuanced and clever. The aim is intimidation. Isolating the discloser is a natural result of how SLAPPs work. Nine out of every ten SLAPP suits are brought against an individual rather than the organization to which they belong. Journalist John Carreyrou described the text of the twenty-three-page letter his newspaper received as they planned to go public on Theranos: 'That letter is essentially a searing indictment of me as a journalist and of my methods as a journalist. It's an attempt to really get the *Journal* to disavow me.'[62] By targeting the disclosers rather than their employers, the aim is clear: to maximize stress and ensure isolation.

Even with his newspaper's support, John's work on Theranos was not without personal consequences. He learned about a chant that emerged at Theranos, with employees yelling, 'Fuck you, Carreyrou' at a staff meeting held after his articles criticizing their company appeared. John got wind of a video game, space-invaders-style, which featured him as the target of the player's bullets:

The invader in this version of the game is me ... And the machine gun at the bottom of the screen is Theranos' mini-lab blood testing device. And the bullets that it's shooting are its little nanotainer vials. You know, it's another one of the crazy twists in this crazy story that has essentially consumed the past three and a half years of my life.

Individual whistleblowers can find their personal support networks wither in the face of expensive legal threats. Tyler Shultz and his family had paid out almost half a million dollars in legal fees by 2016, likely a lot more since. This brings stress and tension. With family means and no dependants, Tyler Shultz was able to pay for the help needed to continue his struggle, and he was able to refuse the settlement Theranos offered in exchange for his silence.[63] Other Theranos whistleblowers were unable to sustain the financial burden of legal fees. Alan Beam, described by Carreyrou as 'middle class and with a family to support', ultimately settled with the firm rather than fight the case for breaching his NDA.

In whistleblowing cases, I have seen couples brought closer together, facing a common challenge. Relationship break-ups, however, are just as common, if not more so, for whistleblowers.[64] The problem whistle-blower has now been placed in the position of being a problem for their significant others too. The temptation to abandon one's principles is strong.

Other aspects of SLAPP strategies include choosing criminal rather than civil cases: these tend to drag out for longer, thus enabling the maximum exploitation of the money–time advantage. Time can be used as a tactic in other ways too, for example to heighten the feeling of fear evoked by the law. The CEO of Transparency International Ireland, John Devitt, described to me what it is like to receive the letter from the lawyer, 'usually Friday evening, through the letterbox. Often on a bank holiday, so you are left to stew'. In the case of Erika's former director at Theranos, Avie Tevanian, the timing was hardly accidental. Avie had been a high-profile prize when he left his role as the head of software engineering at Apple in 2006, invested $1.5 million in Theranos and joined its board. He repeatedly challenged Elizabeth Holmes' decisions as CEO and was eventually asked to resign, which he did. But Avie refused to sign an NDA. Shortly after, he received an email. It said that, if he did not sign, then he would be sued, because by speaking out about Theranos he was damaging the firm's reputation. The email arrived at 11 pm on Christmas Eve, just in time for the family holidays.

We saw how sometimes public-interest disclosures can negate NDAs and offer protection against prosecutions for disclosing secrets. But the point is many workers will not even bother testing this. Signing contracts has a chilling effect, and notice-posting only goes so far to alleviate this chill, regardless of the font size used. Here is what people know: I signed a secrecy agreement, and it said I would be liable for prosecution if I break it. And for any employee digging a little deeper, they find information about potential loopholes that might – only might – be taken into account by a judge feeling sympathetic on the day. None of this instils comfort. Even if it is legally possible to break one's NDA, why risk it? The upshot is a choice between leaving or defaulting to silence, and, ultimately, complicity in whatever it is that you are not speaking up about.

This 'chill effect' is a phrase you hear over and over again at the many events and webinars that people hold to draw attention to lawfare. It reflects the most insidious aspect of this kind of practice: that the mere spectre of lawfare is enough to scare people into silence. When we see others held up for years in lengthy and expensive legal battles, when we watch the impact this has on the whistleblower – the stress written on their faces, the families borrowing money to pay fees, the need to find a different school for the kids when moving house to a cheaper district – the message is loud and clear. The stories of whistleblowers who bear the brunt of lawfare tactics are read by colleagues as a single clear message: say nothing, because whistleblowing is painful and dangerous and should be avoided at all costs.[65]

The strategies described here are the tactics of people whose game is more than just the law. Taken together, it is not difficult to see why 'lawfare' is the term that has emerged to describe such uses of our legal systems. I am not sure things are improving. Ever more weight is given to the legal perspective, but from the perspective of attacking, rather than facilitating or protecting. We are seeing employers across the world becoming more dependent on the legal side in issues of compliance; lawyers are called in at ever earlier stages in disputes of all kinds.

It is not difficult to see this rush to the law as a social defence on behalf of those senior managers who do it. Lawfare is the externalization of fears and anxieties in action. We recall that social defences are collective arrangements engaged by organization members to protect them against the disturbing emotions to which perceived outsider threats – and the nature of their own work – give rise. In times of extreme threat, we can be drawn to tactics that help us suppress the upsetting reality of the situation, so we may gain a sense of safety, even if this is based in fantasy and denial of a real-life mess.[66] The law in such cases is more than just the law: it is a powerful shield against having to realize the deep-seated impossibilities in the work we are doing. This extends far beyond Theranos of course; shared social defences spread across institutional and organizational settings,[67] something we are seeing today in the rush to lawfare across the globe.

And when the lawyers are called in, things can get contentious. The legal voice becomes more prominent in how companies are run. Theranos did not just depend on David Boies's firm for legal advice, he had a seat on the board. Employers are increasingly tending to pursue through litigation when they find themselves entrenched instead of seeking out other methods.[68] They get into the business of silencing. And there is a lot of ammunition at their disposal.

Reprisals Creating 'Criminal' Subjects

In Chapter 1, we saw how anxious and defensive organizations can actively try to defend the boundary between inside and outside through silencing techniques. These involve creating certain kinds of subjects: workers speaking out are considered illicit and unacceptable, and thus they are represented as legitimate targets for punishment. At Theranos, we see how law was similarly used to create subject positions for workers. This time, speaking out was not just unacceptable: it was illegal. The whistleblower would not just be an 'invalid, abject' worker, but an all-out criminal – with all the frightening consequences this brings for oneself and one's dependants.

And all this power, working through the creation of new kinds of subjects, functioned passively, behind the scenes. Just enough information about the real consequences of transgressing the rules around knowledge-property had been shared with staff. The law at Theranos operated as a kind of panopticon – an institutional structure that controls people's behaviours simply by letting them know it is watching, and letting them know that punishment will be harsh. This knowledge can radically change people's behaviour, because it changes the range of subject positions available to them: it changes how workers see their potential selves. Disclosure ceases to be any kind of option, if survival is a priority. Senior management at Theranos clung to the law. It was powerful in upholding a culture of fear, through creating new, criminal, subject positions. The law was a powerful, imagined buffer against chaos.

During her trial, prosecutors asked Elizabeth Holmes how she felt about how Erika, then twenty-two, had been treated. As well as the threat letters, it turned out that Theranos had hired investigators to conduct surveillance outside her home. Elizabeth acknowledged that every disclosure made by Erika had been correct. 'I sure as hell wish we treated her differently and listened to her', Holmes said. The prosecutor pushed her further: 'You know today that Ms. Cheung was right, isn't that fair?' 'Yes', Holmes replied.

The *New York Times* called Erika Cheung's testimony, alongside that of other whistleblowers, pivotal in the decision to convict Elizabeth Holmes of four counts of fraud. The appearances of the Theranos whistleblowers, Erika, Tyler and countless others, were the star moments of an extraordinary trial. What made these accounts so powerful, it seemed, was the picture they painted of a company where well-intended attempts to question things were so aggressively suppressed. Alongside all the evidence of faulty machines, lies to investors and patients duped, it was the way these workers were treated, the way these scientists, these young graduates, had been shut down with such force, that made a big difference. The whistleblowers were proof that a culture of secrecy and conformity was deliberately enforced from early on, with serious consequences for those who spoke up.

Technically, as whistleblower cases go, Erika's was just about as effective as you can get. Within days after her disclosure to CMS, their teams descended on Theranos. The laboratories were closed, charges were levied and federal indictments made against Elizabeth Holmes and Sunny Balwani. Yet Erika had ended up in danger – both legally threatened but also professionally vulnerable because her name was out there, exposed as a whistleblower.

Organizational attacks on whistleblowers operate through prefiguring potential disclosers as criminals. The law and lawfare enhances the arsenal for the anxious, defensive employer, making life almost impossible for an exposed whistleblower. At the same time, we saw another side to this: Erika had found a connection with a colleague Tyler who shared her concerns and her determination, showing she was not alone. And she gained access to an attorney even she could afford, with expertise that could help her protect herself. The relationships Erika formed had helped this young, broke worker navigate what was among the most precarious situations a whistleblower could encounter. Can such relationships between colleagues work on a bigger scale in whistleblowing claims?

Notes

1. Cases of securities fraud of this scale are rare, not least when accused parties have already settled with the SEC prior to being indicted, as did Holmes.
2. Receipts for over $150,000 were produced, indicating that private investigator firms had been hired to intimidate other whistleblowers too, although this was denied by Elizabeth Holmes.
3. Tugend (2019).
4. Cheung & O'Dea (2019).
5. Dunn et al. (2019).
6. Dunn et al. (2019).
7. Dunn et al. (2019).
8. Dunn et al. (2019).
9. Dunn et al. (2019).
10. Dunn et al. (2019).
11. Dunn et al. (2019).
12. Somerville (2021).
13. Ioannidis would in early 2015 publish an article in the *Journal of American Medicine Association*. If Theranos's breakthrough is so

radical and important, he asked, why on earth is the technology not subject to peer review in the normal way?

14. Rogal (2021).
15. Dunn et al. (2019).
16. Gabriel (1999).
17. Gabriel (1999, p. 227).
18. Transparency International Ireland (2017).
19. Dunn et al. (2019).
20. Dunn et al. (2019).
21. Rogal (2021, p. 1687).
22. In the UK, the organization Public Concern at Work (now called Protect) estimates that over 75 percent of claims brought under the PIDA legislation are settled before they are heard in an Employment Tribunal. It is difficult to assess the prevalence of settlements because some are informal and involve cases withdrawn without details given.
23. Best practice whistleblower protection law includes a ban on such 'gag orders' resulting from any 'rules, policies or nondisclosure agreements that would otherwise override rights in the whistleblower law and impose prior restraint on speech', according to the International Bar Association (IBA, 2021), with some US laws (SOX, WPA), Ireland's PDA 2014 and the 2019 EU Whistleblower Directive examples of this. Some employers deal with this by requiring an employee to confirm in writing that they are not aware of circumstances that would give rise to a protected disclosure at the time of signing an NDA, effectively trying to bind the employee to their own words. In other cases, NDAs are found within the text of written work policies that employees are told are binding (Rogal, 2021, p. 1686).
24. Carreyrou (2018).
25. Rogal (2021, pp. 1693, 1671).
26. Rogal (2021, p. 1668).
27. Cheung & O'Dea (2019).
28. Dunn et al. (2019).
29. Cheung & O'Dea (2019).
30. Rogal (2021, p. 1668).
31. Smith (2014a).
32. Ouriemmi (2023).
33. Rogal (2021, p. 1693).
34. Dunn et al. (2019).
35. Dunn et al. (2019).
36. At that meeting, Tyler was threatened to sign another NDA on pain of appearing in court with two days' notice. The meeting took place at his grandfather's house, where a team of Theranos lawyers were waiting.

37. Rogal (2021, pp. 1679–1681), Van Portfliet & Kenny (2018).
38. The issue has parallels with other sectors in which we are seeing increases in the kinds of information that are deemed secret. At its most extreme, national security organizations around the world are classifying more and more documents (Immerman, 2020). When I met John Kiriakou, NSA torture waterboarding whistleblower, he joked, 'My wife and I would be emailing where to meet for lunch: those things are classified.' The widespread classification of all kinds of benign information grows. And disclosure of classified information is forbidden and punished far more strongly in government and national security organizations than of non-classified.
39. Rogal (2021).
40. ICNL (2020). See also Appendix 2 for discussion of changes in the law that introduce penalties for bringing 'vexatious proceedings', including SLAPP suits against whistleblowers.
41. Dunn et al. (2019).
42. Dunn et al. (2019).
43. As another example, a few years earlier when US talk-show host John Oliver received a SLAPP suit for comments made about Bob Murray, the then CEO of Murray Energy, he too was able to fight the frivolous lawsuit. HBO stepped in to pay the cost of fighting the challenge and the subsequent appeal. The TV network had the resources to do this, but it took years to resolve. After it was all over, Oliver, shaken, used his late-night platform to explain to the public the 'scourge of SLAPPs'. People are scared of criticizing Murray, he pointed out, 'because even if they are baseless, his lawsuits can do major damage'. He went on to detail how the suit cost more than $200,000 in legal fees, 'even though our insurance covered part of it, and we were lucky that HBO stood by us . . . [t]his lawsuit was infuriating, took up a lot of time and resources, and resulted in a tripling of our libel insurance premiums. Despite the fact that, to reiterate: we fucking won this case!' It seemed to him, he explained, that Murray's goal was never to win, it was to exhaust the other side, financially and emotionally. 'The whole point is to put the defendant through a difficult, painful experience and even if cases fail in lower court, as they often do, the plaintiffs can find ways to extend them through intensive discovery requests, depositions and appeals that drain the defendants' time and resources.' It is important to note that HBO was not the target of the Murray SLAPP – it was served to John Oliver.
44. Ceva & Bocchiola (2019), Tsahuridu & Vandekerckhove (2008), Vandekerckhove & Tsahuridu (2010).
45. Cheung & O'Dea (2019).

46. Rogal (2021, p. 1666).
47. Tugend (2019).
48. Cherry (2004).
49. Rogal (2021, p. 1673).
50. Whistleblowers prevail in about one in five cases worldwide (IBA, 2021).
51. Tyler Shultz and Erika Cheung were unusual in that they researched the rules around proficiency testing but even that did not fully protect them, as shown here.
52. Note that other jurisdictions have more inclusive criteria for whistleblowing protection. In Ireland and the UK, for example, workers must simply hold a 'reasonable belief' that wrongdoing is occurring. This means that, even if a worker is mistaken, they are protected as long as they have an honest belief that is objectively reasonable. No detailed knowledge of the law is required.
53. Rogal (2021).
54. Rogal (2021, p. 1674).
55. Rogal (2021, p. 1685).
56. Today, whistleblower and free speech protection laws override secrecy agreements in court. When the disclosures in question involve public-interest information, for example genuine whistleblowing, NDA contracts are not enforceable. Laws tend to state that trade secrets can justifiably be disclosed in certain cases: public-interest whistleblowers are protected from both civil and criminal liability. The point is that organizations are not allowed to ask staff to sign away their free speech rights in cases of serious wrongdoing. And if they do this anyway, courts are there to call it out. But in practice it is not so straightforward, as detailed here.
57. Rogal (2021, p. 1689).
58. Devine (2015), Lewis (2008). For a thorough discussion with reference to whistleblower cases, see also Mueller's *Crisis of Conscience* (2019), Chapter 6.
59. This was true for both California law and Federal law. See Rogal (2021, pp. 1694, 1698).
60. Rogal (2021, pp. 1694–1695).
61. See Appendix 2 for details.
62. Dunn et al. (2019).
63. Rogal (2021, p. 1693).
64. K. Jean Lennane's (1993) study of Australian whistleblowers reported negative impacts on the partnerships of more than half her respondents, with approximately one in four breaking up as a result.

65. The deployment of whistleblower reprisals as serious warnings to other workers has been studied in a variety of sectors to date (Alford, 2001, Kenny, 2018, Rothschild & Miethe, 1999).
66. Freud (1936).
67. Bain (1998), Petriglieri & Petriglieri (2020).
68. See Gold (2013) for discussion.

3 | Whistleblowing Subcultures at Amazon

Colleagues in the Break Room

Waiting for the video call to connect, I did not know what to expect. When Transparency International Ireland's Integrity at Work team asked me to host a speaker at the November 2020 Annual conference, I had only one guest speaker in mind. If he would agree to it. I first read about Christian Smalls in the *Financial Times* just six months earlier, right in the middle of the COVID-19 outbreak.

Christian worked in Amazon's largest fulfilment centre of its kind in North America, supervising over sixty staff at the JFK8 facility in Staten Island, New York. Along with colleagues, he began speaking out about life and death dangers they were facing. Within a few days his case had been taken up by high-profile politicians, journalists and activists. His publicized disclosures had attracted Amazon colleagues from across the US to join him, people he had never met in person. Within the year this 'Amazon whistleblower', as the press called Christian, would found the first worker union at Amazon. And all this amid a targeted, personalized smear campaign aimed at silencing him.

Christian appeared on my laptop screen wearing casual sports clothes, a bandanna headscarf. 'Chris does not look like a traditional union leader', the BBC reported in their piece about one of the most influential industrial relations leaders of recent times. 'He does dress urban', his mother had told the programme. 'Some people want clean-cut and a tie, but that is not who Chris is.'[1] I was, by this time, immersed in the literature on organizational power and domination in whistleblowing cases: the unequal playing fields between worker and employer when disclosures go public and things turn ugly. I had a lot of questions.

A Dangerous New Virus

Christian Smalls told me about first joining Amazon in 2015, working in warehouses in New Jersey and Connecticut before transferring to Staten Island in 2018.[2] He had been, he said, a dedicated Amazon worker prior to the events of March 2020. Despite lengthy commutes, unsocial hours and frustrated hopes of advancement, he stayed with the firm.[3] An experienced supervisor of more than sixty colleagues at JFK8, Christian was never promoted beyond the role of 'hourly associate' to a more formal management position. I asked him about this. He said he tended to stand up for his supervisees when disputes arose with the employer, which did not help his cause. He had, for example, been dismissed following a dispute in its Connecticut facility but later reinstated.[4] And, he noted, Amazon had a preference for white managers over black and other ethnicities.[5]

Amazon's own research speaks to this racial stratification. The firm's 2018 report calculated that seven out of ten people working as 'labourers and helpers', including warehouse workers, were people of colour, while, conversely, seven out of every ten top executives and senior-level employees were white.[6] In his accounts of his time in JFK8, Christian describes his colleagues as an 'extended family'.[7] As they worked together in long shifts of over twelve hours, close relationships formed.

When COVID-19 hit the US, growth in demand for Amazon products shot up. Pressure on its warehouses to fulfil the orders increased accordingly. Things were changing fast. New York was battling its first wave of the pandemic; warehouse workers had worries at home. But things were stressful at work too, and the company was not providing adequate personal protective equipment to help stop the spread of the virus in shared spaces. And social distancing did not seem to be a priority. This was despite multiple cases – both confirmed and suspected – emerging every day. Even when a worker tested positive, the building was not being cleaned. Office-based executives in the firm had been sent off to work from home as soon as things got bad, but conditions in the warehouse were worrying. And all this a full year before any vaccine was to arrive on the scene.

When we spoke, Christian told me about how, in the early weeks, workers were worried health guidelines were being ignored: 'It was just the fact that we were in the dark. We didn't know what the hell we was doing or what was going on with the virus. Because we're watching it on the news and the company is doing something else.' Management, he recalled, were being more or less silent on the issue: 'So it was something "off" in there, something off in the building with managers, with the communication. And I'm like, "what the hell is going on here?"' Meanwhile, colleagues were feeling under pressure to come into work. Workers with a positive COVID-19 test were not allowed to take paid time off. A doctor's note was needed, and this took a long time. Workers with COVID-19 could stay home – unpaid – for as long as they wished, he recalled, 'but what about the bills?' Christian could see the effects all this was having on colleagues: We're in the break room sitting shoulder-to-shoulder. Derrick can tell you, we were sitting there joking: We're all going to die because we're sitting shoulder-to-shoulder. And we're watching CNN and they're telling us we need to be six feet apart with masks.'[8]

Christian's accounts frequently refer to his friendship with his JFK8 colleague and fellow organizer, Derrick Palmer. Derrick also related the fear and disquiet among workers within the facility: 'I was scared. The energy in the building was just like, everyone was quiet, and no one knew what the next steps were. We didn't know what Amazon's plans were. So that was the energy that was going on at that time.'[9]

Christian first tried to raise his concerns within the organization itself, approaching HR:

As a supervisor, I felt it was my responsibility to say something. So, I went directly to HR just by myself. Asking questions. Trying to do the right thing but keep it in-house, saying 'hey, look, what are we doing as far as COVID? We're coming to work. What are we going to do for people that have children at home – schools are closing, senior citizens at home,' et cetera?

Christian recalled a dismissive reaction. 'Their response was, "oh, we're following the CDC guidelines. You have nothing to worry about. If you want to leave, you can leave"'. For Christian, this solution was not very helpful, '[b]ecause they were offering us – they were telling us that we can go home, and no time would be deducted. "You can go home if you don't want to [work], but you're not being paid."'[10]

Escalating Concerns as a Collective

Foiled in these efforts, the situation deteriorated when it emerged that Christian and his colleagues had potentially been exposed to COVID-19 by a visibly sick worker who was in the centre despite testing positive.[11]

'So, I had to take further action. You know I took further action by taking some time off to put together some emails.' Christian recalls using the time to write to politicians, medical authorities and media outlets in the New York area, to draw attention to the situation faced by workers. He was reaching out to potential helpers, powerful allies, asking for support.

I sent emails out to the health department of New York, the CDC department, the governor – Governor Cuomo's office, some senators, even Mayor DeBlasio of New York, I even tried to contact some media outlets of New York area. Just to try to get some attention drawn to the company about what was going on because I felt like, you know, something's not right here.[12]

New York had, by now, become the epicentre of the US COVID-19 outbreak, and Christian's emails went unanswered. Together with Derrick, they decided to escalate their efforts to raise the alarm within the organization: 'So, the next day I came back to work, and Derrick came with me. We went straight into the break room at 7 o'clock, 7:15. And at the top of our lungs, we're yelling around, "Yo, we need to do something", in the break room, telling the workers like, "somebody's been here positive".' They found many others who felt the same sense of immediate danger. 'And now, workers are panicking like, "Oh, my god. Yeah, I've seen such and such sick. Oh, I don't feel good". Even somebody was like, "Yo, I'm sick right now". We had one woman that was like, "I'm sick. Stay away from me". That's what she said, like, "stay away from me".'[13]

For four days, Christian and colleagues stationed themselves in the cafeteria, 'off the clock, on our own free will, telling every employee the truth, that you are possibly working next to somebody that tested positive (for COVID-19). And (that) we need to voice our concerns'.[14] Christian and Derrick began organizing workers to demand answers: 'Every morning around 9 o'clock, we interrupted the general manager's meetings. We walked groups of associates into the main office, and we voiced our concerns.' But these efforts came to nothing.

Christian, Derrick and a group of co-workers petitioned the general manager for a two-week closure and cleaning of the facility in line with the medical guidelines at the time. But the next day, 28 March, Christian – alone – was sent home on quarantine. He was only the third person to be quarantined in a workforce of more than 5,000 at JFK8.[15] And while quarantine was meant to occur within two weeks of exposure to the virus, Christian was being sent home after three, after the threat had passed. There seemed something wrong with the order to stay home.

Around this time, the colleagues learned of news that led them to escalate things even more. Amazon warehouse staff across the country in Kentucky, in similar circumstances, had actually walked out. The state's governor had been prompted to close that facility: 'We saw Kentucky did a walkout; "why aren't we doing that?"'[16]

Reflecting on this period, Christian describes the excitement generated among those conspiring to defy the employer. 'We had been organizing all weekend. I started a group chat with the workers that I was organizing in the break room with. And they were passing out the signs in the bathrooms.' The shared energy so fuelled by fear just a few days earlier was being galvanized into something else. 'We kind of had like a secret "Mission Impossible" thing going on. We wrote secret notes to each other. We talked on social media and private messages, and everybody knew that at 12:30 to walk out of the building at lunchtime.'[17]

The official channels for reporting concerns, it would seem, had failed. New options needed to be found. When whistleblowers end up escalating to people outside the organization, it is generally because of a negative response – or the lack of response – they received when they disclosed inside.[18] External whistleblowing is typically a last resort: a full nine out of every ten 'whistleblowing' workers will choose to speak up first to a manager or colleague, or use a speak-up policy, only going outside after these attempts prove useless. Sometimes it just cannot be avoided: in emergency situations where waiting is not an option. Workers then start searching for a sufficiently independent audience to take their disclosure seriously and do something about it.[19] With Christian and his colleagues, we see a life-or-death situation in which escalation seems to be the only option. They made their plans, to walk out on 30 March 2020.

This was more than one person acting alone. The escalation impulse was driven by a palpable sense of fear spreading between colleagues. While Christian and Derrick appeared as leaders, this was not their singular cause. The generalized sense of injustice shared between workers and prompting this action came from a collective distress for people's bodily safety that flowed from one colleague to another as they sat, as Christian described, 'shoulder-to-shoulder'. They were forced into this situation. It was necessary to earn money and support their families, and, with no paid leave for positive tests, the options were few. It was this shared dread of an impossible situation that sparked them to speak up more – not alone – but together: approaching the managers' meeting, through a petition and now, it would seem, staging their protest via their very bodies, removing themselves from the physical space in which they were needed to work.

Public Whistleblowing and the Media

The walkout was happening. But without any media attention, it was unlikely to have any impact at all. Christian was candid about his inexperience in this area. He had written to some newspapers, but beyond this, 'I did not know what the hell I was doing. I was not an activist or organizer.' So, he improvised. 'I told the media like, "yes, we are going to have a protest, a walk out on Monday March 30th about what's going on: the health and safety concerns" … I sent out emails to all the media that I can think of.' He recalled fear of the potential for retaliation if the company learned he had tried to involve the media: 'And when they showed up, I was definitely heart-pounding, nervous, because I'd never done anything like this before. And I knew that it was going to be some type of repercussions, but I didn't know what it would be.'[20]

Listening to Christian describe his tactics, despite his nerves and inexperience, it does appear he has a knack for this kind of work. He intuited the media would need some kind of spectacle, something newsworthy to report.

I knew the media wasn't going to come if I would have said five people [would be there]. … 'Two hundred,' I said. 'About to be 200 people outside.' And I knew that it wasn't going to be. But I knew I checked the weather. I played chess. I checked the weather. I was like, 'Yo, it's going to be 60 degrees': I know, as an Amazon worker myself … I'd be outside eating lunch. So, I said, 'the perception is everything'.[21]

Christian told me how, in the end, around sixty people joined the walkout. But it appeared a larger crowd because of the sunny day.

I remember the newspaper coverage. It had all been about the bus stop: meeting at the bus stop, passing out food at the bus stop.

I wondered why the bus stop was such an attractive spot. Well, he told me, it's how lots of people get to work so it is a good place for organizers to meet workers. But more than this, the bus stop is public property; it is owned by the City. It is a few square feet of public ground in the vast sea of private Amazon-owned concrete paving, car parking and warehousing. The bus stop is a place where protesters cannot be called up for trespassing.

Major media outlets sent reporters to cover the scene of the walkout, with CNN and CNBC broadcasting interviews with Christian in advance. Supportive messages started to come in from people watching reports. Next, we learned that, just two hours after the walkout, Christian was dismissed by phone call and his colleague Derrick Palmer was given a formal warning. Christian hung up on management in anger before they could give a full explanation of his dismissal, he later recalled.[22] That same evening, New York Attorney General Letitia James was responding, condemning Amazon's firing of Christian 'as immoral and inhumane ... It is disgraceful that Amazon would terminate an employee who bravely stood up to protect himself and his colleagues.'[23] Coverage tended to juxtapose walkout leader Christian, a mere warehouse worker, with Amazon owner and 'world's richest man' Jeff Bezos. Christian was the brave defender. And newspaper articles cited him word-for-word, as he described the alarm inside JFK8: "'We have plenty of workers that haven't been to work for the entire month of March because they're scared for their lives ...'", he told readers of Common Dreams, "We have people that have Lupus, we have people that have asthma, we have people that have infants at home, that have people that's pregnant".'[24]

Within three days of the walkout, an army of supporters lined up behind the Attorney General, all demanding formal investigations into Chris's dismissal. He was a whistleblower. He should not have been fired. Congresswoman Alexandria Ocasio-Cortez and Senator Bernie Sanders publicly condemned the decision, along with the Mayor of New York. An open letter was directed at Jeff Bezos and his executives, signed by the leaders of seven nationwide unions and forty elected officials from New York State.[25]

Public declarations of solidarity for whistleblowers are relatively unusual. But here we had even distant observers lending support. It seemed as though the resistant, passionate energy so evident in the warehouse workers' break room, and in the WhatsApp messages between angry colleagues, was spreading. It had begun as fear but was becoming something else. The infectious force was prompting others to act, to speak and to advocate. And the media spotlight enhanced the momentum.

But what of Amazon? As we have seen, large firms do not like to lose control, especially when so much is at stake. And at Amazon, there was plenty at stake. The company enjoyed a unique advantage during the pandemic. A significant proportion of the US population had been ordered to stay at home. Children needed schooling, people wanted to work out, set up home offices, style their hair. Demand for all the things quarantining people need spiked. Profits at Amazon would reach a staggering $26 billion during the year.[26] Desperate for staff to meet demand, a hiring drive saw the company offer $2 more per hour to attract workers. Newspaper coverage had styled Amazon as something of a hero-company during the lockdown. The firm so many people depended on.

And suddenly, we learned, Amazon was risking workers' lives. And forcefully punishing those who protested. So far, Christian had experienced the playbook of whistleblower reprisals. He had been warned to be quiet. He had been placed on trumped-up sick leave and, when he would not give up, he was fired. But here he was. Still talking. And making powerful allies. Whistleblowers who disclose in public tend to face much harsher reprisals than those who keep their protest inside the organization.[27] We can only imagine what might happen to whistleblowers who start phoning up the *New York Times*, are quoted in the UK *Guardian* and whose faces appear on the TV screen each evening after work. And who, despite warnings, won't stop talking.

Amazon Reprisals and Backlash

In the weeks after the walkout, powerful people continued to support the workers – their voices heard on mainstream media but also on social media platforms. Senior Amazon executives were called on to respond to the emerging scandal of a whistleblower fired for speaking out about imminent threats to colleagues' lives. The official reason given to the media was that he had been dismissed for violating Amazon's two-week quarantine policy: he had returned to work too early.[28]

Some executives publicly denigrated the whistleblower at the heart of the scandal. Senator Bernie Sanders had been posting on Twitter supporting Christian. Senior Vice President of Worldwide Operations and Customer Service, Dave Clark, responded in kind. 'You have been misinformed again Sen. Sanders', he tweeted. 'Mr. Smalls purposely violated social distancing rules multiple times and on 3/28 was put on Paid 14-days of quarantine due to COVID exposure. 3/30 he returned to the site. Knowingly putting our team at risk is unacceptable.'[29] Just one hour later, another Amazon Senior Vice President was on the platform. Former White House Press Secretary Jay Carney's tweet was almost identical in phrasing '@SenSanders, I'm confused. Thought you wanted us to protect our workers? Mr. Smalls purposely violated social distancing rules, repeatedly, & was put on Paid 14-day quarantine for COVID exposure. 3/30 he returned to the site. Knowingly putting our team at risk is unacceptable.'[30] The use of cut-and-paste reflected that there was a clear party line being followed by some members of the Amazon senior team.

Two days later, on 2 April, we learned a little more. A leaked memo with notes authored by Amazon General Counsel David Zapolsky emerged. The notes came from a meeting of senior executives, including CEO Jeff Bezos, to discuss Amazon's communication strategy responding to the JFK8 walkout. The memo described the planned choreography of responses that had been discussed and agreed. This is typical of course. Employers must respond quickly to crises, especially those appearing in the media. But something was unusual in this one.

The notes pointed to the deliberate discrediting of Christian Smalls, as a central pillar of the planned response: 'We should spend the first part of our response strongly laying out the case for why the organizer's conduct was immoral, unacceptable, and arguably illegal, in detail, and only then follow with our usual talking points about worker safety.'[31] The memo went on to instruct Amazon's communications teams to place Christian at the centre of responses issued to the media. 'Make him [Christian] the most interesting part of the story. And if possible, make him the face of the entire union/organizing movement.' The 'movement' was a wider unionizing effort among Amazon workers at JFK8 who had been trying to organize since 2018 but was resisted by the company.

As well as linking Christian to this failed historical effort, the memo went on to describe him in the following terms: 'He's not smart, or articulate, and to the extent the press wants to focus on us versus him, we will be in a much stronger PR position than simply explaining for the umpteenth time how we're trying to protect workers.'[32]

This is the kind of memo that normally stays in-house, under wraps. Not this time. By mistake, an executive emailed the memo to a thousand colleagues at Amazon. It was leaked to Vice News, and then to other outlets. The response, from a media still focused on the life-endangering treatment of warehouse workers at Amazon, was not positive. It was read as a senior Amazon executive clearly stating that – in his opinion – to link all claims of worker dissatisfaction with Christian Smalls would grossly undermine their arguments.[33] The statement was interpreted as racist as well as demonstrating overt and targeted whistleblower reprisal.

The company moved to defend itself. The unfortunate author of the memo made a statement downplaying its import: 'My comments were personal and emotional. I was frustrated and upset that an Amazon employee would endanger the health and safety of other Amazonians by repeatedly returning to the premises after having been warned to quarantine himself after exposure to virus COVID-19. I let my emotions draft my words and get the better of me.'[34] Amazon's spokesperson backed him up, stating again that Christian had 'violated its social distancing policy'. Moreover, they emphasized, 'the executive did not know he was black'.[35]

Christian Smalls was asked to respond. 'They're digging their own grave', the *Daily News* reported him saying. 'It's borderline racist. These people are disgusting. They should be ashamed of themselves. It's like a vendetta against me. ... For what? For doing the right thing?'[36] Later, when a *New York Times* journalist asked him how he felt after reading the memo, he responded, 'I just said, "Noted". You know: "not smart or articulate: Black man". That is the stigma. That is how they try to stigmatize us. We are not smart enough to be on the same level.'[37]

Others agreed. For many, Amazon was clearly placing its concern for its own reputation over that of its workers, and now it would seem over a racism problem among executives. It was, as one commentator noted, a weak attempt to defend 'brutally insensitive remarks ... where the focus was on defending Amazon "talking points" regardless of the situation'.[38] 'Hundreds of Amazon workers are telling the public about the risk Amazon poses to their health, their families and the communities they live in – and we've got Amazon execs, working from home, trying to fix the PR problem instead of the public health problem.' Dania Rajendra, the director of Athena, a coalition of labour and community groups campaigning against Amazon, was being quoted in the *Guardian*. 'Amazon top brass chose tired, racist insinuations and snarky tweets. A better choice would be to make a plan that takes worker and public health seriously.'[39] Within twenty-four hours, Alexandria Ocasio-Cortez was calling out Amazon's 'dismissal of a black warehouse worker as "racist", describing how leaked notes revealed senior executives had planned to publicly discredit him'.[40] Zapolsky's retraction did not seem to be working.

The details of senior Amazon executives' responses, behind closed doors, exacerbated public outrage in relation to Chris's case. This outrage was heightened some months later, in media coverage of Amazon's public relations response as the #BlackLivesMatter movement gained momentum in summer 2020 after the murder of George Floyd, and again in coverage of the successful union drive that Christian Smalls and allies went on to lead in 2022.[41] 'Actions speak louder than words', a spokesperson for *Amazon Employees for Climate Justice*, a group of employee activists at the company, was quoted as saying. 'The company's track record with non-white employee organizers has … proven to be in conflict with its public statements regarding racial equity …. Amazon's words mean nothing when they are firing black employees organizing for better working conditions.'[42] From the *New York Times* to the UK *Guardian*, the racist reprisal against whistleblower Christian Smalls was cited and re-cited.

Christian by now seemed to have an unassailable platform. With each conflict, newspapers would report Amazon's official line, typically immediately followed by Christian Smalls, who was granted the last word. 'Amazon says employee Christian Smalls was fired last month for breaking social distancing protocols', began an editorial in the *Daily News*. 'Smalls says he was organizing a protest of unsafe practices at the company's Staten Island facility, including the undercounting of employees testing positive', it continued. Editorials like this made a critical link between health workers on the front line of the COVID-19 pandemic, and Christian's colleagues in the warehouse: 'It's not just health workers being forced to choose between silence and potentially subjecting themselves, their co-workers and the public to risk.'[43]

All this happened in a mere three weeks. By now, it was still April 2020, the very early days of the pandemic. And Amazon was still, according to many insiders, failing to protect its warehouse workers from exposure to the virus. Meanwhile, Amazon's shares were up a whopping 70 per cent as people around the world turned to online shopping to furnish their newly quarantined lives.

Amazon's Defence Backfires

When a whistleblower's campaign reaches this kind of media exposure, retaliatory smear campaigns are not uncommon.[44] But normally, they work like they are supposed to. A large employer has all the advantages in the battle for public opinion: name recognition, professional PR and legal firms on retainer, access to a worker's records, emails and other sources of potentially damaging information about their history. Employers like Amazon can be confident that a well-orchestrated crusade to publicly negate a whistleblower's claim will speedily achieve the goal of discrediting them so that their disclosure is ignored.[45] In this case, the plan failed. More than fail, the campaign backfired.

Well-known voices had already expressed outrage, in public, at the perceived injustice of Chris's firing. But now there was the memo. The racist undertones and dismissive language, set out in a document not meant for sharing, started something new. The empathy people already had for the warehouse workers seemed to be set alight by this glimpse into the cold, bureaucratic language used to plan Christian's downfall behind the scenes. And by the sheer discrepancy in power between executives and workers.

Derrick recalls reading about it all:

I was appalled. You know . . . How can you guys sit down at a meeting, and you are probably making millions of dollars, and Chris who is only making, what, 25 dollars an hour? So, I just knew that they wanted to – pretty much – silence the whole effort. Anyone speaking out: that was how they were going to treat them, moving forward. Including myself.

Derrick resolved to continue helping organize the movement. After the memo was leaked, he received emails: 'from people from all over the country – Amazon workers, non-Amazon workers, that just want to help advocate as well'.[46] In the weeks that followed, demonstrations took place at Amazon facilities across the country, with some protesters holding placards declaring, 'we stand in solidarity with Chris Smalls', and 'we stand in solidarity with JFK8'.[47]

With Theranos and the ESB, we have already seen how employers respond when backed against a wall by a whistleblower determined to go public. But this case took a strange turn. We saw – through information leaked digitally – what happens inside a retaliating organization. This kind of scene is rarely if ever available for scrutiny. This rare peek at what happens inside an organization was as compelling to people as it was enraging. It was impossible to turn away.

From the company's perspective, it was the deep-seated fear that the organization's boundary was fatally cracking, that the outside was bearing down on the inside, enabled by the rapid spread through email, that led to this happening. Leaky, digital technology had violated the safe backstage area that normally remains hidden. But in the weeks that followed, we would find out just how fragile that 'internal' space really was.

Insider Solidarity

From April 2020, Chris's whistleblowing actions, his colleagues' resistance and the reprisals against them began to inspire others both outside and within the organization to speak up. As it turned out, there were more than just warehouse staff among the 'in-house' supporters who empathized with Christian and colleagues. White-collar executives were beginning to take notice.

When Christian was fired, he told all the journalists who would listen that it was wrongful dismissal: he had not violated quarantine, he had been sacked for being a whistleblower.[48] Later, it would emerge that some executives at Amazon had privately agreed with him. Again, a leak. Internal messages between Amazon HR personnel from this period were leaked and reported to the *New York Times*. The newspaper's podcast host, Michael Barbaro, ran an episode on the whole incident: 'So, Amazon's official explanation always has been, and is to this day, that Chris was violating quarantine', he began. 'However, I'm going to read you text messages that were sent between two Amazon HR officials on the same day Chris was fired. They are saying things like, "Come on. They were social distancing, as requested. It was a peaceful protest. His right to organize is protected. This is going to be perceived as retaliation. Not a good look.'"[49] The podcast host and his guest, *NYT* investigative journalist Jodi Kantor, chatted about what it all meant. 'These are HR officials within Amazon expressing some real reservations about Chris being fired?' asked Michael. 'Yes. They are saying "This is crazy: I don't even know what to say". So, this is proof that even on that day, there were HR people at Amazon who thought this was a very bad idea.'

There had been internal discord within Amazon about the way Christian was treated. Disquiet with the situation had not remained with him and his warehouse colleagues, but had reached HR executives who felt it to be a 'crazy', inexplicable response by their own management. And this sense extended to other white-collar workers.

Amazon Employees for Climate Justice was an activist group that since 2018 had been organizing thousands of workers in walkouts and petitions protesting the company's lack of climate action. Leaders Maren Costa and Emily Cunningham worked as Amazon user experience designers for many years. Now, in 2020, they were reading about the exposed warehouse colleagues, and the palpable fear for their lives they expressed. Emily recalled: 'We knew we had to do something.' The two began to organize their group in support. 'Warehouse workers are putting their lives on the line and are under real threat right now. We have to do all that we can to support workers on the frontlines, now more than ever.'[50] As well as being angry about the dangerous position warehouse workers were in, it was perceived injustice and inequality between workers at Amazon, making itself clear in the ways in which safety and protection seemed to be prioritized differently for different groups, that prompted Emily and Maren to help. Each reflected on the vast difference between their treatment as white-collar office workers who were paid to work from home, and that experienced by warehouse colleagues when the pandemic began. When cases emerged in warehouses and some workers opted to stay home, 'they just send more bodies in'. This was, Emily was reported in CNBC as saying, simply unacceptable.

Maren and Emily took action immediately. In support of the JFK8 workers, they announced that donations up to $500 would be matched from their own wallets, and that they would support the warehouse staff 'while they struggle to get consistent, sufficient protections and procedures from our employer'. The pair promoted a petition, using their significant influence among Amazon colleagues, having previously organized over 80,000 staff signing a petition to press the company on its climate responsibilities. A full 3,000 employees – in Amazon centres around the globe – had walked out of work in the 2019 Global Climate Strike, again organized by Maren and Emily. These efforts, Maren recalled, were 'widely recognized for bringing about Amazon's Climate Pledge'.

Maren described how their profile came to Christian Smalls and his colleagues' attention. 'When COVID came around, the warehouse workers were asking for our support because we had had good luck changing Amazon in the past ... . And we said "absolutely".' They organized a webinar for 16 April that would feature Amazon warehouse workers from around the globe discussing their employers' pandemic response, with activist and author Naomi Klein as guest speaker. After sending the invitation out on the internal mailing lists, on 10 April both Maren and Emily were fired.[51]

Whistleblowing Subcultures Emerge

We saw how Erika Cheung, Tyler Shultz and other whistleblowers at Theranos offered support for each other. In other large organizations, whistleblowers speaking up about wrongdoing emerge to assist one another. At the US National Security Agency, numerous whistleblowers cite each other, both as inspiration and also as sources of support: Daniel Hale, Jesselyn Radack, Thomas Drake, Edward Snowden and the ubiquitous presence of the late Daniel Ellsberg offering advice and solidarity. When researching my book on whistleblowing in financial services, some of the most rule-averse banking organizations had whole pockets of whistleblowers trying to raise concerns – often unknown to each other that, when they made contact, offered invaluable assistance. In the case of Countrywide for example, Eileen Foster, Michael Winston and others were connected with the help of journalist Mike Hudson, who linked their stories and put them in touch. The odd thing is, therefore, that even in a large, oppressive and dominant corporate culture demanding complicity, where silence is fiercely enforced, the very presence of this power seems to give rise to whole groups doing the opposite: groups of whistleblowers speaking out. A kind of whistleblowing subculture develops.

Something similar was brewing at Amazon: this time among white-collar workers. As Emily and Maren's dismissal reached the news, public support was again mobilized for Amazon staff fired for protesting. Eight Democratic Party Senators, including Elizabeth Warren, Bernie Sanders, Kirsten Gillibrand and Kamala Harris, sent a letter to the company demanding answers.[52] There was a common theme to the complaints: people saw this incident as another blatant retaliation against whistleblowers – a claim Amazon again denied.

But the most remarkable defender was a surprise to many. Three days after Maren and Emily were fired, on 4 May 2020, news broke that a vice president of Amazon Web Services, Tim Bray, had resigned in protest of the treatment of Smalls and other whistleblowers within the organization. He recalled Amazon's official reasons for dismissing Emily and Maren: 'Amazon's justifications were laughable; it was clear to any reasonable observer that they were turfed for whistleblowing.' Bray then described how he raised his own concerns using the official channels. 'VPs (Vice Presidents) shouldn't go publicly rogue, so I escalated through the proper channels and by the book. ... That done, remaining an Amazon VP would have meant, in effect, signing off on actions I despised. So, I resigned.'[53] By sharing with the world the disclosure he had made through internal channels, he was identifying publicly as a whistleblower. By resigning, he underlined his solidarity with fellow whistleblowers who had been unjustly fired. He stated their names: 'The victims weren't abstract entities but real people; here are some of their names: Courtney Bowden, Gerald Bryson, Maren Costa, Emily Cunningham, Bashir Mohammed [*sic*], and Chris Smalls.'

Bray's blog post went on to detail the very different treatment of white-collar executives like him compared with that of workers in Amazon's warehouses. He and his colleagues had been allowed to work from home and were generously provided for by the company. In the end, he noted, whistleblower retaliation, along with race and gender-based discrimination drove his resignation: 'I'm sure it's a coincidence that every one of them [the dismissed whistleblowers] is a person of colour, a woman, or both. Right? Let's give one of those names a voice. Bashir Mohamed said, "They fired me to make others scared." Do you disagree?'[54]

Tim's blog post was shared on social media, and in turn quoted in media articles and in the letter from nine US Senators calling for Amazon to clarify the company's discipline and termination policies regarding workers who raise health concerns.[55] Soon hundreds of comments appeared under the blog post celebrating Tim's action and reinforcing his decision.

While the compelling nature of Christian and colleagues' disclosures drew hundreds of powerful supporters to their side, it seems like when fellow workers – from the warehouse to executive suite – allied to the cause that cracks in the organization's defences really became clear. Paradoxically, it was the very exertion of dominance and quashing of dissent that seemed to precipitate the rise of whistleblowing subcultures where none existed before.

Brian Martin is the Australian professor working with whistleblowers who warned us about the risks of depending on official channels in Chapter 1. In his book *Whistleblowing: A Practical Guide*, his advice emphasizes the importance of connection. Would-be whistleblowers should not, he cautions, act in ways that severely jeopardize their well-being. Sometimes speaking out is not the best option. Sometimes the safest route is simply to leave and, from the outside, lend a hand to activists who are working to expose the wrongdoing you are disclosing. If planning something like this, Martin advises, it is always best to try to get another job first. If, however, a worker feels compelled to stay and fight, he suggests they organize 'on the job' and connect with like-minded colleagues. 'In opposing corruption', he writes, 'there is strength in numbers. The challenge is to build the numbers.' Martin, drawing on years of experience working with whistleblowers in Australia, is frank about the hazards: 'It is not always easy. Finding others who are willing to do something can be risky: some prospective allies might be part of corrupt operations, might inform those who are or simply be indiscreet or unreliable.' Acting too soon to contact others can 'reveal the existence of opposition and lead to a witch-hunt'. But the strength in numbers that comes from working with colleagues can prove decisive: 'A single whistleblower can be ignored or discredited; half a dozen will have far more impact and can provide support for each other. A leaking operation involving a network of workers can be far more effective than a lone leaker.' He concludes: 'The key message is to consider options carefully and prepare thoroughly before acting.'

When I spoke with Christian Smalls some six months later, I asked him what advice he would give to others in a situation like the one in which he had found himself, as a manager trying to defend his reports.

'What worked in my favour was …' He mused before concluding, 'Public opinion is everything.' 'You have to put your issue out there: on front street.' He described how, for him and Derrick, galvanizing the workers was essential to achieving this; 'there is strength in numbers. Do not do it individually', he said, 'do it as a collective.'

From Strategic Alliances to Personal Connections

The experiences of Christian Smalls and Brian Martin speak to one aspect of public whistleblowing: the strategic role of other disclosers, and their importance for a whistleblower's survival. But there is something else occurring. Whistleblowers are typically depicted as isolated individuals: people speaking out alone. In my research into financial services whistleblowing, however, digging deeper into disclosers' experiences, I found this characterization to be wrong-headed.[56] Each whistleblower was intricately embedded in networks of relationships enabling their disclosure and their survival. And it was more than mere dependency at work. We assume a clear boundary between the whistleblowers and others who surround them, but this is a flawed assumption; the relationships involve flows of mutual recognition and passionate attachments. It seemed like the connections went somewhat deeper than mere strategic alliances; these interdependencies worked at the level of personal relationships and emotional connections.

Further empirical research with whistleblowers who had left their employer lent support to this. With colleagues I had the opportunity to survey almost a hundred whistleblowers from across a range of sectors: public, private and non-profit, and in a variety of nations.[57] As part of the research we asked people to report any personal and social benefits that they perceived as a result of their disclosure. This was a question we had been requested to include by the whistleblower activist-lawyers on our project advisory team. Keen to look beyond all the focus on whistleblower suffering, they wanted to bring to the fore what they saw in day-to-day life: the pleasures and satisfactions, as well as the sorrows. Despite the isolation and exclusion their disclosures had brought, just over a third reported 'new friends and connections' had been made as they progressed through the whistleblowing journey, and a full four out of ten had 'empowered other whistleblowers' during this time. Striking findings from a study of what, if we believe everything we read, is normally an endeavour undertaken alone. It is not all good news, of course. Results depicting mental health impacts, blacklisting and financial detriments made grim reading, as did people's first-hand accounts of the effects of whistleblowing on themselves and their families. But an intrinsic embeddedness in others seemed both to help and to drive people forward, as they spoke out; we will explore this later.

Reflecting on her dismissal from Amazon, Maren Costa described how she had since been contacted by lots of people, including a warehouse worker who had contracted COVID-19 at work, and whose wife died because of his passing it to her. He wanted to say thank you. 'What that whole experience taught me', she went on, 'was that when we stand up and speak up together, we can make massive, monumental change. And that's what we did . . . at Amazon.'

By May, pressure was intensifying from external parties showing solidarity with Christian and whistleblowing colleagues. Formal letters calling for his reinstatement came from Senator Bernie Sanders, Congresswoman Alexandria Ocasio-Cortez and many others who earlier spoke up on social media. As she had promised, Attorney General of New York State Letitia James began legal action.[58] Many of these supporters would prove important in the efforts by Smalls to advocate on behalf of Amazon workers through the formation of the Congress of Essential Workers and later the Amazon Labor Union, which he went on to do with colleagues.[59]

Six weeks after he had first spoken out, Christian had connected with powerful supporters and, crucially, with other disclosers in Amazon who were experiencing similar fears and mistreatment. The collective movement granted a sense of legitimacy and credibility. ICT and social media were decisive, both for communication between disclosers and reaching the media. This led to a whistleblowing claim moving from an incident involving a lone individual with a grudge, or a worker that didn't know better and was mistaken, to a collective movement with real power to act.

Of course, blunders by Amazon management influenced this apparent success. Other factors did too. Christian's protests took place at the JFK8 'Fulfilment Centre' in Staten Island, the facility at the centre of his later unionizing efforts. New York State is arguably more open to worker collective action than others. In New York at the time, according to the Bureau of Labor Statistics, more than one in five wage and salary workers were union members. This is double the national average of about one in ten.[60] This doesn't take from Christian's leadership celebrated by commentators worldwide. As Derrick later described, 'Chris is very brave.' His bravery reflected that of his co-organizers, '[a]ll of us on the frontlines are very brave', he added, '[a] lot of workers want to be in the cause, but they're scared'.[61] Still, there was someone speaking out on their behalf.

Nor was Christian and colleagues' campaign straightforward. He had gained a platform, yet his frank accounts of what happened sometimes appeared self-defeating. He described in a public interview how he had intended to leave Amazon soon anyway, because he was not being promoted because of his race and activism in workers' rights, something that might have diminished his claims.[62] Christian was open about having exaggerated the number of colleagues walking out in late March to the media; his frank account shows a tactical awareness of the need for the walkout to be something of a spectacle, or else the reporters would not show. Christian later went on to publicly clash with unions and politicians who offered support that was, in his view, insufficient.[63] He reported slamming down the phone to HR colleagues calling to tell him he was fired. Christian did not always appear as the polished, unflappable leader of the many; perhaps, however, if solidarity between real people is what galvanizes the support needed to address the dominance of employers like Amazon, such human moments are critical.

That said, during those brief eight weeks in spring 2020, change occurred. The following year, in April 2021, Maren and Emily's dismissal by Amazon was deemed illegal by the National Labor Relations Board, a ruling Amazon protested. The case has now been settled. Returning to the source of all this conflict – the warehouse workers – according to Derrick Palmer, by late May Amazon had provided personal protective equipment to workers. Social distancing rules were now being enforced, and temperature checks were happening. But, he stated, 'cleaning procedures remain inadequate'. This was backed up by another employee at JFK8 who wanted to remain anonymous, complaining that PPE only arrived in mid-April, while deep-cleaning was not happening. 'The word she kept using', said the *New York Times* journalist reporting on the story, 'was "facade".' All that said, the day of the famous walkout, regardless of how many actually took part, was now known by 'multiple workers at JFK8 . . . as the moment Amazon started making meaningful changes'. Whatever the case,

Amazon's behaviour towards its warehouse staff was now firmly in the spotlight.[64]

Christian Smalls appears exceptional, in his capacity to lead and inspire others, to read the audience and respond when needed, and to orchestrate the kind of communication campaign that capitalizes upon the affordances of today's print and online media landscape. In what follows, we draw out the learnings from this case as it connects with others. Christian's long-term commitment to his cause shines through. After our interview, I thanked him. I told him the recording would soon be available online. 'Don't forget to tag me on Twitter', he said.

Reprisals as Obliteration or Cracks in the Armour?

There is more to this than the classic 'David versus Goliath' storyline. First, this version of 'David' – Christian – was rarely alone. The presence of others was a constant. In fact, David in this case was Christian, plus Derrick, plus colleagues at JFK8, eventually expanding to encompass Senators, a mayor, warehouse workers and Amazon executives across the country. As I found in the study of financial services whistleblowers, when we look a little deeper, the boundary between whistleblowers and the others they act with and for is blurred. Second, it seems like it was the cracks that appeared in the employer's apparent domination of the scene that made a difference. These were facilitated by new digital technologies. And these cracks seemed to chip away at Amazon's power to control what was happening.

Thus far, when considering the position of the public whistleblower, we have emphasized the unequal power held by employers bent on whistleblower reprisals. Recall C. Fred Alford's warnings that to 'run up against the organization is to risk obliteration ... nothing remains after'. But taking our cases together, we are starting to see other things emerge in the form of cracks and fissures: leaks at Amazon, manic over-reach in ensuring impossible levels of security at Theranos, disorganized, chaotic responses at ESB. It seems that partnerships between people speaking up are critical in the work to expand these cracks: widening them, creating new fractures and new openings. For Erika, it was Tyler, other whistleblowers, journalist John Carreyrou and a generous lawyer friend. Christian and Derrick saw hundreds of people coming out to support them, while Seamus and his wife had the Environmental Protection Agency, newspaper journalists and TV investigative reporters who would spend months researching a documentary to show at prime-time. Are such partnerships unique to these public whistleblowers? Are there commonalities with other cases? And, in exploring this, can we learn more about the other side of the support relationship, particularly the perspective of the newspaper reporters, these cornerstones of public whistleblowing campaigns?

Notes

1. BBC (2022).
2. Alter (2022).
3. Barbaro (2022).
4. The *Guardian* (2021).
5. Author interview; Barbaro (2022).
6. Cited in Alimahomed-Wilson & Reese (2021, p. 59).
7. Linebaugh (2022).
8. Barbaro (2022).
9. Alter (2022), Barbaro (2022).
10. Barbaro (2022).
11. Barbaro (2022), Linebaugh (2022).
12. Author interview, November 2020.
13. Barbaro (2022).
14. Author interview, November 2020.
15. Barbaro (2022); Author interview, November 2020; Wong (2020).
16. Barbaro (2022).
17. Linebaugh (2022).
18. Park et al. (2020b), Vandekerckhove & Langenberg (2012).
19. Vandekerckhove & Phillips (2019), Kenny & Fotaki (2021).
20. Speaking on Linebaugh (2022).
21. Barbaro (2022).
22. Alter (2022), Barbaro (2022).
23. Johnson (2020).
24. Johnson (2020).
25. RWDSU (2020).
26. Herrera (2021).
27. IBA (2018), Lewis (2008), Mesmer-Magnus & Viswesvaran (2005).
28. Evelyn (2020).
29. Quoted in Palmer (2020a).
30. Quoted in Wong (2020), Palmer (2020a).
31. Quoted in Blest (2020), Wong (2020).
32. Quoted in Blest (2020), Wong (2020).

33. Barboro (2022).
34. Wong (2020).
35. Gelles (2020).
36. Kriegstein & McShane (2020).
37. Barbaro (2022).
38. Bray (2020).
39. Wong (2020).
40. Spocchia (2020).
41. Alter (2022), Barbaro (2022), Gelles (2020), Linebaugh (2022).
42. Paul (2020).
43. Editorial in *Daily News* (New York) on 10 April, p. 20.
44. Devine & Maassarani (2011).
45. Mueller (2019).
46. Barbaro (2022).
47. Author interview, November 2020.
48. Evelyn (2020).
49. Barbaro (2022).
50. Palmer (2020b).
51. Paul (2020).
52. Conger (2020).
53. Bray (2020).
54. Bray (2020).
55. Zaveri (2020), Heater (2020).
56. Kenny (2019).
57. Kenny & Fotaki (2019, 2021).
58. Weise (2021).
59. Alter (2022).
60. AP news wire in *The Independent* (United Kingdom), 26 March 2022.
61. The *Guardian* (2021).
62. Author interview, November 2020.
63. Linebaugh (2022).
64. Michael Sainato writing in the *Guardian* (London), 1 May 2020.

4 | *The Facebook Whistleblower and the Journalist*

Holding Facebook to Account

In 2022, President Joe Biden's State of the Union speech had a word for a whistleblower:

As Frances Haugen, who is here with us tonight, has shown, we must hold social media platforms accountable for the national experiment they're conducting on our children for profit. Folks – thank you, thank you for the courage you showed. Thank you. Thank you for the courage you showed.[1]

I must admit, I agreed with Joe. There was something cathartic learning about what Facebook's platforms were doing to our children. There had been lots of discussion but now we knew. And more than this, we knew that they knew, the people in charge of Facebook: they had known for some time. In September 2021, the *Wall Street Journal* and later other newspapers ran stories showing platforms like Instagram knowingly impact the mental health of users and in particular of teenage girls. Facebook was also aware it endangers public safety and democracy in many countries because of poor control over what gets posted. Its algorithms actively facilitate radicalization because extremist views and misinformation are automatically amplified to the user. There were links to incidents of ethnic violence and genocide in India, Ethiopia, Myanmar and other places. In countries where Facebook is the only social media platform supporting the local language, Facebook simply is the internet. It is often those countries it focuses upon least, when it comes to moderating disinformation and hate speech. And these stories were all coming from inside Facebook. All this information was – as Joe Biden would later celebrate – coming from Frances Haugen. She had gathered it while working at Facebook.

An Organized Campaign

Some three years earlier, a recruitment agent had approached Frances. How would she feel about working at Facebook? She replied she would join, but only if she could work on projects countering the platform's impact on democracy through the spread of false information. Frances was hired as lead Product Manager on the Civic Integrity team, international section.[2] Her job was to analyse civic misinformation: 'fake-news' content about politics and society that was misleading or false. She studied the power of the algorithms to ignite already tense atmospheres. Demonizing minorities online can cause situations to explode, leading to ethnic violence, and this was happening around the world. Frances particularly focused on 'narrowcasting': when false information 'goes viral', spreading among a small group of like-minded people.

Fake news was top of people's minds at the time, with the 2020 US elections coming up. Scandals had shown up the role of social media platforms skewing previous election results. People were nervous. Facebook had wanted to respond, so it put together a team of people to research and deal with this. Just after the elections, however, the team was disbanded. The official reason given was to enable team members to take positions in departments across the firm. They were, the firm said, to share what they had learned. Team members read it differently. Many felt the unit, whose stated goal was to prioritize public safety ahead of Facebook's profits, had too much power.[3] As Frances later joked with a reporter: 'We're not going to get regulated for messing up the election for at least four more years.'[4] It did not look like dealing with misinformation was a priority for Facebook any longer, now that the spotlight was off. But political polarization had not gone away. No longer operating together as a unit, former Civic Integrity team members were unable to do anything about the organization of the 6 January riots in Washington DC, just a few weeks after the polls. Many left the company. Frances decided she would have to speak up.

Things moved so fast in the months that followed. When the first articles began appearing in the *Wall Street Journal* in late September 2021, there was no whistleblower named. But within three weeks, Frances came out as the source, in the most public way possible: a *60 Minutes* interview at CBS News.[5] That was early October, and on the very same day, the *Wall Street Journal*'s podcast series released an interview with her. Just two days later, she was on C-Span in a televised testimony to the US Senate Commerce Subcommittee. The European Commissioner in Brussels, Thierry Breton, wanted her number. Members of the UK Parliament were in touch: would Frances appear in front of a joint committee of a draft online safety bill? She set a date for the end of October. It was a mere three weeks since the first article emerged when the *Financial Times* told us how her disclosures 'have pitched the social network into its biggest crisis since the Cambridge Analytica'.[6] The following week Frances was in Lisbon at the Web Summit, publicly calling for Zuckerberg to resign.

It seemed like newspapers and politicians were all on the same page, as Frances Haugen's whistleblowing disclosures swept across the globe. It felt as though an audience had been waiting for this kind of evidence. And, when it arrived, people were quick to act. By mid-November the state of Ohio was using the information she had disclosed to file a suit against Facebook, while the cosmetics company Lush announced it was shutting down its Facebook, Instagram, Snapchat and TikTok accounts, citing the new knowledge about mental health impacts of Instagram that Frances had brought to light. In the months that followed, more lawsuits were filed against the company. Aspects of new regulations and practices have since been attributed to her disclosures, including the Digital Services Act in the UK, the introduction of a stronger 'Whistleblower Law' in Europe and increased parental controls on Instagram. And Facebook's moderation of information in non-Western contexts – or its lack thereof – has been especially under the spotlight. By January 2022, Frances was joining with other whistleblowers, demanding the firm release its report on the impact of Facebook in India.

It was around this time she was invited as a guest of First Lady Jill Biden to attend the State of the Union address in US Congress; that evening in March 2022, Frances was mentioned in the President's speech. By now she was authoring opinion pieces for the *Guardian,* directly targeting Nick Clegg, newly promoted Facebook President for Global Affairs, for the *Financial Times* calling for provisions for civil society organizations to access platform data in the European Union's upcoming Digital Services Act and for the *New York Times* telling the US they ought to emulate the protections for citizens in that same Act.

Among the most respected thinkers and writers on big tech's unprecedented gain in dominance over the past thirty years is Harvard

University's Shoshana Zuboff. She has serious concerns about the power of these corporations, and the fact that this power keeps growing, unchallenged. Zuboff warns that 'Facebook reached trillion-dollar status in a decade by applying surveillance capitalism – a system built on the secret extraction and manipulation of data – to Zuckerberg's vision of total human connection.'[7] This 'vision' is decisive, she argues; you have to understand the ideology behind these firms. There is – apparently – an inherent assumption that connection is always good. Thus, more connections, more interactions, more engagements ought to be the goal. This is the unquestioned fantasy put forward to defend much of what goes on in social media platforms. And it is a fantasy harnessed to make unprecedented amounts of money for their owners. Zuboff's *The Age of Surveillance Capitalism* is unique, a 700-page tome setting out, step by step, the history of the sector, the business models, the political influences, the user dependencies and crucially a detailed anatomy of how we, and the data we produce, are exploited for profit.

The book demonstrates how Facebook's 'success relies upon hidden machine operations and corporate rhetoric designed to conceal its trail of social wreckage: the destruction of privacy, poisoned social discourse, defactualised information and weakened institutions'. Zuboff has repeatedly argued that Facebook knows all about this stuff because it does its own research: carefully designed, expertly executed research by teams of skilled analysts, with unique access to the data. But the company absolutely refuses to let either these analyses, or the underlying data, go outside of the firm. This is, by all accounts, stellar research with no outside scrutiny and few meaningful outcomes. No recommendations can be taken up by lawmakers without Facebook's vetting. So, such firms maintain an information monopoly: Zuboff's phrase is 'information warfare'.[8] The more knowledge they have, the quicker they develop the tech. The more the rest of us are in the dark, the more we struggle to regulate.

The 1990s, according to Zuboff, was a tragic decade. These things were just kicking off, with the kids in Silicon Valley pitching their businesses for the first investors to come on board. They were small firms whose business plans were there for all to see. But, as they grew, regulators did not know enough or care enough to take action: 'While democracy was lulled into complacency, Facebook and a handful of surveillance capitalist giants achieved control over global information flows and communication, unconstrained by public law.'

When the *Financial Times* asked Zuboff to nominate someone for its feature on 'Women of 2021', she had plenty to say about her choice. Frances Haugen's 'courageous gift to the world has been an ice-cold shower of incontestable facts smuggled from the heart of the Facebook empire'. This shower of facts was, she told us, 'written in the words of its people and shining an unflinching light on the destructive powers of its supreme leader, Mark Zuckerberg'.

In just six months, Frances Haugen had delivered this 'gift', shining a spotlight on the dangers of this poorly understood, weakly regulated and ubiquitous technology. She started out as a source, then a named and public whistleblower and, like Christian Smalls, swiftly took on the role of activist. One woman had become a vital source of both information and explanation and advice. And it seemed as though the rollout of the information was seamless. Today, Frances continues to point out the lack of progress on Facebook monitoring of content, in non-English-speaking countries in particular. She has, according to many, been a successful whistleblower.

Responding to the Whistleblower

Whistleblowing is not a one-way street. Facebook executives were going to have to respond. Frances and the *Wall Street Journal* had moved fast. But people were moving fast over at Facebook too. The day after her *60 Minutes* interview, 4 October, Facebook, and its other platforms Instagram and WhatsApp, suddenly went offline for six unexplained hours. And their stocks tumbled. Next morning, CEO Mark Zuckerberg was posting his response to Frances's disclosures on his own Facebook page: 'At the heart of these accusations is this idea that we prioritize profit over safety and wellbeing. That's just not true', he wrote. 'The argument that we deliberately push content that makes people angry for profit is deeply illogical. We make money from ads, and advertisers consistently tell us they don't want their ads next to harmful or angry content.' He went on to explain that Haugen's statements made no sense: why on earth would a firm ignore its own research findings? Zuckerberg reached out to his staff to comfort them after what, he said, must have been a difficult time for them. 'I'm sure many of you have found the recent coverage hard to read because it just doesn't reflect the company we know', he soothed. Haugen's disclosures were painting a 'false picture' of their firm. Oddly enough, just two weeks after his heartfelt defence of all things on Facebook, the false and illogical claims of Frances Haugen appeared to have precipitated a full rebrand. The company ditched its old name in favour of Meta.[9]

Frances had shaken things up in the most powerful and profitable industry. As we have come to expect by now, the next move is for the company to do its best to destroy the whistleblower and negate their message. And this firm was known for its record of successfully silencing whistleblowers. Libby Liu, CEO of Whistleblower Aid, describes how Facebook has, over time, systematically worked to 'close off avenues of support' for workers needing to speak up. According to big tech whistleblowers, Facebook's critics can struggle to find good lawyers because many of the best firms will not engage, citing conflicts of interest because of prior contact with, or work for, Facebook.[10]

For Frances, the backlash was on the way. But in her case, it did not work. Despite the extent of the firm's power and influence, it did not seem able to silence her. In 2021, Facebook was the sixth biggest company in the world.[11] But there was something about Frances Haugen's whistleblowing that seemed to take this size and strength and turn it to her advantage. And critically, she used the media to do this. How did it happen? How did this data scientist-turned-whistleblower become an authoritative source of information about the world's most powerful social media platform? How had she gained a level of credibility that, in my reading, was almost unprecedented for an individual whistleblower? How was she able to counter the defensive response that came next? And why did the media come so quickly to her aid?

The Playbook

'Haugen has managed the rollout of the revelations as if it were the invasion of Normandy', Kara Swisher wrote in the *New York Times*.[12] She expressed what many people watching the story unfold were feeling. 'The effort has been highly coordinated', Swisher went on, detailing the events that had happened in the previous four weeks. It wasn't just the documents, she pointed out, although they were incendiary. Frances 'has also projected moral clarity. Testifying before a Senate subcommittee and British Parliament, she said enough to be devastating but not so much that she tarnished her sincere and pristine image.' Frances had even been clear about who was bankrolling her whole effort, we learned. She had some support for travel expenses but the fact that she was paying her own way 'because she made some well-timed cryptocurrency investments', Swisher wrote, 'is the chef's kiss of the whole affair'.[13] By disclosing to institutions like Congress and the SEC, Frances also had legal protections. But her campaign points to many other important aspects of public whistleblowing.

What Frances Haugen seemed to understand – at a deep level – was something many whistleblowers and onlookers do not.[14] She knew that speaking the truth was never going to be enough. Going public as a whistleblower is incredibly risky. The relationships one has with the journalists involved are critical: but not many people understand this. Journalists must be able to work with the whistleblower in a very particular way. Ideally, one builds up a relationship of trust over a period of time; the journalist must have some commitment to the whistleblower while maintaining an objective position and journalistic integrity. There have been many Hollywood films about the dance of mutual attraction between whistleblowers and newspaper reporters. But they don't show the nuances of this complex relationship. There is usually some tension, we have the 'will they, won't they?' moment as the whistleblower gets cold feet, or the manager of the newspaper threatens to shut it all down because his pal the politician is threatened. But, in the films, it comes good in the end. The reality is a lot more complex, especially when it comes to high-stakes disclosures.

If the information being disclosed goes to the heart of what it is the company does, criticizing the underlying business model, for example, or implicating senior executives, the backlash is going to be bad. And these days smear campaigns turn ugly quickly. As Erika and colleagues at Theranos found out, weaponizing the law in the form of a SLAPP suit is just one method. As Christian Smalls at Amazon learned, personalized attacks planned at the most senior level can and do occur. Yet here is the thing that stands out about Frances's case, the thing Kara Swisher pointed out. For each potential obstacle, Frances appeared to have an answer. And she seemed to plan it all in advance. Frances appears to have known not to trust in the Hollywood ending – not to assume that a couple of published articles would be sufficient to get her message out, and to protect herself. It would all have to be extraordinarily well managed. And she would have to be the one doing the managing. Frances had help; from early on, we learned that an experienced behind-the-scenes team was advising on legal matters as well as media relations.[15]

Commentary like Swisher's implies a seamless, military-style 'roll-out' of revelations. But to describe what occurred only in this way is to simplify the reality of what it was to be a whistleblower in this situation: to downplay Frances's struggles, the challenges encountered and sometimes overcome but not always. It is helpful, in our exploration of how whistleblowers prevail, to look a little closer at this exemplary case. Two things in particular are important to examine: how Frances portrayed herself as 'the whistleblower', and how she dealt with the reprisals that would inevitably come her way.

Presenting Frances Haugen

The Journalist-Partner: Frances Haugen stayed anonymous when the first articles came out. When she did emerge in public as the information source, it was hand-in-hand with the *Wall Street Journal*. Key to this relationship was the reporter Jeff Horwitz. The scale, timing and impact of the events that followed his first article in September 2021 had much to do with this choice.

As the US Presidential Election of 2020 approached, Frances was still at Facebook. And Facebook was under a media spotlight. How would it address the potential of the platform to enable voter manipulation and election rigging? Its answer: the Civic Integrity team. This group had a somewhat unusual mission. Upon joining, each member took an informal oath, promising to 'serve the people's interest first, not Facebook's'.[16] The aim of the Civic Integrity team was to objectively assess the impact of the firm on the people using its products, and work towards defusing misinformation and polarization. Frances and colleagues had been researching intensely to learn the potential dangers of the platform for democracy and public safety in the US and globally, and other concerns. Right after the election concluded, when the team was scrapped, its members were dispersed to other roles. Frances described watching the chaos of the 6 January riot in Washington, DC, when Donald Trump's supporters stormed Congress to stop the results of the election being ratified. Frances understood that the events were organized through social media platforms, especially using video and live-stream media that are difficult to detect and screen. She knew Facebook's platform was at the heart of this, and she knew the team that might have been able to do something had been disbanded. She and her team members felt powerless.

When the message had come through to Facebook staffers from technology reporter Jeff Horwitz, it came at an opportune time. He wanted to talk to some insiders. He had contacted forty or so people hoping for an answer. Frances studied his profile. Jeff had won awards as a financial and enterprise reporter for the Associated Press in Washington, DC. With a long-term interest in Facebook, at times publishing weekly on the firm's exploits, he had detailed its dangers for users before. He appeared to understand the topics deeply. He had written about an area of particular concern for Frances: the role Facebook played in inciting violence relating to Hindu nationalism in India. He had not been afraid to criticize the firm. He knew, he said, about her team and the implications of its being scrapped.

Jeff was also based near San Francisco. It was still a time of COVID-19 restrictions, so he met with Frances outdoors. There was no talk of document sharing at the start, they just talked. For four months these meetings continued, discussing the concerns Frances was having. She began gathering documents in secret. This was not easy. According to Frances, she always assumed she was going to be found out. Document tracking would make sure of this. The question was: how long could she keep gathering information before she was stopped? To mitigate the impacts of surveillance, Frances took photographs of the documents on her laptop screen, assuming her actual devices were under surveillance. In May 2021, she resigned her position, and nine months after their first meetings, Jeff Horwitz's articles first began to appear.

We may assume going to the press with a big story has automatic results. A good scoop can be published to the world the following day. Not so. The newspaper must ensure its position is watertight, and the onus is on it to prove everything is true. The background research and legal input can take a long time. The series of articles dubbed the 'Facebook Files' needed this kind of patience and care before printing was possible, as Jeff later described. The result was the textbook rollout of disclosures that stunned onlookers. Seasoned whistleblower lawyer and supporter Tom Devine earlier wrote about the ideal situation for a public-interest disclosure with significant potential impact delivered in a manner that protects the originator: 'an entire campaign involving a stockpiled series of stories released over time so that each reinforces the effects of the one before it'.[17] This was such a campaign.

Frances describes the care she took choosing Jeff as the person to write the stories she needed to have written. 'I auditioned Jeff for a while', she told a reporter, '[a]nd one of the reasons I went with him is that he was less sensationalistic than other choices I could have made.'[18] As many whistleblowers find to their detriment, not all journalists are the same. A reporter without the technical knowledge of the area under the spotlight may not know exactly what stories to write, what parts of the information are significant, what is new and how it can be made interesting. They may not be able to produce it in a way that keeps the story in circulation, in a busy news cycle with a lot of competition for the attention and imagination of the desired audience. And in sectors like tech, it can be difficult to make the details compelling. All this takes time and expertise. The eventual series of stories appearing in the *Wall Street Journal* were, according to Jeff, the result of lengthy collaborations between the two: Frances had the information, and Jeff knew what would land and how to write it. He asked her directly about things like the impact of Instagram on teenage body image and mental health, a significant concern for the public. 'I knew there was something there, and she came back to me and said, "Damn straight there is"', he later explained. In turn, she ensured her particular concerns about the impact of the platform on the Global South were also highlighted.[19]

More than technical expertise, given the delicacy of the relationship and the vulnerability of a worker whistleblowing on a firm like Facebook, a reporter who cares for their sources is essential too. One proof of the care this journalist showed was how Frances's identity was managed. At the outset, she did not want to be a public figure. Facebook would certainly know who she was, she acknowledged, because all the documents she held would be traceable to her. But the public did not need to know her name.[20] As things progressed, public relations experts and others she was working with advised her that, to gain the maximum impact for these stories, a face would be needed. If she, with her experience, integrity and professionalism, could be the one making the arguments, the impact would be much more powerful. For these reasons, Frances reflects, she decided to become an advocate and activist as well as a source. Here again, the *Wall Street Journal* and Jeff in particular played an important role. The unveiling of Frances's name and identity were timed carefully so that her narrative, her public persona and her account of the disclosures could be curated in the way most likely to deter reprisals.

Most public whistleblowers struggle to find any journalist to help them. Many who succeed seem to simply stumble upon reporters who will help them go public. Some are lucky. But others can lose control of the story, finding themselves exposed in the press by a journalist revealing more information than they are comfortable with. The whistle-blower can find themselves the source of a one-off exposé containing just enough information to properly antagonize their employer, but not enough to generate wider interest and the protection against reprisals that whistleblowers can gain from being surrounded by new-found supporters as part of a robust campaign. Frances was different. Her partnering with the *Wall Street Journal* was not just a chance happening in which she scored the right partner. She actively researched and vetted the person with whom she would work. And she shaped how the work proceeded. A month into the furore she reflected on this decision. 'Now that I've met so many journalists, and I've seen how hard Jeff works, I feel more grateful for the media than when I started.'[21] Having decided on her media partner, it was now necessary to manage how she was portrayed.

A Moral, Independent Critic: In early October, when Frances decided to go public, media organizations scrambled to answer the questions inevitably posed of high-stakes whistleblowers. The world's most recent and famous discloser criticizing the world's most powerful social media platform: why on earth would someone come forward like she did? Why is she the only one speaking up? And, particularly, who on earth is Frances Haugen? It is helpful to examine exactly how she answered.

We began to find out more about the woman behind the stories in the days after she was named. A *Wall Street Journal* podcast episode introduced Frances Haugen 'as poised, incisive and intensely moral'.[22] This message was reinforced over and over in subsequent articles.

Just when her name was released, Frances had a personal website prepared and ready to go online. Here she explains her motivation for speaking out. The reasons are emotive and personal, yet told in the third person, which gives them an authoritative feel. 'As a last resort and at great personal risk, Frances made the courageous decision to blow the whistle on Facebook', begins a concise summary of her journey on the landing page of the website. The podcast allowed her to expand upon this. She was asked by host Kate Linebaugh about her time at the ill-fated Civic Integrity unit. 'Yeah, it was extremely frustrating', France responded.

'One of the most painful things a person can experience is living with a secret with intense consequences.' She went on to paint a picture of what it was like for her, drawing the reader into her story: 'So, here I was, inside of Facebook. I thought I was well-informed before I joined Facebook about misinformation. Now I know that the problem is way, way worse than anyone outside knows. And I'm staffed with a team that I have no faith can actually address this problem.' What is palpable to the listener is the sense of deep dilemma, an inner struggle that was raging. 'I know that no one outside knows these things. I'm walking around holding this information, trying really hard,' Frances, one felt, had thought this through.

This narrative rang true for many influential commentators who took it forward. Print journalists reproduced elements of this self-presentation, citing Frances's moral courage and drawing quotes from her personal website. Others drew on the podcast as the source. She was quoted verbatim when writers discussed why it was that she spoke up. The identity she had presented solidified further when powerful voices with whom she apparently had no connection spoke up in her favour. They shared the assessment of Frances Haugen as moral, and a deep thinker. According to the *Financial Times*, 'People who know her say the person who appeared on TV and in the Senate was authentic ... [a] crypto entrepreneur who said that he met her in San Francisco, described her as "thoughtful" and "a giver". Another says that she is deliberate, purpose-driven and analytical.'[23] Harvard professor and leading tech researcher Shoshana Zuboff was frank in her assessment that this was no immoral business school graduate: 'Despite her Harvard MBA and career in Silicon Valley, Frances retained the humanity, common sense and moral bearings to feel outrage at Facebook's economic logic that pits profits against "what was good for the public".'[24] The culture of big tech, Zuboff suggested, does not lend itself to independent critique. But Frances was different.

For a public whistleblower, being able to voice a public-interest motivation is of critical importance in winning wider support. Yet many find that simply having a website and well-wishers who praise them is not enough. Whistleblowers at this level can be viewed with suspicion. For some, they have gone against norms of loyalty to the firm, revealing insider secrets. This is often seen as a reason not to trust them. And this can seep into how their case is reported. As an example, when Frances's story was first breaking in early October, a *Guardian* author described how '[t]he 37-year-old leaked tens of thousands of internal company documents after becoming frustrated that Facebook was not publicly acknowledging the harm its platforms could cause'.[25] Framing the disclosure as leaking internal documents, rather than public-interest whistleblowing, casts a shadow. Other commentators rushed to ask questions of who was funding this whistleblower: was she merely a puppet of covert interests with an axe to grind?

Firms engaging in smear campaigns typically emphasize such aspects, in order to diminish the credibility of a whistleblower. Being able to directly communicate, in one's own words, an alternative reason for speaking is simply essential to defend against this potential lack of trust. In Frances's case, her emphasis on professional experience and, crucially, her tendency towards analysis and deep reflection lent an authentic air to her depiction. She was given a platform to emphasize her morally driven, thoughtful, intolerance of the employer's wrong-doing. She discussed her finances openly. Frances Haugen was convincing. The timing of all of this helped greatly. Thanks to the *Wall Street Journal's* techniques, support was marshalled almost immediately upon the unveiling of her name in public. From the very start, the narrative around 'who is Frances Haugen' was hers to control.

A Channel of Authority: Frances's website describes that she was born in Iowa City, Iowa, as 'the daughter of two professors'. Academics are generally considered trustworthy; in a battle for legitimacy it does not hurt to channel the authority of the university. Frances 'grew up attending the Iowa caucuses [political meetings] with her parents, instilling a strong sense of pride in democracy and responsibility for civic participation'. Thus, we are told, an early interest and passion for justice was instilled. Her professional credibility is also emphasized, through both educational qualifications and practical experience, across a range of big tech firms. Her degree is in Electrical and Computer Engineering from Olin College, her website tells us, which she followed with a Harvard MBA. Her specialism is algorithmic product management, and she worked on ranking algorithms in firms such as Google, Pinterest and Yelp before joining Facebook. As its lead Product Manager on the Civic Integrity team, she analysed concerns around democracy and misinformation, and later counterespionage.[26] This upfront listing of qualities and experiences further counters any smear attempts by a retaliating firm claiming that she does not know what she is talking about. But also, it channels the authority of a variety of powerful institutions, both academic and corporate: they all are brought in to help shape her public presentation.

To top it off, just after Frances's *60 Minutes* interview, reporters were keen to discover what her former colleagues thought of all of this. One sourced internal messages circulating within Facebook. It appeared there was also a lot of support, with words like 'amazing' and 'hero' used to discuss her. One worker said that Frances was simply 'saying things that many people here have been saying for years' and argued the firm should take heed. She should, noted another, be asked to speak at the next company-wide meeting. A *Guardian* piece emphasized how Frances's claims backed up what many had already been saying: 'While Haugen became the face of internal dissent at the company, unrest has been roiling beneath the surface for years. In June 2020, hundreds of employees staged a walkout to protest against the company's content moderation policies relating to former president Donald Trump.' Other protests, including by content moderators, were described as part of a wide-scale discontent in the firm.[27] Frances, we were told, was channelling the voices of many former colleagues.

Calm and Rational: Frances Haugen's disclosures were, first and foremost, based on facts. A remarkable aspect of her campaign was the sheer volume of documented evidence behind it. Reportage on the Facebook Files frequently evoked a single image: pages and pages of documents. *Vogue* described the 'more than 20,000 scanned pages of internal corporate documents' she amassed, while the *Guardian* and *Times* readers were invited to imagine the 'tens of thousands', and 'thousands' of pages she revealed create a striking picture in the minds of their readers.[28] All this gave the sense of claims based on concrete evidence, not just her testimony.

More than this, Frances would frequently state that, now the Files had been released, the only rational way forward was to move from criticizing Facebook towards working together on a better kind of social media, armed with the research and the documents. 'If people just hate Facebook more because of what I've done, then I've failed. I believe in truth and reconciliation – we need to admit reality', she told the *Wall Street Journal*, '[t]he first step of that is documentation.'[29] Documentation thus supported her claim, but also enabled, she hoped, a constructive conversation about what was to be done.

Frances consistently maintained this persona. Even as the stress built, a general absence of hostility towards Facebook was notable. In fact, she often expressed her fondness for the firm, her admiration for the talented colleagues she had worked with, and her hopes for its future restitution. Again, such sentiments were echoed throughout media coverage, as we will see. As experienced whistleblower advisers tell us, this kind of healing perspective can be critical for building credibility, but also, and more immediately, for surviving the experience.[30] As Tom Devine notes, becoming vindictive can be a disaster; even in the face of serious reprisal, one must try to 'view conflict as a last resort'. For all the reasons set out here, this is not easy.[31] And in Frances's case, she did get angry at times, for example discussing Mark Zuckerberg's counterclaims.[32] Overall, though, she was in control of how she was presented as a person. From the start, Frances was described as 'deliberate, purpose-driven and analytic', and her commitment to a rational, calm persona continued to uphold this image.

Watching this case unfold, I found it hard to fathom what we were seeing. I had carefully studied countless whistleblowing cases. I was accustomed to all the things that can go wrong. I was used to seeing loyal employees devastated when disclosures made in good faith drew aggressive responses aimed at keeping them quiet. The haphazard search for a lawyer, or a journalist, who might help. The constant firefighting as each new, unexpected, disclosure-related crisis emerges, while one's finances, resilience, relationships and reputation all come under attack. This was, I had come to accept, the unfortunate landscape of whistleblowing. But here was a level of cool professionalism I never thought I would encounter. I had viewed Edward Snowden as a well-organized and impressive whistleblower, lining up journalists at world-leading newspapers, planning to walk out of the Hawaii NSA facilities with all the required information on a USB key in a Rubix cube and a plane ticket out of the country already reserved. But Haugen was something else again.

Empathetic and Accessible: The organized, fact-driven and calm Frances Haugen that appeared on the world stage might have struggled to engage people. She could have been seen as somewhat cold and technical, without empathy or ordinary human fragility. But we quickly learned about her personal struggles. These included for example a relationship that underscored her need to disclose. In interviews she spoke about a 'family friend' who had turned to the alt-right under the influence of social media platforms like Facebook. Disillusioned with politics, '[h]e got really, really radicalized. ...

I don't blame Facebook for what happened to him. I blame more 4chan and Reddit. But he was making crazy claims about George Soros running the world economy and things like that. Things that are just super easy to invalidate.'[33] The *Guardian* reported how watching this unfold was transformative for Frances. 'It's one thing to study misinformation, it's another to lose someone to it', she had explained. 'A lot of people who work on these products [social media platforms] only see the positive side of things.'[34] She had personal experience – 'someone I was incredibly close to, who was really important to me: I lost them to misinformation on the Internet, and I never want anyone to feel the pain that I felt'. It was this, she said, that drove her decision to accept the recruiter's invitation to join the Civic Integrity team at Facebook. It fuelled her, insisting that she would only work on its integrity initiatives, not the growth side of the firm.

When I first heard the story of Frances's friend lost to misinformation, it felt almost too good to be true: too conveniently related to the content of Frances's disclosures. Jeff Horwitz, it seems, had felt the same way. He describes contacting this friend as part of his thorough vetting process and verified this compelling tale. Frances was speaking from a personal experience.

Frances described the subsequent decision by Facebook to dismantle the Civic Integrity unit as another emotionally charged turning point triggering concerns about the platform's effects on people. 'I remember the incredible anxiety I felt. By six months in, I had learned so much about the consequences of the problem and felt so powerless to actually make progress on it that I was starting to have panic attacks.'[35] As she noted, '[m]y inflection moment: where I was like, "Oh, I'm going to need to probably tell someone", was when they got rid of Civic Integrity'. It was then, she recalls, that she changed her mind about corporate Facebook's intentions and capacity to make things right, and messaged Jeff Horwitz back.

Frances's struggles and anxieties in negotiating this dilemma counter the image of the cold, rational and fact-driven tech analyst. As she tells it, her key moments, her inflection points, were driven by personal attachments and care for specific others. This sense of care and connection is evident throughout her interviews. It even extends to the friends and colleagues she left behind at Facebook. She was keen to emphasize how many of them cared deeply about the negative impacts their company was having: 'I feel a huge amount of empathy for the people inside the company who are very distressed right now.'[36] At the Civic Integrity unit there remain 'many incredibly conscientious people who come in, learn what's actually happening at Facebook, and push themselves almost to the point of burnout because they know ... they know what's going on'. Putting herself in the position of former colleagues, Frances emphasizes the impossibility of the position they are in: 'And once they leave, they won't be able to help with the problem.'[37] She describes people who are currently grappling with the same indecision that had plagued her. Big tech firms like Facebook do not share their data and research outside the organization, and hence are very difficult to regulate and oversee. It is easy to see how change from the inside is believed to be the only real way forward for those interested in mitigating its impacts on public safety and democracy.

Frances even expressed empathy for those planning to retaliate against her. 'Some people at Facebook may see your decision to release these documents as betrayal', her *Wall Street Journal* podcast host said. 'Oh, I totally can ... I know that's going to happen', responded Frances. 'I totally see how they could come from that perspective.' In another interview she describes how a sense of responsibility for others has intensified since disclosing. With the chance to meet parents who lost their children, through her advocacy work, she has come to 'care a lot more' about the importance of mental health issues for young users of social media. Was whistleblowing worth it? she was asked. 'There's nothing in the world that feels as good as giving another person hope', she replied.[38]

Frances does not present herself as infallible and she is open about her own human frailty. She suffers from coeliac disease and entered an intensive care unit in 2014 following a blood clot in her leg. In one podcast episode she mentions how the dietary demands of this condition posed a challenge to her activities as a whistleblower, due to difficulties of travelling away from home.

With all the vulnerability Frances expresses, would this damage her position in the eyes of the public she is trying to convince? In February 2023, I convened a panel of investigative reporters and journalists experienced in writing about public whistleblowing. I asked them this question. Vulnerability, it turns out, is critical. The audience simply must be able to empathize with the person at the centre of the revelations. 'You need to see yourself' in the whistleblower, RTÉ's Aoife Hegarty explains, 'to be able to relate'. When Aoife's Investigations Unit broadcasts exposés, they ensure there is a person at the heart of the story: 'I am a firm believer in having people tell their stories as much as they can. ... That is how you have the greatest impact.'[39]

Presenting Frances Haugen was an exercise in emphasizing her calm, rational approach, the scale of information she brought forward, her capacity for independent, morally driven thinking, her empathy and her own vulnerability. And it seemed to have worked. But a company being criticized to that degree is going to have to respond. And the first step in responding is to neutralize the threat.

Targeting the Dissenter

Whistleblowers often must make decisions as they go along; there are few blueprints, and each disclosure is unique. Employers retaliating against serious threats, on the other hand, have a well-established playbook of tactics to use. The history of planned whistleblower reprisals goes back to the Nixon administration, when a director of the White House Personnel Office issued the 'Malek Manual', a secret set of instructions on how to remove a public sector worker who was threatening the informal code of silence and obedience.[40] Making an example out of a whistleblower is an important step, for example, if the goal is to deter others from speaking out. Today's employers have a range of methods to choose from.[41] Such strategies normally work quite well. Here, however, they did not. Again, Frances was different. Uniquely, she appeared to have a coordinated set of responses to deter the inevitable attacks.

Isolate the Whistleblower: Painting a worker as a disloyal outlier, a 'lone wolf' acting alone, is powerful. Reinforcing the boundary between the thousands of insiders working at the firm, and this single detractor, drives a clear wedge between the one and the many, damaging the credibility of the inexplicable lone speaker.[42] After Frances had come forward in October 2021, newspapers rushed to find Facebook employees who would talk about her, and about how they felt now that she had disclosed to the world. The *New York Times* reported on these effects a mere week after the 4 October *60 Minutes* appearance in which her name was revealed. Many former colleagues were supportive, it seemed, but some believed she should not have done it.[43] She was being disloyal. In fact, said one worker, she should be 'sued for breaking her nondisclosure agreement with Facebook'.

'Workers questioned Ms. Haugen's motives, her background and her credentials', the article ran.

In one internal message, an employee said Ms. Haugen was 'clueless'. Some said she lacked technical knowledge. 'She didn't know how basic stacks worked', wrote one Facebook engineer, referring to a term used by the engineering team to describe how data is structured in computer programming. He said all of her testimony should be disqualified. . . . Some employees also speculated that Ms. Haugen was motivated to leak because she was not allowed to work remotely from Puerto Rico, where she had moved during the pandemic.

Mark Zuckerberg was posting online about Frances's disclosures: they were 'just not true', 'deeply illogical' and made little sense. It seemed as though many workers agreed with him, and the media reported this.

This whistleblower was being portrayed as an isolated, poorly informed worker with a grudge. Two things were noteworthy about the response of Frances and her team to these claims. First, the content of her critique is consistently neutral, even constructive. It is not that Facebook is evil at the core, she said, it is actually a matter of conflict between two different priorities. And this had led the firm to struggle: 'Facebook has been struggling because a lot of the problems it needs to solve are about conflicts of interest, right? Conflicts of interest between public safety and profits and growth. Those are problems that Facebook cannot solve alone.' Her appeal is to let the outside in: 'Once it starts solving those problems together [with others], it'll be so much more constructive, and the path forward will be so much easier.'[44]

Second, Frances appeared to actively resist any notion of an 'us versus them' divide. She always insisted that the boundary that was being drawn between her – the outsider – and Facebook's insiders was false. Rather, she said, we are all in this together. Frances styled herself as, very much, a 'Facebook person'. Yes, she was very disappointed in the firm, but she was hoping for a brighter future for it and was willing to help work towards this. In media appearances, she repeatedly stressed the hope she had felt when she began working for Facebook. When asked by Kate Linebaugh what she remembered about her first day at the firm, she replied: 'I remember looking at my badge photo and it just represented so much hope to me. I just remember how much pride I felt.' She describes the sense of connection she still feels towards her former colleagues and even, at times, her empathy for

Mark Zuckerberg.[45] The mainstream media echoed and amplified this 'I am Facebook' identity; as the *Guardian* reported it, 'Frances Haugen . . . is adamant that she wants to help the social media company and not foment hatred of it.'[46] Haugen had, according to another reporter, 'faith in the potential of the company to bring people together and enable positive social movements – and actually, she still thinks this. "I really believe that social media has the power to do amazing things in our lives", she tells me. "I hold a slight fantasy that one day Facebook will rehire me to work on something in integrity".'[47]

The *Wall Street Journal* podcast focused on this attitude. Knowing what she now knows, enquired Kate Linebaugh, '[h]ow do you feel about Facebook now? . . . You have strong feelings about the company. Do you hate Facebook?' 'Oh, no, no, no, no, no', Frances responded, '[a] thing that I want people to remember is: to do this project, I had to do a lot of work to document the things I documented at the level I documented. It took a lot of work.' This hard work, she explained, could only be driven by the desire to make things better at the firm: 'You can't do those things if you're driven by hate, because hate burns you out. If I could work at Facebook again, I would work at Facebook again, because I think the most important work in the world is happening at Facebook because we have to figure out how to make social media safer.' Frances went on to appeal to former colleagues at Facebook. In her final message on Facebook's internal system, posted when she left in May, she wrote: 'I don't hate Facebook. I love Facebook. I want to save it.'[48]

Third, Frances deflects the discussion away from her, the Facebook whistleblower, towards the bigger issues in tech and social media. Her own website reinforces this position. It describes her as neither an anti-Facebook campaigner nor an opponent of platform capitalism, but rather as an 'advocate for accountability & transparency in social media'. This was then amplified by supporters in the media.

In summary, in dealing with the personalized attacks she received, rather than responding in kind – with aggression – Frances dismantles the apparent us-versus-them divide, evokes a deep sense of togetherness with colleagues at the firm and calls for collaboration to solve the bigger issues. Instead of allowing herself to be painted as separate and distant, she reached out. Her words extended an embrace to former colleagues, and an offer of help to her – hopefully temporarily – misguided employers. That said, it was not all warmth; at the same time, she has expressed anger at their media response to her disclosures, and mentions feelings of anxiety and frustration while working for them. But overall, these responses to the classic strategy of isolating the whistleblower were powerful. They negated the impact of being a lone voice against a powerful firm.

This response was also, to my knowledge of whistleblowing cases, highly unusual. Frances simply refused the boundary between herself and her former employer – insisting on her attachment to its mission, its workers and its products – placing herself firmly on their side of the table.

Diminish the Whistleblower's Credibility: Attacking the whistleblower's credibility is another classic reprisal strategy. Frances's experience and expertise were questioned, with former colleagues cited in support. Employers often paint the whistleblower – just one person in a complex structure – as being ignorant of the bigger picture, having only a partial view. This, as we saw earlier, was pre-empted by her emphasis on skills and expertise.

Facebook management also countered Frances's credibility by painting her as having misguided principles, particularly in relation to the overall position of the firm in society. An ideological argument centred on the rights of people to have free speech was put forward. Calls for Facebook's platforms to be reined in were painted as censorship, and an infringement of those precious rights. 'Every day our teams have to balance protecting the right of billions of people to express themselves openly with the need to keep our platform a safe and positive place', a Facebook spokesperson told the *Wall Street Journal*.[49]

In some cases, Frances was portrayed as merely driven by ego, seeking the limelight, and thus not credible. A *Vogue* magazine piece equated her 'rollout' to the marketing of a new product: 'Haugen seemed determined to coordinate her own rollout, managing it as tightly as she would a product launch.' The piece suggested at times that it was her ego at work driving her disclosure campaigns. The author wondered whether her publicizing her own credentials was 'crusading grandiosity. ... It occurs to me that Zuckerberg is nearly an exact peer of Haugen's: they're the same age, both entered college the same year, both with software engineering backgrounds. I wonder to myself whether Haugen – who has never met Zuckerberg but calls him "Mark" – perhaps thinks that she could manage the ship better than he has.'[50]

Interviews, including one hosted by a *New York Times* podcast, enabled Frances to pre-empt these criticisms and rebut them. She countered suggestions that she didn't know her topic, responding at length with technical details supporting her claims. Challenges to her position on free speech were also dealt with; Frances explained patiently how moderating the impact of social media on people's lives need not automatically lead to the stymying of democratic free speech.[51] She was also given the opportunity to respond to accusations that she sought the limelight and was nothing more than a 'crisis actor' staging events for the media. Again, she was calm, batting away such claims with humour.[52]

The speed of her responses is what really negated Facebook's capacity to diminish Frances's credibility. As reporters flocked to Facebook employees seeking opinions and quotes relating to Frances when the story broke, management at the firm felt the need to intervene. The situation was so disruptive that they found themselves appealing to workers not to speak to outsiders about Frances, even in negative terms. A *Times* reporter claimed to have seen a memo detailing how 'the discussions became so intense that Facebook's internal communications department issued a directive last week for workers not to disparage Ms. Haugen'. The memo stated: 'We have had employees specifically ask if they can defend the company by referencing experiences they had with her. PLEASE DO NOT ENGAGE in these conversations.'[53] This is just one example of the panic inside the firm that the disclosures elicited.

This panic stood in stark contrast to the consistent calm exuded by the intended target of the firm's reprisals. While Facebook seemed in chaos, Frances was mild. 'No matter what, keep your cool', advises Tom Devine when speaking to whistleblowers targeted by a smear campaign. Especially when dealing with the media, 'the calmest person in the room is usually seen as the most credible. ... Stay poised.'[54] This battle over poise and hence credibility was clearly being won by the worker disclosing. Central to this was the fact that Frances had resigned four months before her disclosures emerged. Many whistleblowers speak up while they are still employed, making them much more vulnerable to reprisal.[55]

Emphasize Suspicious Motives: Some commentators told us that Frances had darker motives. Someone this well organized was just too good to be true; she must have supporters behind her with nefarious intentions. 'The polished rollout, including Ms. Haugen's Oct. 3

appearance on *60 Minutes* and congressional testimony days later, has led to dark hints from Facebook and its allies that there's something a little too good to be true about her', noted the *New York Times*. This whistleblower, went the argument, might be credible, but she could not be trusted. This was simply an 'orchestrated "gotcha" campaign', according to social media posts by one Facebook executive.[56]

Indeed, the polish and poise with which she was presented was unusual. Having researched whistleblowing for many years, when examining individual whistleblowers' cases I normally encounter at least some degree of chaos, as unexpected events occur and unanticipated levels of reprisal are unleashed. Clear goals are rare, as are pre-planned responses to the employer's attempts to fight back. Indeed, research bears this out; whistleblowers famously do not foresee the retaliation that accompanies their disclosure; some say that, if they knew in advance, they would have chosen to stay silent. Frances was so different. As it turned out, her campaign was indeed orchestrated with the help of experts.

When the *New York Times* described Frances's campaign of whistleblowing as being managed 'as if it were the invasion of Normandy', they were not far off the mark. Or, at least, it had certainly been managed and not only by Frances. She described how she had the resources to pay for public relations support, so she secured it. Bill Burton was her PR representative in the US, supporting her appearances on the media there, and her testimony before the US Congress. President of communications firm Bryson Gillette, Bill had acted as a Deputy Press Secretary for the Obama administration between 2009 and 2011. His biography describes him as a 'renowned political and communications strategist', acting as 'senior adviser to political leaders, corporations and non-profits in California, Washington, D.C., and around the country'[57] Bill worked with lawyers to create 'successful messaging campaigns around important cases and issue areas'. Messaging was his business and now he was helping Frances. It may have been on Bill's advice that Frances deleted all earlier social media profiles in the months prior to going public and created a new personal website. It may have been that his team helped with the other aspects of her campaign: her focused talking points delivered with near-identical phrases, consistent responses to questions across interviews and speaking engagements albeit with very different audiences.

Perhaps taking on a firm of the size of Facebook was not something she wanted to do solo. But the fact that Frances Haugen used a PR team fuelled accusations of other agendas at play. Detractors sought to turn her strengths in public speaking and polished media skills into a weakness, representing her as a puppet for behind-the-scenes actors bankrolling the whole spectacle. In the winter of 2021 following the first appearance of Facebook Files articles, Frances travelled to various countries in Europe. Her travel was funded by the Pierre Omidyar-founded charitable foundation Luminate. The engagements were coordinated by an associated European lobbying group 'Reset Tech'. Her critics used the support of these groups to question Haugen's authenticity.

Criticisms focused on two aspects: Frances's association with the US Democratic Party through the partner groups she worked with, and the impact of her disclosures on the free speech versus censorship debate. Journalists Glenn Greenwald and Matt Taibbi were among those making links between the two. The Democratic Party supported by billionaire partners were, they argued, interested in censoring social media, having been wounded in the 2016 election campaign. Greenwald described a 'craving for censorship' on the part of those political actors, but also by their corporate media allies: the newspaper organizations most loudly amplifying Haugen's disclosures. For those newspapers, unfettered social media threatens their 'stranglehold on the flow of information by allowing ordinary, uncredentialed serfs to challenge, question and dispute their decrees or build a large audience that they cannot control'.[58] With Greenwald's international renown as a journalist who had helped Edward Snowden disclose US state surveillance of citizens at home and abroad, and Taibbi's reputation for upholding and defending the rights of whistleblowers for many years, these statements were not inconsequential. For her part, Frances appears to have openly discussed these criticisms, answering questions about the funding she received for travel, and emphasizing her independence as a speaker. Her claims were backed up by others who have sought to clarify these issues.[59]

The Work of Defenders

Overall, Frances was given a platform to speak back and defend herself. But often she simply did not need to. A striking aspect of this story is the way in which – from the start – retaliatory claims by Facebook were immediately turned against the firm by members of the media who called them out for being just that: whistleblower reprisal. They did this work on her behalf.

The *New York Times* for example wrote about Facebook's internal response to workers reacting to what was happening. An article detailed the 1,500-word memo circulated by Nick Clegg, Facebook's President for Policy and Global Affairs. The memo set out his view that Frances's forthcoming appearance on the *60 Minutes* TV programme would involve 'misleading' accusations about the firm.[60] This memo was, according to a *Guardian* opinion piece, a pre-emptive defence, one in which 'Clegg rejected any responsibility for Facebook being "the primary cause of polarisation", and blamed the prevalence of extreme views on individual bad actors, like "a rogue uncle".'

Clegg, it was claimed, was not interested in dealing with the substantive criticisms, rather his aim was to provide simplistic advice on how to respond to irritating questions about the disclosures; his memo 'provided talking points for employees who might "get questions from friends and families about these things"'.[61] The memo apparently featured accusations that the *Wall Street Journal* reports included 'deliberate mischaracterisations', accusations that were 'lobbed in without supplying any specific details or corrections'. The *New York Times* authors were clear in their dismissal of Clegg's exhortations, taking Frances's side in this battle for public opinion on the matter of the Facebook Files. Clegg's memo was, the writers asserted, 'all spin, with no substance. A trained politician deflecting accusations while planting seeds of doubt in the public's mind without acknowledging or addressing the problems at hand.'[62]

A *Financial Times* writer depicted Facebook's dismissive response to Frances's claims as merely something to be expected – a rote retaliatory response not to be taken seriously. It was textbook counter-whistleblowing strategy at work: '(Step) 1. Rubbish them [whistleblowers]. Facebook's approach to the criticism from its former product manager Frances Haugen was to paint her as junior and ignorant – "worked for the company for less than two years, had no direct reports, never attended a decision-point meeting with C-level executives".[63] This was standard stuff, in other words; the smear campaign was simply part of the whistleblower reprisal playbook. Soon it began to appear that anything Facebook said or did to defend itself against Frances Haugen was going to be interpreted as mere reprisal. This was significant in terms of the firm's capacity to respond: it powerfully neutralized its options.

Even basic damage control, to be expected from any firm involved in scandal, was dismissed outright. Aware of the impending publication of Jeff Horwitz's articles, Facebook 'front ran' the story by the *Wall Street Journal*. This was an attempt to get ahead of the narrative. The firm selectively published documents related to her disclosures, detailing how it was already dealing with problematic uses of its platform.[64] In August, Mark Zuckerberg had given the go-ahead to a new initiative designed to convince the public that Facebook was, overall, a force for good. Leading journalists were having none of this. An opinion piece in the *Guardian* appearing days after Horwitz's Facebook Files set out its views on what had been dubbed Project Amplify: '[it] aims to use Facebook's news feed "to show people positive stories about the social network", according to the *New York Times*. By pushing pro-Facebook stories, including some "written by the company", it hopes to influence how users perceive the platform.' According to the writer, this could not be interpreted as a benign PR exercise: 'Facebook is no longer happy to just let others use the news feed to propagate misinformation and exert influence – it wants to wield this tool for its own interests, too. With Project Amplify under way, Facebook is mounting a serious defence against the WSJ Facebook Files.'[65] Writers in the *New York Times*, for example, made no secret of their assessment of this strategy: 'Facebook tried to pre-emptively push back against Ms. Haugen.'

Within mere days of the first articles appearing, Frances Haugen's profile had grown to one of such strength and legitimacy that she found journalists doing the job of defending her, without her needing to utter a word.

Tension among Supporters

Frances wanted her story covered by more than just one media organization. The *Wall Street Journal* had broken the Facebook Files but wider reach was the goal. Soon after the first pieces emerged, Haugen and her PR team invited Jeff Horwitz and editors at the *Wall Street Journal* to a video call. There would be up to seventeen other outlets at the meeting. Frances outlined plans to share the documents with academics in the countries most vulnerable because of lack of regulation, including India and parts of the Middle East. 'The reason I wanted to do this project is because I think the Global South is in danger', she said. The aim of the call was to coordinate how this would all unfold and to outline plans for sharing more redacted documents with the press. As the *New York Times* reported, this was something of 'an uncomfortable moment'. 'This is a little awkward', an editor at the *Journal* was reported as saying. Frances had given them the scoop and they had worked hard to publish. There was, according to the *New York Times*, some disquiet among the other journalists in this new network. While the *Wall Street Journal* wanted all references to the story to cite the 'Facebook Files' tag it had started, others such as the *Times*'s Mike Isaac protested this would be 'free advertising for the Journal series'. Competitive pressures between different parties meant that many outlets went their own way in the months that followed.[66] Again, however, Frances and her team were executing the playbook to the letter. As seasoned whistleblowing experts advise, working with multiple media outlets over a longer period of time is important. It sustains the pressure on one's opponent and increases the impact of disclosures.

The Impact of Frances Haugen and Her Media Partners

Frances's appearance on the world stage was a well-coordinated campaign. We got to hear the plain speaking of this whistleblower, to learn about her moral sensibility and care for the company. We found out what she wanted us to know about Facebook's practices. And it worked. The disclosures reached their hoped-for audience.

At the same time, it was a campaign that enjoyed unprecedented levels of help, from media organizations and a PR firm. She had a team of supportive news outlets that worked to amplify her voice, and experts to help her plan and execute. Was she a calculating strategist, or a passionate worker who finally could take no more silence? Perhaps she was both. The point, for our project here, is that she achieved the impact she sought. And, while not many have her resources, her campaign has lessons for how we understand whistleblowing.

Successful Disclosures

Frances has been invited to speak at the US Congress, UK and EU Parliaments, the French Senate and National Assembly, to name just some. Across the globe, lawmakers in charge of internet and tech regulation still seek her views on what to do about the dangers of social media platforms.

Her goal, she had told us, was to open up the debate on Facebook's practices and social media more generally: to get people talking about them and questioning them. And, now, politicians and journalists world-wide were keen to join in. But perhaps the strongest measure of her impact was that vocal critics were engaging with her claims on her own terms. Even her would-be detractors were drawn into her own agenda.

As an example, Frances's statements galvanized a Facebook share-holder into writing to the *New York Times* with a spirited reflection on the core issues. Mr Brautigam from Tallinn criticized 'Frances Haugen, a do-gooder', for ignoring the fact that she was a 'Facebook employee who owed a duty of loyalty to her employer … Ms. Haugen is not a whistle-blower or a hero', his letter stated. 'She is a disloyal employee.' He went on to emphasize that, in his view: 'I am a Facebook shareholder, and I expect Facebook and its employees to run Facebook in a legal way to maximize shareholder value. She claims she wants to fix Facebook – by not giving its users what they want? Profit over safety? Safety from what?'[67] While the letter was pitched as criticism, the core conflict of interest Frances sought to highlight – between shareholder profit and safety – was front and centre.

Another letter, this time a professor of communication at Cleveland State University, questioned the assumed causality between use of social media platforms and violent behaviour. We need more data before we rush to judge Facebook, he argued.[68] 'Well', Frances might have responded, 'exactly'. A central tenet of her revelations was Facebook's own – hidden – empirical research into the impacts of its platforms, results of which it kept secret preventing analysis by aca-demics and others who might learn from it. The professor's letter prompts the reader to start asking why we don't have access to the information needed to answer the questions about causality he poses. The strongest measure of the success of Frances's disclosures may be that even her critics engaged in the very debates she was calling for. The content of their criticisms acted as support for her claims.

Self-Inflicted Wounds of the Retaliating Employer

In public whistleblowing disputes, the right kind of media coverage can prove essential when the stakes are high.[69] According to Tom Devine of Government Accountability Project, it can simply be the difference in whether the whistleblower gets to 'turn information into power' or not.

The media can help secure a level of public attention and support that lessens the power differential between whistleblower and employer.[70] But it is a dangerous game to play. The media is useful because it has high credibility, says Brian Martin.[71] But the whistleblower has little control on how it is going to work. People should always consider other options. Whistleblowers can live to regret going public in this way, agrees Devine, because it is difficult to turn back. People can find alternative avenues to reconciling with the employer shut down 'if it finds itself shamed and on the defensive'. There is nothing like a public scandal to help this feeling along. All in all, Devine advises, media exposure 'should be a last resort, not the first'.

But for Frances Haugen, the media 'game' seemed to have been pre-engineered for a win. What was remarkable was that the media, in their turn, seemed mostly to play along. Frances was given a platform to introduce herself on her own terms. She repeatedly reiterated her gratitude towards her supporters within the media. She described how she was 'incredibly honoured' by how hard journalists worked on material she provided,[72] and particularly her 'extreme amount of gratitude' for Jeff Horwitz – who, for example, gave her insight into what topics would be of public interest.[73] Indeed, she had been treated well. As one commentator noted, the media response 'amounted to white-glove treatment of a treasured source'.[74]

Frances's public profile was, we were told by experts like Kara Swisher, just enough and not too much. There was nothing that would risk her being tarnished as unhinged or corrupted by outside interests; her financial independence was emphasized. As soon as the reprisals began, she was given the space to defend herself, and to sit back and let others do the defending. It is one thing being able to rebut accusations of untrustworthiness and being tarnished as less than credible; most whistleblowers can easily defend themselves but only get to do so in private. What was unique about Frances's case was the platform she was offered to refute each accusation, point by point. Powerful media organizations granted her this stage.

Larger organizations are hotbeds of anxiety and uncertainty. Blame and scapegoating are commonplace. People on the front line dealing with customers and outsiders know this very well. Responsibility is pushed down to them without the capacity to make changes if this responsibility proves unbearable. In the case of Frances, this responsibility was untenable. Speaking out, she was then scapegoated, her vulnerability and isolation the source of an attempted campaign to discredit her words. But, unusually, it was this very act of organizational self-defence that provided the undoing of Facebook's position. Frances turned the anxiety of the defensive firm around: first, by empathizing with it and then offering herself as counsellor for it. As Tom Devine puts it, '[I]f done successfully, the company's deepest wounds will be self-inflicted.'[75] Frances had managed to create an advantage out of whistleblower reprisal, effectively rendering the company powerless. Digging deeper into this shows something new; what is often not foregrounded in discussions of Frances Haugen is the desire we have for care and connection with others, and how these can shape the way things turn out.[76]

A Relationship of Care

'I have never seen a source work harder in my life', Jeff Horwitz told *Vogue* magazine in November 2021.[77] This was one of a number of interviews he has done, in which he is asked all about his work with the famous Facebook whistleblower. A trade reporter, Jeff says he is not used to this kind of attention. On one such media appearance, he caused something of a stir with his laid-back dress sense; he wore a thick grey headband on 'Meet the Press', wild hair peeking out of the top. 'It was COVID, and I needed a haircut', he later explained, somewhat bemused. Being the focus of a media story is 'really weird', he told a podcast host.[78] In interviews, Jeff is frank, matter of fact, often describing the journey to disclose in terms of a typical journalist working with a source. But there's more to it. There is a sense of care that comes through.

Listening to his accounts, Jeff seems reluctant to answer the numerous questions he gets about 'what Frances is really like'. He tends to divert the focus of the conversation towards the serious dangers she revealed. When pushed to answer, however, he describes her as, first and foremost, 'an extremely smart person', with significant experience in tech, and significant knowledge of Facebook's practices.[79] Frances had really quizzed him, he recalls, after he first contacted her. They did not know what stories might emerge when they began meeting, but she was adamant that the information would come out in a way that was helpful and constructive. That she chose to come forward while forty of the colleagues he contacted would not is 'kind of impressive'.

Moreover, Jeff recalls, 'there were 50,000 people working at Facebook who could have done what she did . . . with the access and knowledge to do what she did. But they didn't.'[80]

Some of Horwitz's interviews have been with other journalists, for a journalist audience. Here, especially, interviewers tend to describe Frances's response to Jeff's initial request as some sort of windfall. They often stress Jeff's good fortune in landing this scoop. The world's most famous whistleblower, one podcast host began, what was it like to work with her?[81] How did you get this fantastic source to talk to you? asked another: 'what a prize', he went on.[82]

What is striking about these interviews is how uncomfortable Jeff sounds when his work with Frances is described in this way. Rather than the 'prize source', he describes a real person. Jeff speaks in detail about the challenges Frances encountered. At one point during the initial months when they were mainly 'just chatting', he recalls, 'there were definitely points when she just went dark on me for a few weeks'.[83] He was resigned to the idea she had changed her mind. He regretted it but understood. Disclosing in this way was going to be such a life-changing move. Jeff later found out that she had been 'really struggling with consciously being a mole inside Facebook. That she was very confident that she was doing the right thing, and that this was information that just absolutely needed to get out of the company. But it still sucks.' It was, he recalls, the fact that she would be making life very difficult for those left behind that gave her pause. 'She was unable to be honest with the people she was around about what she was doing',[84] he reflected, 'and she has colleagues, and she likes her colleagues, and it is not a fun situation.' The thought of speaking up like this was painful; there was 'a lot of dissonance there. That was hard for her.' Jeff has empathy for the dilemmas she faced.

Jeff also shows insight into Frances's personal philosophy.[85] Having studied in the past the work of the Civic Integrity team, he understood the complex feelings Frances and her colleagues had on learning of its disbanding. 'These were the people asked by Facebook to not just study the problems in the world but fix them.' The company had let them do the first but fired them before they could do the second. This, Jeff argued, left them in an impossible position. He recalled how Frances had talked about the concept of 'moral injury' in relation to this; where one is forced to do tasks at work to which one has serious moral objections. This is, he notes, one of the reasons she spoke up. 'She viewed that as basically . . . if she had left Facebook without having done something about this, she was going to be complicit.'[86]

Jeff also describes the difficult labour of collecting so many documents. In his droll manner, he recounts how it was 'not a lot of fun for her ... I am aware of the effort that went in here. She was trying to hold down a job and simultaneously trying to make the most of her waning days at the company'; it was, he noted, 'pretty brutal'. Jeff describes his initial sense after first meeting her, how he found himself thinking: 'wow, this woman is pretty fearless actually, and she is talking a game in which she is not going to be afraid of getting caught, in the end. She seems to be ok with the idea that this is her job, that this is her mission.'[87] From Frances's side, she told the *New York Times* that she 'got the impression that he would support her as a person, rather than as a mere source who could supply him with the inside information she had picked up'.

That said, Jeff Horwitz's support was, as he describes it, conditional and limited; it needed to be this way. He observes that Frances has a lot of people in her life that care for her. 'From a source protection point of view, I am really glad there are people in her life who are supportive, whether that is friends or allies ... or obviously lawyers have their place in that too.' He is, he notes, 'thankful that she was very mindful of this' need to take care of herself. Because, he stresses, as a reporter, he cannot be part of this. He is not fully on her side: 'As much as I may think highly of her, I can't be on "Team Frances" in the same way as those people.' 'Candidly', he says, 'she is really credible and really knows her stuff; it seemed like her motivations were really good. She wanted information out and was really not looking for a high-profile role for herself.' He notes that this may sound strange because of the limelight she has received, but he stresses her stated preferences, early on, for anonymity. He also describes understanding her choice to go to other media outlets in the months after the first articles appeared. Jeff understands her role is more than that of a whistleblower or a source, he notes, because of the choice she made to become an activist advocating for change. This kind of arms-length collaboration was how Erika Cheung had described her work with journalist John Carreyrou: 'There had to be some distance there; you can't have a good personal relationship with the journalist who needs to be objective to get the story out', she told me, noting that 'a lot of whistleblowers struggle with this'. Erika and John were friendly, but professional. As she summed it up, 'this is not a person I can lean on for emotional support'.

Public whistleblowers generally struggle to secure any mainstream media coverage at all. For those that prevail, research emphasizes the importance of the choice of journalist, both for effective disclosures and for the protection of the whistleblower. Yet this in-depth glance into Frances Haugen's case shows that this is about more than expertise and experience. The importance of care – long term – is evident. Having gathered a panel of investigative journalists to discuss whistleblowing work, I asked them about this.[88] They talked about all the things that are important when working to develop a story that will land: taking time to build trust, discussing how a whistleblower's name would be used if at all, planning the timing of articles to keep the issues alive in public consciousness and the other aspects seen here. But more than this, the nature of the relationship must be of a specific kind: 'I think there is an element where the person has to like you, and see that you're in it for the right reasons', reflected one journalist, '[a]nd that you're doing it. ... They come to you when they see what you do.' The panel described how sometimes the norms of journalistic work obstruct this kind of care. Traditionally, the primary duty of a journalist is not to the source, but rather the story. But, as they noted, the custom of never discussing the details of what is going to be published with the source, for example, can amount to an abuse of the power the author has over the person being interviewed. Despite being normal practice, when a source is vulnerable, it is not the right thing to do. In this, and in other aspects of working with a whistleblower, the panel agreed, a journalist must prioritize commitment and care for the human at the centre of the story.

Dana Gold explained the whistleblower's perspective to me, based on years of experience representing such clients. What most people do not realize, she pointed out, is that a journalist has no formal duty of care to a source. Lawyers have a duty to all of their clients, including whistleblowers, but journalists do not. This can place reporters who find themselves under pressure from competing interest groups in a tricky situation. And it can inadvertently place the whistleblower at risk. All in, despite the planning and orchestration that went into Frances Haugen's campaign, it seems that, without the care her journalistic partners showed, the story was unlikely to have unfolded in the way it did. As with Erika Cheung, however, it was a tempered, professional kind of care that marked the relationship between the whistleblower and the reporter.

One question remaining is whether this kind of successful campaign is available to all whistleblowers, something explored in Chapter 6. Before moving on, we must acknowledge that not all lessons from such cases are positive.

An Ideal Discloser?

'Frances's revelations delivered shock and awe precisely because surveillance capitalism is secret', Professor Shoshana Zuboff wrote in the *Financial Times*. At last, she was saying, we have an insider to tell us what we have long known, but needed definitive company research to demonstrate fully. There was something more to Frances's explosion onto the world scene, beyond mere credibility or information. She filled, as Zuboff said, a space we needed to be filled. More than this, perhaps she was the right person to do the filling. The extraordinary level of support and celebration she attracted is rarely seen in whistleblowing cases. It may have helped that she fit the bill of what a credible speaker looks and sounds like.

A psychosocial perspective shows us how we can become invested in public figures in times of chaos and crisis. Elements of fantasy come into play; we project unconscious fears and desires onto those appearing to represent a solution.[89] Public figures often draw supporters and followers because they are in fact both reflecting, but also amplifying, the fears and the ideals of these followers. While these investments may be, to some degree, fuelled by fantasy, they have a very real reality because the sense of meaning they grant us, in times of uncertainty, draws us to them.[90]

As Freud pointed out, this dynamic is particularly potent in groups, 'when people come together in numbers, they are more likely to be swept up in a shared fear or to be enthused by a common faith than they are to engage in reasoned problem solving'. Being in a group injects a unique force to the desire to seek a person who can provide solutions.[91] A social response to the need for order and stability is thus to create a figure to fill this gap. This is how leaders emerge, and, for our purposes, it offers a view on how certain public whistleblowers, as in the case of Frances and also Christian Smalls in the case of Amazon, can become lightning rods for the desires and fears of onlookers.[92] Their presence, their certainty and their apparent representation of the principles and preferences of their audiences allow us to escape the anxiety felt about the present circumstance.

Fantasy is a potent deterrent against whistleblower reprisal, because the force of investment creates a powerful screen of protection around the person at the heart of the fantasy. Idealization of a public figure means that those who follow will reject any sign of dysfunction in their chosen person: 'Not a single negative word or critical comment is allowed to spoil an image of sheer perfection', as sociologist Yiannis Gabriel tells us; the figure becomes part of our 'ego-ideal, the set of idealized images against which [we] measures [ourselves]'.[93] This, then, offers a screen against retaliation.

Frances started out with much less power than this firm. She used what she had. The excitable and unprecedented nature of support speaks to how well this worked. A *Vogue* profile described how '[a]t 5 feet 10 inches, with blonde hair, blue eyes, and a heart-shaped, strong-jawed face, Haugen looks a little like Reese Witherspoon's much taller cousin.'[94] So here we had a smart Reese Witherspoon with an MBA and big tech experience, who could tell us things we had longed to hear.

Of course, the darker side of this projection is that the very traits that made Frances such a convincing and powerful voice are the same that might exclude others from this playing field. Recent studies of whistle-blowing describe how, in specific whistleblowing scenes, a discloser occupying a relatively lower position of power can find it far more difficult to speak up and secure an audience.[95] Studies show how race can shape a whistleblower's experience. A quick online search of 'whistleblower' images shows us just how white the label is perceived to be.

The same kinds of fantasy-based projections that place certain people in leadership positions unfortunately influence the kinds of bodies we then find in those positions. When it comes to credibility, possessing a body most associated with authority and leadership works in one's favour. NSA's Edward Snowden, male, white, educated, articulate and straight, was celebrated across the world for his mass disclosures on citizen surveillance by his employer. Meanwhile, Reality Winner, a female NSA whistleblower who leaked a mere half-page document disclosing Russian interference in US elections to *The Intercept* and was punished, received little media attention and public support. Even Snowden himself spoke about the difference between how he was received and how her – equally newsworthy and important – information fell into silence.[96]

This situation is by no means set in stone; crises give rise to fears and desires that can be projected onto those who represent a solution, regardless of race, class and gender: some whistleblowers emerge at the right place, at the right time, even as they work hard to bring about the changes they see are needed, as we saw with Christian Smalls at Amazon. And the capacity to plan and strategize can mitigate obstacles for whistleblowers who begin from a position of relative powerlessness, discussed in Chapter 6. Nor is it easy to generalize across settings: different situations have different landscapes of how power and domination work: in some places, one's class, race, gender or sexuality, or a combination of these, can influence who gets to speak up, while in other settings these same traits will not make a difference.

'Successful' whistleblowers, if success is gaining a media platform, are often the kinds of figures valorized in a given society at the time, according to political scientist Lida Maxwell. Here, we can safely say that the authority Frances was able to channel – the Ivy League schools, scholarly upbringing and financial independence – are not usually accessible to people from the working classes. Her whiteness was useful in a country not known for successful racial integration. Perhaps only someone who looked and spoke like she did could properly take the space in the way she did. This all points to a subtle, informal system in which whistleblowing acceptability is graded. This is the value of what Lida Maxwell calls 'outsider truth-telling'. For some disclosers, their experiences reveal more than just wrongdoing: they reveal a system of exclusion of certain kinds of bodies. Perhaps only a figurehead that aligned with people's desires – for both the truth and the truth told in an acceptable package – could counter the control and authority of such a powerful organization as Facebook in 2021. This is not to detract from Frances's revelations but rather to make it clear that race and class likely play a role in their acceptability, as Chapter 5 explores.

Overall, a whistleblower does not go against a powerful big tech firm and expect to win. A firm that controls one of the most powerful information platforms in the world is unlikely to let that happen. Yet Frances Haugen did. She called out Facebook/Meta for misleading both the general public and its own investors about how issues from misinformation and hate speech to children's mental health are being handled. Her cause was not, she said, to shut down social media but rather to open up debate on how it might take form that 'brings out the best in humanity'.[97] All that said, a real woman remains behind the media fanfare. Today, Frances Haugen lives with the aftermath of whistleblowing. She continues her advocacy, writing books, defending her legal case. She has had to make her private life public, to robustly defend herself, to have a thick skin. Stress on the part of whistleblowers is a well-known part of the process, and she has to manage it. We must remember this.

Notes

1. The *New York Times*, 1 March 2022.
2. www.franceshaugen.com/.
3. Perrigo (2021).
4. Nast (2021).
5. Broadcast on 3 October 2021.
6. Stacey & Bradshaw (2021).
7. *Financial Times* (2021).
8. Zuboff (2022).
9. The firm was known as Facebook when Frances Haugen worked there, changing its name to Meta mid-way through her disclosures. For consistency Facebook is used here albeit that Haugen's disclosures refer to the other platforms run by Meta too.
10. The Real Facebook Oversight Board (2021). This webinar points out that a lot of the help available for Frances (e.g. mental health supports) was not available for them.
11. By market capitalization; see PWC (2021).
12. Swisher (2021).
13. Nast (2021) gives details of Haugen's self-funding via cryptocurrency investments.
14. As well as Devine & Maassarani's *Corporate Whistleblower's Survival Guide* (2011), see Brian Martin's *The Whistleblower's Handbook* (1999). (Note: Updated version = Martin (2013, p. 101).)
15. Birnbaum (2021). Legal advisers helped Frances pre-empt retaliation by securing legislative protections. She shared disclosures directly with the SEC and Congress; these moves are protected whistleblower activities.
16. Perrigo (2021).
17. Devine & Maassarani (2011, p. 109).
18. Smith (2021).
19. Nast (2021).
20. Nast (2021).
21. Smith (2021).
22. Smith (2021).

23. Waters & Murphy (2021).
24. *Financial Times* (2021).
25. Milmo (2021).
26. www.franceshaugen.com/.
27. Paul (2021).
28. Nast (2021); see also Callum Jones in *The Times* (London) 5 October 2021.
29. Milmo (2021).
30. Devine & Maassarani (2011).
31. Mueller (2019, p. 62).
32. *Digital Insider* (2022).
33. *Wall Street Journal* podcasts (2021).
34. Milmo (2021).
35. *Wall Street Journal* podcasts (2021).
36. Nast (2021).
37. *Wall Street Journal* podcasts (2021).
38. Pivot (2022).
39. 23 February 2022, with panellists Mick Clifford, Ian Fraser, Aoife Hegarty and Conall Ó Fátharta, view at www.whistleblowingimpact .org/news-and-events/whistleblowing-and-the-media/.
40. Devine & Maassarani (2011, p. 19).
41. Devine & Maassarani (2011), and Brian Martin's *The Whistleblower's Handbook* (1999). (Note: Updated version = Martin (2013).)
42. Kenny (2018, 2019).
43. Isaac, Mac & Frenkel (2021).
44. *Wall Street Journal* podcasts (2021).
45. Pivot (2022).
46. Milmo (2021).
47. Nast (2021).
48. Milmo (2021).
49. Linebaugh (2022).
50. Nast (2021).
51. Pivot (2022) at approx. 30 min.
52. Pivot (2022) at approx. 10 min.
53. Isaac, Mac & Frenkel (2021).
54. Devine & Maassarani (2011, p. 116).
55. See, for example, the case of Andrew Wilkie, www.bmartin.cc/pubs/ 05overland.html.
56. Smith (2021).
57. www.brysongillette.com/divi_overlay/bill-burton/.
58. Greenwald (2021).
59. Luminate's senior management have stated that the firm's decisions are independent of their funder's influence, decisions including support of

Haugen. The organization also stated the limits of their help on a blog post: 'Our support helped cover the travel, logistics and communications costs of Frances' team' (Scutari, 2022). See also Politico on Haugen's relationship with Reset and alleged links to the Democratic Party (Politico, 2021). See Smith (2021) for discussion of her disclosures from the perspective of censorship versus free speech alongside questions on who funded her travel and expenses in her trips to Europe.

60. Mac & Kang (2021).
61. Sadowski (2021).
62. Sadowski (2021).
63. Braithwaite (2021).
64. *Digital Insider* (2022), approximately 16.25 minutes.
65. Sadowski (2021).
66. Smith (2021).
67. Michael G. Brautigam, Tallinn, Estonia, in the *New York Times*, 6 October 2021, Pg. 20; LETTERS.
68. Richard M. Perloff, Cleveland, in the *New York Times*, 8 November 2021, Pg. 18; LETTERS.
69. Devine & Maassarani (2011, p. 109).
70. Devine & Maassarani (2011, p. 109).
71. Martin (1999, p. 97). (Note: Updated version = Martin (2013).)
72. Pivot (2022) at approx. 12 min.
73. Pivot (2022) at approx. 15 min.
74. Smith (2021). He was reflecting on the somewhat unusual move for a whistleblowing story: releasing a podcast episode to coincide with the publication of the first Facebook Files articles.
75. Devine & Maassarani (2011, p. 110).
76. Insights from psychoanalysis are 'indispensable for understanding the operation of social norms and power', Fotaki et al. (2012, p. 1114), Ekman (2012, p. 1177), Glynos, West, Hagger & Shaw (2014), Stavrakakis (2008).
77. Nast (2021).
78. Listen Notes (2021a).
79. Listen Notes (2021b).
80. Listen Notes (2021b).
81. Listen Notes (2021b).
82. Listen Notes (2021a).
83. Listen Notes (2021b).
84. Listen Notes (2021b).
85. Listen Notes (2021a).
86. Listen Notes (2021a).
87. Listen Notes (2021b).

88. 23 February 2022 with panellists Mick Clifford, Ian Fraser, Aoife Hegarty and Conall Ó Fátharta; view at www.whistleblowingimpact.org/news-and-events/whistleblowing-and-the-media/.
89. For discussion of a psychosocial perspective, see Appendix 1. Fantasy can shape people's search for people to solve problems in times of crisis. 'When we go to work, we take these fundamental desires', write Kets de Vries & Engellau (2010). The lack that such situations create give rise to a frustrated desire or 'a person or an institution – who can safely contain all our internal contradictions and give us a sense of wholeness' (Miller, 1999, p. 101); see also Kenny (2010), Gabriel (1995, 1997, 1999), Picard & Islam (2020).
90. Gabriel (1999), Kets de Vries (1979), Petriglieri & Stein (2012).
91. Kets de Vries (1988), Petriglieri & Petriglieri (2020).
92. Kets de Vries & Miller (1984).
93. Gabriel (1997, p. 321).
94. Nast (2021).
95. See Agostinho & Thylstrup (2019), Maxwell (2018, 2019), Rehg et al. (2008), Tavares et al. (2021).
96. Da Silva (2019). Military whistleblower Chelsea Manning, a trans woman, was perceived to have less credibility. Discussing this, Lida Maxwell (2020) points to the journey Daniel Ellsberg took to win credibility in the eyes of the US public. His disclosures were essential. But also, being white, handsome and well educated did not hurt.
97. www.franceshaugen.com/.

5 | Advocates and the Immigration Detention Centre

Supporting Dawn

High numbers of female detainees, detained immigrants, at an ICE detention centre in Georgia received questionable hysterectomies while in ICE custody.

I was listening to a podcast from the *New Yorker Radio Hour*. It began with a clip from a story from back in September 2020: '*Chilling breaking news today ... an alarming new whistle blower complaint*'. A for-profit detention facility in Georgia was the focus: Irwin County, run by a private prison company on behalf of the US's Immigration and Customs Enforcement (ICE). There had been allegations of medical mistreatment of immigrant women.

And one of the central faces you may have seen is the face of a woman named Dawn Wooten, who was a Nurse at the facility where all of this was happening.

I had heard of Dawn. She had blown the whistle on failures to provide necessary medical care to detainees at Irwin County Detention Center (ICDC). The failures were many: guidelines to control the spread of COVID-19 had not been followed. Women had been sent for unnecessary hysterectomies and other gynaecological procedures without informed consent. Along with some of the women survivors, nurse Dawn had spoken out about the abuse. In her forties, the podcast told us, Dawn had five children and was now living in Tifton, Georgia, a small town about three hours from Atlanta.

In the interview, Dawn reflected on the conditions in which the women were held: 'It was more of a place of ... a kennel, or I would say an animal centre. It was not clean, to the point they did not have adequate, at times, water. It was not adequate for them. The food: I have seen maggots in the food.'

Dawn's voice is upbeat, light-hearted as she tells her podcast host about her choice to speak up.

138

I'm coming home one day in my truck, and my eyes are full of water, and I'm like 'Okay, God, what do you want me to do? You've got a sense of humour. This is not funny. What do you want me to do?' And I'm 20 minutes home, I pull in my driveway, and I sit. And I was like 'Now I understand the assignment. You want me to speak for those (women) … so now I see what it is.' So now I go to work.

Her mind made up, she began to raise concerns in her workplace.

I come back and I'm asking questions. Supervisor's up here: 'Oh, you're going to leave that alone. Oh, you don't want to touch that. Oh, you don't want to bother that. Oh, you don't want to talk about that.' So, now I'm getting that type of treatment now coming through, and I'm like 'There's got to be something that's going on here.' So now I've turned from LPN (nurse) to private eye, because I just can't let this go.
Dawn was true to her word.

Filing a Whistleblower Complaint

In September 2020, a group of organizations filed a formal complaint on behalf of the women detainees and Dawn.[1] Led by grassroots advocacy organization Project South, the complaint focused on widespread medical neglect taking place at ICDC. It included detainee interviews, results of a 2017 ICE inspection of the facilities, and other sources. The complaint included a claim that Dawn's whistleblowing rights were being violated: 'Ms. Wooten has witnessed other employees be reprimanded for doing "what's right," and she has been reprimanded and retaliated against, herself', it stated. Having formally lodged the documents with the Office of Inspector General of the Department of Homeland Security, Dawn and the women waited for action.

News of the complaint, it appears, was first broken by *The Intercept* on 14 September. The story went viral, with a follow-up released the day after. Articles with headlines declaring 'mass hysterectomies' were shared rapidly. The concerns raised by Dawn and the women tapped into a long-standing scandal centred on ICDC. Just three months previously, the *New York Times* had reported on hunger strikes and protests by detained migrants fearful for their lives because of the facility's refusal to respond to COVID-19. *The Intercept* articles were followed up by interviews with Dawn on *MSNBC, Democracy Now* and other outlets. 'It just exploded', she reflected of this period. 'September 14th, I'll never forget, 2020. You can find me now on

Google [laughs]. You never could type my name in. But [now] you can type my name in.'

Dawn and colleagues' original complaint was primarily highlighting the response to COVID-19 within ICDC, yet it was a secondary disclosure that became the focus of the media and subsequent investigations. The rate of hysterectomies performed upon detained women led some to raise the alarm; all had been referred to the clinic of a single doctor. Their concerns formed part of the formal complaint. 'When I met all these women who had had surgeries', one detainee was reported as saying, 'I thought this was like an experimental concentration camp. It was like they're experimenting with our bodies.' All these women had been sent for treatment by Dr Mahendra Amin, who practised gynaecology in the nearby town of Douglas, and was described by ICE officials as the detention centre's 'primary gynaecologist'. As Dawn reported: 'We've questioned among ourselves. Like, "goodness he's taking everybody's stuff out … That's his specialty".'[2]

My *New Yorker* podcast episode went on to describe the impacts of whistleblowing for Dawn. Her disclosures had spread quickly, leading to passionate demands for change from vocal medics, politicians and activist groups. The UK *Guardian*, the *New York Times* and others had covered the story of ICDC. Multiple women had come forward validating their concerns and filing a class action suit. Finally, ICE had been ordered to end its contract with ICDC. Despite all this, the host was telling us, Dawn was not doing so well. It was now two years later; she was out of a job and blacklisted in the small town she lived in.

As I listened, it all sounded depressingly familiar: the successful whistleblowing but the grim aftermath for the whistleblower. Yet something felt different. Here was the whistleblower, on the *New Yorker Radio Hour*, explaining her situation, in her own voice, directly to thousands of listeners.

The podcast host was explaining the background to the episode:

Recently I got a call, after all this time had passed, from Dawn Wooten's attorney. And she said, you know, so many people followed that story in the news, it sparked congressional investigations, it sparked a civil lawsuit and a criminal investigation about all the misconduct that Dawn had helped to reveal. But what very few people know is what happened to Dawn after she blew the whistle on this place.

What happened to Dawn – the reprisals she still suffered – formed a significant part of this *New Yorker* episode. Prompted, it seemed, by this phone call from Dawn's attorney. What was going on here? As it turned out, a years-long advocacy campaign by dedicated and knowledgeable supporters was now helping Dawn's own story reach the public. How did they manage this?

Information Matchmaking

I had met Dawn's attorney several times. Dana Gold works with Government Accountability Project. This Washington, DC-based legal firm was founded in 1977 and has focused on representing whistleblowers who disclose abuses in immigration detention settings since June 2018. I asked Dana for some expert advice on a research project I was doing with a colleague, on how whistleblowers survive post-disclosure. We exchanged emails. Hers are direct, immediate, detailed. They describe current campaigns, the crises in the US political landscape and its impacts on whistleblowers, and what needs to change. Her work is intense, her days are busy and yet she always takes time to share with people researching whistleblowing. It was through Dana and her colleagues that I encountered information matchmaking.

The people I meet from Government Accountability Project are a little different from regular whistleblower lawyers. They call themselves activist-lawyers. It was from Dana's colleague Tom Devine that I first learned about the strategy behind the work they do. Tom is quietly spoken. He wears a suit, but with a Grateful Dead tie. I first heard him describe information matchmaking at a seminar at a London university.[3] The room was full of historians and political theorists. They were there to discuss the legacy of overt secrecy in national security and intelligence agencies, and the challenges for those who blow the whistle. Unlike the other speakers, Tom was not from a university. Nor did he have any notes, not even a PowerPoint presentation.

When his talk was introduced, Tom rose from his seat, walked to the whiteboard and drew a single black dot. He pointed to it. The audience stared. 'That's the whistleblower. That's the worker trying to disclose something really serious.' Tom then drew a circle around the dot. The circle, he told us, is the organization they are in. As long as the whistleblower is not seen as a threat, the information can get out of the circle to people on the outside who can do something about it. But once the whistleblower is spotted, they become trapped on the inside of the circle. They can be isolated and punished if they keep trying to speak up. Tom rapidly drew arrows from the edge of the circle, all pointing at the lonely little dot in the middle. Once they are in the spotlight, the project becomes about targeting and silencing them. The information flow stops.

The critical thing, he told us, is to stop this happening; to help the whistleblower stay under the radar, to keep a low profile. But if they gain public attention and become a target, here's what we need to do. Another, bigger, circle surrounding the employing organization. More rapid dashes on the whiteboard, this time arrows pointing from the outer circle to the inner one. The public must surround the employer and focus on it. The public's attention can make the employer – and the retaliation it is engaged in – the new focus of the story.[4]

The room was silent. Tom went on to give examples of how Government Accountability Project has helped over 8,000 whistle-blowers in this way since it began in the 1970s, highlighting issues from government abuse of power with Edward Snowden to the United Nations' failures to protect civilians, to exposing dangerous chemicals used in the BP oil-spill clean-up. From the early days of working with US government disclosers like Daniel Ellsberg and Ernie Fitzgerald, targeted for retaliation by the most senior members of the administration, the organization had learned a lot about protecting whistle-blowers. Working with whistleblowers is, for them, a package: litigating cases is a core part, of course, but whistleblower support, educational outreach, lobbying for legislation change and research into corruption are the activities that go hand in hand with this.

I had never thought of whistleblowing cases in this way. 'The dot philosophy', I scribbled in my notebook, beside some arrows and circles. Things began to make sense. The email I had received from Dana a few years earlier in response to an *Atlantic* piece I wrote claiming whistle-blower success was merely about luck. I now saw why she had rebutted this so strongly. This dot philosophy. 'In my experience working as an activist-lawyer with other activist-lawyers at Government Accountability Project', Dana had written, 'whistleblowers are most successful if they have the support of a knowledgeable advocate (often working behind the scenes) who can help them turn their information into power and essentially "turn the tables" on those responsible for the disclosed wrongdoing (and the likely retaliation against the messenger)'. It was now becoming clear. A lot of the whistleblowing cases I studied were failing or prevailing depending on how well that little dot was being protected by supporters. But it wasn't just that there were similarities across cases. The way Tom was describing it, it was more than a pattern. It was a practical method evolved into a generalizable framework. The idea that all this could be orchestrated was new to me. Information matchmaking was the phrase he used.

Solidarity, Tom stressed to that London audience, is crucial to survival. Society – and by that he meant civil society, NGOs, journalists and ordinary people – must surround the employer. The way to make this happen, according to Tom, is through 'information matchmaking'. When he takes on a whistleblowing case, he first gets in touch with as many public-interest stakeholders as possible. These are people who have an interest in the truth of the matter being uncovered. They can include law enforcers, prosecutors, journalists, local activists, community leaders, public-interest groups or professional associations – basically any party with a specific interest in the whistleblower's information. Politicians on a crusade can be particularly helpful. In fact, Tom reflects, sometimes it is a good idea to involve politicians from opposing parties who want to out-do each other and be the first to uncover a scandal. This can trigger government investigations at different levels. Sometimes, even a firm's competitors can be encouraged to get involved; or opposing factions within an employing organization. Competition like this can really galvanize stakeholders, Tom explained, leading to more revelations, more credibility for the whistleblower and more of a chance for the wrongdoing to be addressed. Regardless of who they are, partners cannot be people who are easily bought off or intimidated. The energy and action they generate brings light to a previously hidden issue, making it so much more difficult for an employer to engage in a cover-up. Being a legal representative of a whistleblower for Government Accountability Project, therefore, involves a lot more than the law: information matchmaking with strategically helpful stakeholders is essential. And it is not always easy: author Tom Mueller describes this complex yet delicate process involving so many stakeholders as requiring 'the timing and finesse of an orchestra conductor'.[5]

All this doesn't just happen by chance, Devine went on. The key thing is to make a clear plan to strengthen those arrows and keep them trained on the employer for as long as possible. This gives the whistleblower's case the best chance of success. My email from Dana Gold had added more detail: 'When Government Accountability Project works with whistleblowers, we are able to provide not only legal counsel and protection to the employees but to use our expertise and credibility to reach out to journalists.' Her colleagues do more than just let reporters know about the situation, however. Their very interest lends credibility to the discloser. The journalists, Dana explained, 'know that we have rigorously vetted the whistleblower and verified the information disclosed, which is half the challenge and an obvious barrier to media coverage'.[6]

Government Accountability Project has a research arm too, which helps extend the reach and impact of the disclosure: 'We can also do things like analyse and further investigate the whistleblower's disclosures', thus these activist-lawyers do some of the journalist's job for them. Moreover, they are often found going beyond the simple case surrounding the whistleblower's claim, actively 'turning that information into white papers, or letters to agency officials, or members of Congress to generate hearings and investigations into the underlying whistleblower concerns or even into workplace cultures that chill disclosures'.[7] Media coverage, Dana stressed, can drive reform. 'So, working effectively with investigative journalists can be one of the most powerful components to a whistleblower's success. Sometimes, too, just the threat of media attention can be an effective means of creating "success" for a whistleblower. Sometimes so can the threat of a lawsuit, or an actual lawsuit.' Threat and reality – providing solid information while also understanding the power of perception, it seems information matchmaking involves a complex strategy based on relationship building and communication as well as legal supports.

When I first heard about information matchmaking, it resonated with something I had been seeing more and more in whistleblowing cases, but that I had no words for. I was increasingly aware of whistleblowers arriving on the scene, seeming to have their campaign already designed and ready to execute. Each of them seemed to know the law inside out, so much so that they were able to predict what the other side would do and counter it in advance. They appear to know precisely the value of allies. They know which supporters to approach, when and how to do it. They are attuned to the errors employers make, and are ready to exploit them. Although few if any manage to avoid reprisals, these planned campaigns look a whole lot different to the typical whistleblower story.

These are emphatically not the haphazard, reactive struggles for survival by a worker suddenly thrust into the public gaze, desperately trying to defend themselves in a new and perplexing landscape where law and the capacity to pay for it seem to be all that count. Frances Haugen's approach was somewhat like this. To a certain extent, Edward Snowden's premeditated removal of data, flights to Hong Kong and choice of world-respected journalists who would meet him there suggested a good deal of premeditated strategizing.[8] The Trump White House whistleblower of 2019 seemed to know in advance how the game would play out; commentators observed their securing of legal protection, maintaining confidentiality and explicitly avoiding the post-hoc classification of 'secrets' that had so badly damaged former government dissenters' defence cases. Watching each story unfold, I felt the same thing. These people, it seemed to me, came to play. These cases were extraordinary because of people's apparent understanding of what lay ahead, and capacity to withstand the challenges. Now I could see the tactical impulse behind all this.

Even as they exemplify information matchmaking, however, these pre-planned campaigns are not those of ordinary workers and the people with whom groups like Government Accountability Project work. In practice, whistleblowers who benefit from the kind of tactical approach taken by activist-lawyers can be in much more precarious positions. The reality is, while information matchmaking is powerful, real-life settings reveal the challenges that accompany its use, as we explore next.

Information Matchmaking in Action

Nurse Dawn Wooten had certainly experienced life as the 'dot' in Tom Devine's whiteboard sketch. She described to the *New Yorker* podcast what had happened when she began asking questions on behalf of the women detainees who were bringing concerns to her during her work. In the first half of 2020 she had been raising issues to her managers. It all came to a head in June. 'The moment I realized I was being retaliated on, [was] when I was written up. I hadn't been written up out of the twelve years I've been nursing ... out of the three cycles I had been through that place. I automatically knew that they were building a case.' Having never received a formal complaint about her conduct by any employer, suddenly Dawn had become a target. Her supervisor wrote her up, falsely, for a 'no-call, no-show' failure to turn up at work without a reason. But Dawn had been certified ill on the day in question. She queried this with senior management.

When I had the conversation with the Deputy Warden, he said, 'Dawn, just take it. It's just a write-up. That is all you have to do.' I said, '[b]ut it's a lie. It's not the truth. I have a doctor's excuse for the day she's claiming that I was a no-call no-show.' I went outside to my car, came back with the doctor's excuse for the time. His response was that it was out of his league: 'Well you might want to take this to the Warden.'

Dawn asked what was actually happening, requesting more clarity. 'I asked him, I said, "What is going on? I've never been written up. I've never had a problem in this place. You've never had any issues with me." He said he'll call me when he needs me.'

Like many nurses in similar institutions, Dawn did not have secure tenure of employment. Yet she was a valued member of staff, consistently working full-time hours. After that conversation, however, she was immediately demoted to the status of an 'as-needed' colleague. She waited to be called for a shift she could take, but she never again worked in the centre. The arrows, it seems, were pointing at Dawn. In the final version of the complaint she would file two months later, she described how

You put two and two together. I'm asking for these things and I'm speaking for these detainees. I'm a problem. I'm being seen, and I'm not supposed to be seen or heard. It makes it look like you're not doing your job . . . It [ICDC] has driven away so many people who work there whenever they go to speak up and they go to do what's right.[9]

Having become a problem, help was needed.

Driving Whistleblower Support and Focusing on the Employer

Dawn worked with activist-lawyers who did what they could to drive the focus away from the whistleblower and onto the employer at fault. Along with Project South, she was represented by Government Accountability Project when the September 2020 complaint was filed.[10] In the following days and months, her attorneys issued multiple press releases and communications in support of Dawn and her disclosures. Her legal representatives came with her to the interviews she was asked to do with oversight agencies, Congress and the press.

Follow-up investigations by journalists from the *New York Times* rapidly verified Dawn and her co-complainants' claims. Reporters interviewed sixteen women and arranged for reviews of the files of seven who were able to gain access to their records.[11] By 16 September, just two days after the complaint was filed, formal inquiries were being ordered by members of US Congress and the Department of Homeland Security into the disclosures. ICE offices in New York were picketed the following day. Four weeks later, the findings of a study by 'nine board-certified OB-GYNs and two nursing experts', investigating the cases of nineteen women who had been referred to Dr Amin, were sent to members of Congress. The report warned of an 'alarming pattern' in which the doctor allegedly subjected the women to unwarranted gynaecological surgeries, in most cases performed without consent.[12] By December more than forty women submitted testimony in a federal lawsuit against Amin. Within a year, ICE formally ended its contract with ICDC. They cited the revelations made public by Dawn and the detained women, and the activists that had helped them.

As the story of the inmates' treatment at ICDC exploded across the US and global news media, whistleblower Dawn remained relatively unknown. Articles mentioned how the disclosures came to light via a whistleblower. But where her name was mentioned, it was in terms of her profession and her actions only; she was simply 'whistleblower, Nurse Dawn Wooten'. There were some supportive statements. Joaquín Castro, the Congressional Hispanic Caucus chairman, praised Dawn's 'courageous choice to speak up' and said 'these horrors must not remain hidden' as he joined the calls for an immediate investigation. A personal website was created, clearly setting out Dawn's motivation for speaking out and giving some detail on her background. But, researching her case with colleagues, I found little of the typical media scrutiny, the 'who is the whistleblower' articles with extended biographies and deep dives into personal histories. The spotlight to which other whistleblowers are subjected appeared to be absent. If there had been an attempt by her employer to smear her name and negate her disclosures, this does not appear to have reached a national audience.[13] Dawn, in short, was not a major part of the story. The focus seemed to be on the employer ICDC and its wrongdoing.

In the end, the disclosures Dawn made with other detainees led to multiple investigations: the ending of referrals of women detained by ICE to a doctor carrying out multiple hysterectomies without cause, the ultimate ending of ICE detentions at ICDC and ongoing legal actions by the women who had suffered the medical abuses. It is important not to overstate the role of activist-lawyers. Dawn's journey was no means facilitated by Government Accountability Project alone. Project South played a key role. And the women detainees at the heart of the story collectivized in the face of medical abuses by Mahendra Amin and the facility's lack of response to COVID-19.[14] The detainees had made use of social media and digital technology creating videos drawing attention to their conditions. It was they who drew Dawn Wooten's attention to the scale of the abuses in the first instance. The women, as Dawn describes in her blog, had come to her. They were at the centre of the efforts to disclose.

In Dawn's case, the information appeared to have reached those who needed to know about it. Government Accountability Project's information matchmaking seemed to have worked. The outer circle, public scrutiny, had done its job. Yet at the same time, when it came to whistleblower reprisal, there was only so much these activist-lawyers could do. As the *New Yorker* podcast was detailing, Dawn had been struggling since speaking up.

Blacklisting and Impacts on Livelihood

Despite all the attention on the wrongdoing and ICDC, and despite her relatively positive media profile, daily life for Dawn and her family was getting much worse. As the case began to gain wider publicity, she recalls: 'My emotions were everywhere. I was depressed. I should have been excited; I had done a good thing.' Dawn may have done a good thing, but she was also now out of work, with five children to support. She was not being contacted by her former employer, nor by any others. Dawn had a strong employment record and there was a nursing shortage across the US because of COVID-19. She describes her response: 'Angry. And I'm fearful at the same time. So, if doing a good thing costs me my job, and doing a thing costs me now my life, now I also have people on the reverse end that want my throat.'

Even though she was not being targeted in the national media, her name was still out there, especially in those months following the disclosure: 'I would wake up every day for a certain period of time and have to hear it and hear it and hear it and hear it and hear it and hear it. I never thought that it would be to this degree. I was everywhere.' This attention, she felt, had antagonized some powerful people in her town. Irwin County Detention Center was known for paying relatively high wages. It was a big employer in the area, and many local businesses supplied the facility. Dawn recalls how she was perceived: 'Now I'm messing with the commodity, in a small hick town city, [how] they make their money, it's the biggest industrial part ... flourishing in the city. Now I'm messing with that economically. So, now I don't know who wants my head on a platter.'

Dawn found work at a local hospital's nursing home facility just twenty minutes from her house. There were no obvious links with ICDC. But, one day, she was informed she had been taken off payroll. She was not given a reason: 'My Supervisor there at the time didn't even have the decency to call me and say, "Hey, Dawn, they took you off. You're a liability", whatever, whatever.' She felt she knew why it had happened. Having spoken out publicly about the big local employer, it now seemed like she was blacklisted. More than this, she was a target. Dawn described how her children were threatened via anonymous phone calls, how unknown cars sat outside their school waiting for them. Dawn had been forced into hiding with her family, with Project South helping them shelter in hotels in the two months following the story breaking.

Dawn's options were limited. Her whistleblower complaint languished as part of a significant backlog in the Department of Homeland Security's systems at the Office of Inspector General. All she could do was wait and wait. Meanwhile, she tried to find work, applying for over a hundred jobs. She tried everything: COVID vaccination jobs, jobs doing nasal swab testing, jobs in palliative care and nephrology.[15] After more rejections, Dawn took a practical approach, 'I'm thinking "Okay, so". And here I am, going to McDonald's. I went to the McDonald's here in Tifton, was going to flip some burgers, as a nurse!' Even at McDonald's, however, it turned out she was known. At the recruitment meeting, 'the girl recognized, "You're so and so's Mama." So, she calls my daughter's name, I was like, "yeah!" So, the manager comes out, and was like "Uh, well I'd better call the main office." So, I never heard anything back from the McDonald's. I was like "Well darn, I can't even flip burgers?"'

Dawn describes being called for numerous other interviews that went well, but, once the employers' staff found out who she was, she would receive a phone call saying the job was gone. After yet another such rejection, she decided to test the level of blacklisting involved. 'So,

I waited a week and I called back, and I pretended to be somebody else. I said "Hi, my name is Melissa. I'm calling from Tifton, Georgia, and I'm an LPN (Licensed Practical Nurse) and I've been nursing for about 12 years. Do you have any open positions?"' The response was enthusiastic. 'Yes, yes, yes, yes! We need nurses, like today. We need nurses like today!' Once Dawn's name was revealed, the job disappeared. It seemed the media attention had set this relatively small community against a whistleblower wrongly identified as the source of the problem.

The Office of Inspector General of the Department of Homeland Security finally published one of two reports into conditions at ICDC in January 2022.[16] It vindicated her claims but was not much use to Dawn and her family. As had happened to Seamus in Chapter 1, the claim for whistleblower retaliation had been separated off into another investigation, the findings of which were never issued, while the wrongdoing had been split into two investigations: detracting from the overall extent of neglect and abuse at centres like this.

The Private Costs of Whistleblowing

Financial struggles had been the feature of Dawn's life since speaking up. Even while Congress and international newspapers were loudly proclaiming their disgust at what was happening, and celebrating the whistleblower, she was not able to pay her bills. A support fund had been set up to help with this by the author Jordan Ifueko:

there was a Go Fund Me out there first ... It did, it helped me catch my rent up, so I was caught up with the rent here, a few bills, I was able to catch my vehicle up, because they were getting ready to drag it, or repossess it, and then not knowing ... was not thinking that I was not going to be employed, so [I] paid things up, paid things off, got things, bought things, because I didn't want any overhead. Things that the kids needed.

With all the expenses she incurred in daily living with a family of six, the fund could only offer so much assistance: 'So that money just kind of went, like the wind blowing a grain of sand.' It was difficult to make ends meet. 'I'm like, "I don't know what I'm going to do." So, I'm falling further and further and further and further behind financially, and (extended) family is like "Well, we're kind of needy ourselves." It's not that you can go to family and say, "Hey, I need my lights", or "$1,100 is not a lot to come by."' Even as Dawn was recording the podcast with the *New Yorker*, she was having difficulties. Her old car had broken down, she told the host.

While Dawn's situation is not unique, there is relatively little focus on these day-to-day challenges of surviving after whistleblowing. In 2018, frustrated by the lack of attention to the tangible costs suffered by whistleblowers, I researched this with colleagues. Interviewing and surveying over 150 disclosers and experts, we wanted to figure out how much money whistleblowing costs people: the financial impacts of speaking up.[17] We focused on people who, like Dawn, had to leave their jobs as a result of whistleblowing. Two out of every three whistleblowers reported a reduced income after disclosing. The same proportion reported being blacklisted either formally, where instructions not to hire them are written down, or informally, where potential employers are verbally discouraged from hiring the whistleblower. Speaking out brings new and unexpected expenses like legal fees, travel costs, health supports due to stress and income depletion due to career change. On average, we found respondents incurring total costs of over 240,000 euros directly relating to whistleblowing. For those who had lost the capacity to earn a wage, costs were double this. We found struggles to meet living costs, which naturally has an effect on physical health and mental well-being, and heart-breaking impacts for families. Dawn's children found themselves living in hotels just after the disclosures and suffered from the constant stress of being without a family income due to their mother being blacklisted in her profession, unable to find secure employment.

So, Dawn is not alone. Loss of income is common in such cases. But people who are less well able to withstand this kind of financial upheaval are in a particularly difficult place. Dawn's situation stands in stark contrast to some of the famous white-collar whistleblowers we might recognize from news stories: those who have savings, family resources and other means to withstand a financial onslaught. Interviewing whistleblowers who lost their job, I was struck by the number of people who openly reflected on their good fortune, having a partner or spouse who was in a different industry, thus immune from reprisal, and could keep the family afloat. This, many said, is what made the difference in their capacity to survive the experience. Others cited savings. Some mentioned being close to a well-pensioned retirement, hence less exposed. And there are whistleblowers, as we have seen in this book, who can rely on well-resourced supporters to help with expenses. But as Dana Gold told me, 'Dawn's case puts a spotlight on how most whistleblowers actually aren't so "lucky" as to have a wave of individual donations flowing in as expressions of support to compensate for the lack of income from retaliation.' Whistleblowing support organizations running on a charity model can do little to help. 'Foundations that support non-profits, and the non-profits themselves, aren't structured to easily cover the post-disclosure costs for individual whistleblowers', Dana explained.

Responding to this reality, Dawn's activist-lawyers at Government Accountability Project worked to keep their client's cause – as a whistleblowing survivor – in the public eye in order to secure support. The aim was to draw attention to the injustice of her current situation. Two years after her disclosure, in October 2022, the *Guardian* reported on her case, with a headline: '"I'm back on food stamps": Nurse who exposed "uterus collector" still faces consequence.' The *New Yorker* podcast I was listening to had been released earlier that year, in January 2022.

Dawn won the First Amendment award later that year. She was chosen as a portrait subject for the *Americans Who Tell the Truth* series unveiled at an event at the National Portrait Gallery in Washington, DC. These are rare examples of amplifying the voice of a whistleblower despite the news cycle having moved on. Along with these honours, the podcast also made a difference to Dawn. 'To be actually asked: where am I, how am I faring, means the world at this moment to us, and I'm going to include the babies too, because we have been on a topsy-turvy downward spiral', she told the host. The discussion gave Dawn the chance to describe how, even after all the attention has blown over, '[t]his year was kind of rough. This year, this whistleblowing is rough.' It is often difficult to gain public support for a whistleblower related to an old news story. But Dawn's allies are trying to stall this.

Dana Gold and her team continue to keep the focus on Dawn's story. And now their attention has also turned to another part of their work: fighting for legislative change. In some countries, Ireland for example, whistleblowers whose cases are pending can apply for interim relief. This means they keep getting paid until the case is resolved. Interim relief makes a huge difference, financially, when employers are trying to drag things out. Dana and colleagues at Government Accountability Project have been fighting to change federal policy. The current protections in place for whistleblowers, they argue, are just not enough. Dawn's case shows this clearly.

Inequality and Whistleblowing

The costs of whistleblowing are not equally shared across those who speak up. Whistleblower reprisal is a form of attack against workers speaking out, and it tends to draw on all the available tools. As we saw in the previous chapter, in a setting in which gender, race or working-class identities have already been devalued, systemic bias works against people being believed, and being supported. These labels can exacerbate reprisals against whistleblowers possessing them.[18] Building on this, what we see here is that the very real financial impacts of speaking up can be worse, depending on who is doing the speaking. This is exacerbated in workplaces where power imbalances exist with, for example, women and people of colour disproportionately occupying lower-status positions. Adding to this, the recent rise in short-term and insecure work contracts hampers people's capacity to speak up and survive afterwards.[19] Recall how for people in relatively precarious work agreements – Dawn, but also Christian Smalls at Amazon, and Erika Cheung as a graduate at Theranos – even basic workplace protections were lacking. The difficulties that racism, job insecurity and low-income status create show up important things about the practical inequalities underlying whistleblowing. The point is that, when a worker is considering speaking out, they are doing so against a backdrop in which bias, insecurity and power imbalances, often deeply embedded, may already be working against them. The challenge of speaking up intensifies and multiplies. Put simply, the well-known hazards of becoming a whistleblower are exacerbated by unequal working conditions.

People in precarious jobs, and people who are their family's sole breadwinner, are disproportionately disadvantaged. As a single mother working as a nurse in today's US healthcare system, Dawn is both. As she waits for justice – her complaint about whistleblowing retaliation is still pending as I write – so too are the many women detainees who filed civil lawsuits for the medical mistreatment they suffered. And their situation, many without citizenship, is yet more precarious. It does not sound like the institutions involved are prioritizing these matters. According to the *New Yorker*, in Dawn's case, '[t]he government legally had 180 days to respond, and they blew past that deadline. They asked for more time, and then they blew past another.'

Information matchmaking works well for getting information to those who can do something about it. It can effectively deflect media scrutiny away from the whistleblower and onto the wrongdoing. But it does not simply end there. Even with a successful communication strategy and a supportive network, the aftermath of disclosures can be very difficult for some whistleblowers. Dawn's case showed how, while an effective campaign worked to keep her from being smeared in the media, and successfully drew attention to the issues disclosed, it could not do much about the private costs of whistleblowing that can impact people and their families. Doing the right thing seems to have jeopardized her significantly. Her situation meant the risk to her and her family was severe. As Dana Gold's ongoing interventions show, effective information matchmaking involves a long-term commitment, because, whether we like it or not, inequality is a hidden part of the whistleblowing landscape.

The Organizing Practices of Whistleblower Activist-Lawyers

Dawn Wooten's case shows the care, commitment and hard graft that dedicated whistleblower support can require. For the person providing that support, what is it like? It is useful to examine the nuances of the organizing practices involved, taking Government Accountability Project as one example.

The Organizational Model

Government Accountability Project has a long heritage. Tom Devine got his law degree from the University of the District of Columbia School of Law (formerly Antioch), which he describes as 'a hotbed of public interest law – founded in 1972 in answer to Nader's call for a new breed of lawyer willing to defend the public'. He recalls the passion of both the faculty and the students at that school, where assignments involved defending underserved members of society. These principles informed Government Accountability Project's work since their first clients arrived in the seventies. They have evolved into a structured process for doing the work. At the client intake stage, the information is screened, and the case reviewed. As a non-profit public-interest organization, if a case is to be considered, it must tie in with the mission of the organization to promote government and corporate accountability. Expectations with whistleblowers are managed in advance: the risks are clearly explained. People are encouraged to speak with their family members in the first instance, and source other legal support for non-whistleblowing issues if needed. The staff at Government Accountability Project is not large. The strong relationships and the trust-building required for its brand of legal activism to work takes a lot of effort. At any one time, a lawyer working there might have twenty or thirty cases, but capacity is limited. The organization cannot take on all cases, so those chosen must have a strong public-interest justification, with robust evidence to support. The organization strives to be explicitly non-partisan, when it comes to lobbying for whistleblower rights. They have worked with both right-wing and left-wing groups for policy change.

Today a number of lawyers and transparency experts offer this kind of practical advice and public solidarity alongside legal help to whistleblowers they encounter as part of their work. What is striking about Government Accountability Project is, first, the clear and detailed strategic process they have from start to finish. And the depth of experience they draw upon in executing. Government Accountability Project's model is spreading, with countries from Serbia to South Africa focusing on advocacy as well as legal issues.

Even with the successes it has brought, challenges persist in this kind of work. Those organizations run as charities require constant fundraising. Because both time and resources are limited, if only a small number of cases can be taken on, many worthy causes will be rejected. Whistleblower activist-lawyer groups often hire former whistleblowers, a particularly effective model when it comes to deep knowledge and the capacity to empathize with clients, but one that is not always easy to recruit for.

In general, the organizations doing this work are not well supported by public or philanthropic funding; money is scarce in this space. Awareness of such challenges prompted Anna Myers and colleagues to form *Whistleblower International Network*, a group that supports civil society and NGO advocacy organizations working with whistleblowers, helping them to build capacity for giving effective advice, sharing best practices and working to ensure many countries are involved so that the global North does not dominate our understandings of whistleblower advocacy. Anna described to us how advocacy organizations are often ignored in discussions of whistleblowing cases: 'It's so interesting to me. . . . They are the ones that are often just left out of any of the narrative. You've got the whistleblower and the media, or you've got the whistleblower and the employer, and you may have lawyers in there. But you don't have the organizations that have done most of the work around the whistleblowing.'[20] The civil society organizations working in this space are often overlooked. Yet the lawyers I have met and describe here are rare entities. They have empathy, they have experience and they are in high demand.

Commitment Culture

When we asked Tom about Government Accountability Project's work, winning cases was not the only goal. 'When you're doing this work, you develop priorities. The first priority is the wellbeing of the whistleblowers and their lives. I work at GAP because I want to change the world. But it's crossing the line from a good trip to a bad trip if you start using the whistleblowers and they're just means to an end.' There are many private lawyers who see whistleblowers as simply a case: a potential income stream if their claim succeeds. Similarly, journalists can just see them as a source for a story they can write to please their readers and editors before the news cycle moves on. Tom emphasizes how his work with whistleblowers involves 'professionally intimate relationships. I get real close with them.' Now and then, this closeness requires telling a client not to speak up at all, for example in the case of previous whistleblowers: 'When I've been through intense suffering with somebody and their family and we manage to come out of it with their families, bodies and careers intact and their feet on the ground, partly it's my duty and partly it's from the heart to warn them, "Do you really want this to happen to you again?"'

This closeness and commitment to clients was evoked in Dana's long-term support for Dawn. But what is driving it? Solidarity was the word used by Tom Devine at that event in London. Solidarity typically refers to a connection between people working together to achieve a common goal – a connection that arises from common interests, objectives or principles.[21] Between these activist-lawyers and the whistleblowers they represent, this sense of solidarity and connection appears pivotal. It is what enables them to work together to challenge the status quo in powerful employers and institutions through public whistleblowing. However, when we consider the accounts of activist-lawyers together, there is something more going on, fuelling both the commitment and the common goals. There seems a sense of compassion: a felt compulsion to care for the other. While this compassion is what drives the long-haul dedication necessary to sustain this kind of work, it can spill over into stress and overwhelm.

Danger of Overwhelm

Working as an activist-lawyer is not straightforward. It can take over. I had exchanged emails with Dana Gold, inviting her to contribute a chapter to a book I was writing with friends. It was during the busiest time with Dawn's case. She very much wanted to help, Dana replied, but her work 'had been all-consuming and urgent for months, and anything non-urgent or as important . . . has necessarily taken a back seat'. It was prior to the 2019 US elections and Dana was, as well as representing clients, working with others to counter misinformation being spread, helping found a new 'Democracy Protection Initiative' programme bringing together advice for election workers, journalists, faith leaders and whistleblowers in election-related activities. 'I am looking forward to the challenge of not working insane hours.'

It is not just the volume of the work that can be challenging. The day-to-day of whistleblower lawyer-activism involves encountering painful situations experienced by whistleblowers and those they try to help through their disclosures. And, as we saw with Dawn, it is not always possible to alleviate suffering. Dawn's disclosures had impact, as we saw, yet, as I write, this month has seen further disclosures of abuse and sexual violence at another detention centre, where many ICE detainees of ICDC have ended up. There are few definitive resolutions to many of the situations encountered. For an activist-lawyer, work can sometimes spiral into 'operating in a constant state of trauma and reaction', Dana described. 'It has been hard, exhausting, and deeply sad at times.' But, as she reflected, a person in her role has to live with this. 'The gift of this work has been that I have been able to make a contribution in my own way to fighting to save democracy by supporting whistleblowers, and that has saved my sanity.'

Tom Devine has also spoken of the stress of the job. Some years ago, the labour of representing as many whistleblowers as possible became overwhelming. Working over a hundred hours a week, he developed medical issues and was forced to take a step back. Tom has learned to detach himself from the mundane challenges of each client for the sake of his own health while still empathizing with their struggles, and respecting their values. This detachment is essential for his work: 'I love this job because I get to speak truth to power but also keep the job', he emphasizes.[22] The capacity to detach even a little is, he feels, also essential for the whistleblowers he works with. Over many years, Tom has reframed what his work means: survival – for both the lawyer and the client – as well as trying to win cases.

In conclusion, whistleblower support is a critical factor in enabling disclosures about wrongdoing to come to light. We know little about how it works. But there are lessons from activist-lawyers' work with whistleblowers that seem to hold promise. Information matchmaking offers insight into the strategy deflecting negative attention away from the whistleblower and keeping the public's focus trained on the wrong-doing, even if this is a long-term project.[23] Meanwhile, examining what enables all this to happen – the organization model, the culture of commitment and compassion, and its corollary, the threat of over-whelm – gives us a sense of how these things work in practice. If our goal is to understand a little more about how alliances between part-ners support public whistleblowing, it may be that here we have the beginning of an organizing practice.

Notes

1. Cuffari, Quinn, Giles & Paulk (2020). Project South has a long history in investigating and highlighting the conditions experienced by migrant detainees and challenging the system of detention itself. These grassroots activist-lawyers worked with many women who were directly affected by the conditions at the detention centre. Other advocacy groups involved in filing this complaint include Georgia Detention Watch, Georgia Latino Alliance for Human Rights and South Georgia Immigrant Support Network.
2. Dawn is quoting others here.
3. At Government Accountability Project, this process is referred to as their methodology for developing an advocacy campaign.
4. See also Mueller (2019) for an excellent description.
5. Mueller (2019).
6. Email from Dana Gold.
7. As just one example, a *New York Times* op-ed describes collaboration with lawyer associations to dispute the use of secrecy agreements by companies trying to circumvent reporting.

This involved building a coalition of 200 organizations to petition the SEC to stop such agreements and protect whistleblowers. It was successful, with the SEC bringing enforcement actions against companies, eventually seeing firms comply voluntarily. See Devine & Thomas (2014).

8. Snowden, together with powerful members of the Consortium of Investigative Journalists, saw his disclosures reaching political figures and newspaper corporations across the globe (Munro, 2018).

9. Cuffari, Quinn, Giles & Paulk (2020).

10. Government Accountability Project appears to have originally been co-counsel with Project South. By late 2021, Government Accountability Project's Senior Counsel & Director of Education, Dana Gold, was Dawn's sole counsel.

11. Dickerson, Wessler & Jordan (2020).

12. O'Toole (2020).

13. At the time that ICE's contract with ICDC was ended, some public comments were made, including by local politicians, denying the information she had disclosed or blaming Dawn for the closures. This backlash mostly remained local.

14. Mahendra Amin was not held accountable and, at the time of writing, continues to practise in Georgia, although he remains the subject of numerous federal investigations. See Vasquez (2022).

15. *New Yorker* (2022).

16. The published report focused on allegations relating to COVID-19 protections and other medical failures at ICDC. The second report emerged much later in early 2024: an audit of the way in which surgical procedures are authorized in ICE detention. However, the Office of Inspector General of the Department of Homeland Security did not issue its findings in the claim for whistleblower retaliation, even as DHS acted on Dawn's disclosures and ended the ICE contract. See https://whistleblower .org/press-release/press-release-oig-report-confirms-whistleblower-claims-of-wrongdoing-at-irwin-county-detention-center/, and the latest report finding a third of all major surgeries were unnecessary across ICE detention. www.oig.dhs.gov/sites/default/files/assets/2024-01/OIG-24-16-Jan24.pdf.

17. Kenny & Fotaki (2021).

18. See Miceli et al. (1999) for a study of US public sector federal workers suggesting retaliation was more comprehensive when the whistleblower was not white.

19. During the COVID-19 pandemic, it became clear how agency staff, and people on short-term and precarious work contracts, often struggled to

speak up because of insecurity about their position, particularly in healthcare settings, but also other frontline roles in which exposure to COVID-19 was prevalent but capacities to disclose were limited.

20. Interview with research collaborator Meghan Van Portfliet.
21. See also Vachhani & Pullen (2019), Tonkiss (2021).
22. Mueller (2019).
23. For other examples, see Martin (2012, 2013), Martin & Rifkin (2004).

6 | *Public Whistleblowing as Collective Bricolage*

Our aim in this book was to understand more about the outsiders: the public whistleblowers who find themselves outside the protections of the official channels and the law. Exposed for disclosing deep-seated, systemic wrongdoing that threatens the very mission of their employer and the reputation of its leaders, public whistleblowers can find themselves the targets of extreme retaliation. Experts in whistleblowing policy, consulting and research tend to focus on perfecting the legal and organizational shields for whistleblowers working within the system. For this other group, there are no shields. Some limited research examines support for public whistleblowers, and practical guidebooks describe where workers might access it. But insights into how this all works are lacking. Plus, in practice, effective help is not easy to secure. Workers know this, and it deters many from speaking out.

We therefore began this project hoping to find out more about useful support: what kinds of connections are meaningful, how they come about and how they can help whistleblowers disclose effectively but also survive the experience. The task was never going to be easy. The public whistleblower without protection is something of an impossible subject: there has long been resistance to examining the topic in any great detail.

Addressing this need, the following chapter summarizes what we have learned from our case studies focusing on the work of public whistleblower supporters. Each insight is analysed in turn, before bringing them together in an overall framework termed 'collective bricolage'. Collective bricolage describes the organizing practices of public whistleblowers and their allies, working together outside the official channels to disrupt the status quo, and bringing information about serious wrongdoing to those who can address it. Collective bricolage is how partners generate creative means for resistance, even from surprising sources including the errors and mistakes of a retaliating employer.

Inside Retaliating Organizations

Common understandings of whistleblowing tend to evoke an all-powerful employer with the capacity to crush a whistleblower. Much research into the aftermath of whistleblowing focuses on the downside. C. Fred Alford's book *Whistleblowers: Broken Lives and Organizational Power* is considered a classic in the field. Alford's central point is that we can learn a lot about the exorbitant power of organizations by examining the experiences of whistleblowers. We can understand more about how tribal organizations can be, how intolerant of dissenters and how untouchable their position in society. With the defence of inside secrets as the paramount goal of organization members, the whistleblower automatically becomes a scapegoat who must be cast out so that the tribe can survive. Alford's stated project is to explore this: to 'follow the scapegoat into the desert of his exile and there to study his affliction so that I might learn the sins of the tribe'. This affliction, this exile, is the focus of Alford's work. Aiming to show just how far the employer goes to destroy those who speak up, his psychosocial insights into both the perspective of the whistleblower and the employer are invaluable. *Broken Lives* is a powerful book. I have met numerous whistleblowers who tell me the impact it has had on them. It explains how the mesh of organizational power and influence can fatally surround the discloser. There is a deep learning here: we can know organizations through what they do to dissenters. We know their power because it is mapped out for us by the trouble dissenters experience. Numerous scholars have been inspired by this idea, taking his work forward in different settings.[1]

Certainly, throughout this book, we saw such power at work, from the twenty-something graduates asking simple questions about quality control then aggressively pursued by one of the most well-known legal firms in the US on behalf of client Theranos, to the apparently orchestrated smearing of Christian Smalls at senior levels within Amazon. We saw examples of how hard anxious managers work to cure the organization of the whistleblower, now seen as nothing more than 'an insidious disease, a boundary violator',[2] breaking the rules by bringing the outside in. The work of restoring control becomes about redrawing boundaries to exclude this disease. Desperate measures are sometimes needed. And employers have the resources to engage them.

This idea that the employing organization is all-powerful is compelling. And it is, to some degree, accurate. People who have worked in this area agree. In 2020, responding to a panel webinar discussion of how stronger laws might provide impenetrable shields for all whistleblowers at some time in the future, Transparency International Ireland CEO John Devitt was quick to counter: 'No one can protect whistleblowers and it is unethical to suggest that you can.' Sitting in the audience, I was taken aback. Here was someone tirelessly lobbying for legal change. Had he changed his mind? Devitt went on to clarify that, when an employer is well resourced and bent on reprisal, it will take more than just the law to protect a targeted whistleblower. He was talking about entrenched employers, the kinds we examine here. His point is that, if powerful organizations really want to retaliate, they can and will. '*Reality Check for the Aspiring Whistleblower*' is the title of a section in Chapter 1 of Tom Devine's influential advice guide. 'Because we want you to be prepared', he writes, 'we will not mince words in describing the risks of your decision.' Decent legal advice, he goes on, can help the whistleblower even the odds against an organization hell-bent on reprisal and silencing critique. But 'in terms of raw power, the corporation holds all the cards . . . the deck will be stacked against you'.[3] Forget all those whistleblower role models held up for our admiration in the movies and the magazines: they had it easy.

Alford's *Broken Lives* is just one study among countless examinations of the wide array of painful and debilitating whistleblower reprisal strategies that can be used by the well-resourced organization intent on silencing. 'To run up against the employer is to risk obliteration . . . nothing remains after one runs afoul of the employer', Alford tells us.[4] The message is one of capitulation. The employer can and does destroy the whistleblower, which teaches us a lot about these apparently benign entities in our world. But there Alford stops.

Can we go one step further? Can we see capitulation as neither inevitable nor predetermined? Rather than write whistleblowers off as victims, can we be more ambitious for this group that does so much for us all? Are we, in short, missing part of the picture? Reflecting on Alford's work, through the interviewing and the analysis for this project, and having examined our cases through a psychosocial lens, I find myself agreeing and disagreeing with him. The power of employer organizations can be awesome and all-consuming: devastating for those in their sights. But we must own that there are opportunities and gaps in this power – mistakes and chances that arise, and that people make use of. Both of these things are true. Can we work within this tension?

Anxiety, Errors and Unintended Consequences

To date, few researchers, if any, examine the retaliating employer, to foreground the perspectives of those within it. Few try to understand why they act like they do.[5] This is a unique feature of a psychosocial lens on organizations; it enables a deep dive into what is going on within them, particularly in times of crisis when deep-seated fears, emotions and defences spring quickly to the surface. This lens allowed us to see things a little differently. We witnessed the anxiety pervading employer organizations under threat from a public whistleblower's disclosures, particular in Seamus's and Erika's cases, but also to an extent in Christian's and Frances's. This anxiety led managers to flee to the perceived safety of the shelters on offer: a rush to scapegoat the whistleblower, to seek solace in apparently infallible official channels and to cling to the promise of aggressive laws designed to crush workers speaking out.

Importantly, however, this anxiety elicited gaps and fissures in the apparently monolithic power of these retaliating employers. It caused retaliating managers to make mistakes. And this provides a view of public whistleblowing not often centred in discussions of such settings. Examining these breaches of power more closely, we see investments in management roles, the emergence of subcultures, mistakes and forced errors and digital leaks leading to acceleration of affective forces – all elements that disrupt the well-worn narrative of the all-powerful organization.

Investments in Management Roles: Our work roles can have a powerful impact on us. We become invested in the positions we are given.[6] For workers-turned-whistleblowers, these investments stayed with them, particularly their commitment to the principles of management. This manifested in their capacity to turn the tables on the employer when the time came. Each whistleblower was a worker, and many had been managers. As such, they had each received training, gained experience managing other people and internalized professional norms of management. Throughout their disclosures, the norms and principles they had absorbed on the job shaped their whistleblowing. This was a surprise to me.

Frances Haugen noted that her appeal to Facebook insiders to see the light through what she was revealing, and her request that they all work together to help heal the wrongs of social media, were lessons she had learned during her time at Facebook. Her mentors and teachers there, she recalled, had taught her that 'solving problems together is better than solving them alone'.[7] In Christian Smalls' frequent media appearances in the aftermath of his successful union drive, he has continued to stress how he had been 'invested in the company' and that 'at first, he loved his job'.[8] He reflects on his several years in a supervisory role in Staten Island: 'It's funny, because I say this all the time: Amazon prepared me for this. Even though I wasn't a manager, I was doing the job of a manager for the last four and a half years.' The company's managerial mantras, it appears, continue to inspire him today as an activist and organizer: 'The leadership principles that I had at Amazon made it easier for me to transition over to the activism that I'm doing. I'm using a lot of the principles that I learned at Amazon against them. My favourite one is "have a backbone and commit." They hated the fact that I use that all the time.'

Christian felt the irony of this 'backbone' being both the reason for his lack of promotion success, and his capacity to organize in opposition to Amazon: 'It's probably why I never got promoted: I had a backbone, I stood up for what I thought was right, and I'm committing to seeing change. Another principle at Amazon is "see it, own it, fix it," which is probably one of my original principles – I saw the issues, I owned up to it, and now I'm trying to fix it.'[9] The whistleblowers' investments in the very principles they had been required to internalize were turned against the employer that had taught them.

The Emergence of Whistleblowing Subcultures: There is much written on the importance of organizational cultures. After every scandal, after every public inquiry pointing to organizational failings, we hear the same thing: 'we need culture change'. This idea is thrown about as if culture change was easy. But it is probably the most difficult thing an employer can try to do.[10] That is because, at its core, an organization's culture is ephemeral and obscure. Academics searching for ways to bring this elusive concept to light say things like 'culture is just "the way we do things around here"'. These ways are not easily spotted on the surface of organizations; they are rarely written down and less easily changed. Culture does not exist anywhere we can see it: it is not tangible. It resides in workers' and managers' heads, and it is made up of subtle norms, beliefs and values. These include shared beliefs about who 'we' are, and what 'we' value.

Despite employers' best endeavours, and despite millions of euros spent each year on consultants promising 'culture change', it remains

slippery. A decisive part of this slipperiness involves the formation –
inevitably – of subcultures. Subcultures form among groups of workers
who believe, value and do things a little differently from the official
cultural narrative. We find these pockets everywhere in organizations:
think of the different cultures existing among IT staff and the sales team
in a single firm, for example, or the cultural norms amid blue-collar
warehouse workers and executives on the senior team. These groups
disrupt the commonly held fantasy on the part of senior managers that
a homogenous, easily controlled and tangible organizational culture is
possible.

A fascinating and paradoxical aspect of the public whistleblowing
scenes we witnessed in this book is that, if we look closely, we see
whistleblowing subcultures emerging. These arise in the most surprising places. For each whistleblower who, at first glance, seemed isolated
and alone, shared norms and values developed through connections
with other dissenters within the organization. These norms and values
manifested new, albeit marginal, cultures: where wrongdoing is intoler-
able and speaking out is imperative. Across Theranos, a few people
began talking. They began to learn of each other and of the presence of
more dissenters, subtly normalizing the idea that patient testing practices were wrong, and that their observations were correct. At Amazon,
shared desires to resist the endangering of workers spread between key
people in its warehouse facilities across the US, and even to the executive suite. Beyond our cases, the UK's national health service has long
contained groups of NHS whistleblowers organizing in support of each
other. The US government is another, particularly salient, example.
Whistleblowers emerging from its intelligence and security agencies
refer to others who spoke out previously and connected to colleagues
attempting to whistleblow in the present.[11]

Subcultures of dissent, of whistleblowing, emerge as a paradoxical
feature of anxious and aggressive employers. Such subcultures sustain
and thrive through counter-narratives contrasting the official organizational story about a wrongdoing that continues unimpeded. Stories
encompass collective desires to address it, giving meaning and value to
people's lives even in the face of moral injury they face in their day-to-day
work in a corrupt setting.[12] Not all members of a dissenting subculture
will speak up, but those who do speak from a place where critique
is accepted. Whistleblowing subcultures have practical uses:
people watch what happened to others and make choices about how

to disclose accordingly.[13] But they also offer a different sense of identity. If, as we saw, part of the work of whistleblower reprisal is to threaten subject positions that feel unbearable to those who would occupy them – invalid worker, for example, or lawbreaker – here we see that another identity, 'organizational dissenter', becomes available. And it is just as valid as any other because it emerges from a subculture of others feeling the same. The paradox is, of course, these subcultures emerge precisely where aggression against whistleblowers is inflicted most strongly, thus the employer's own response works in this self-defeating way. If the official organizational culture is promoted as 'how we do things around here', in some places within that organization, a notable, even if marginal, subculture holds that whistleblowing, or working towards whistleblowing, is 'how *we* do things around here'.[14]

Mistakes and Forced Errors: Even the most powerful employer makes mistakes. As we saw in Chapter 1, error is built into the fabric of large organizations which, because of their size and scale, must operate under a fantasy of control – a fantasy maintained for both workers and stakeholders. Particularly in contexts that are at best fast-changing and unpredictable, at worst chaotic and crisis-ridden, a fantasy that the organization is in charge must be upheld at all times. But this is, finally, a fantasy. Since Max Weber's publication of *Economy and Society* at the turn of the last century, in which he details the 'ideal type' bureaucracy, many studies have shown all the ways in which real-life large organizations depart from this ideal. And one of these ways is the ubiquitous presence of unintended consequences. Given the multiple variables at play in organizations, the many people working there with their different interests, agendas and personalities, no plan or strategy is executed without the unexpected, imperfect, the defective. Mistakes and errors are inevitable given the size and complexity of these entities. Amazon's leaked memo accidently sent to around a thousand users precipitated an outpouring of support for one of its loudest critics. Facebook's clunky response to Frances Haugen drew ire from commentators deriding it as mere whistleblower backlash, while for Theranos, senior management seemed unaware that extreme practices of silencing could never have worked for long, particularly in such an early stage of the company. In each case, these errors were capitalized upon by dissenters.

Brian Martin, writing with Will Rifkin, bemoans the lack of attention researchers typically give to this aspect of whistleblowing.

Were we to examine scenes of speak-up and reprisal more care-fully, they argue, we would see how the very irrationalities of bureaucracies, even authoritarian and domineering ones, produce fissures and gaps that can be exploited by dissenters.[15] We would better understand how the same dynamics – chaos – that give rise to the desperate fantasy of control leading to the whistleblower being scapegoated are those dynamics that throw up errors – errors to be utilized as part of a whistleblower's strategy of dissent. Building on this idea, more recently, Martin urges activists fighting injustice to consider what he terms the paradox of repression: extreme repression of protesting voices can be counterproductive and backfire against the employer engaged in them.[16] While most activists don't focus on the point of view of the 'other side', he argues, they should. They ought to carefully watch and study the responses to protest. Examining the potential fruitfulness of back-fire is a critical part of the tactical thinking that is invaluable for effective resistance strategies. But few do it.

Digital Leaks, Affective Forces and Rapid Connections: The land-scape of whistleblowing disclosures is transformed through new infor-mation and communications technologies. Digital leaks were a feature across our cases. At Amazon, the instantaneous nature of email allowed the inadvertent sharing of normally secret documents, includ-ing leaked messages from one HR worker to another. It is easy to imagine how this might have gone differently. A powerful and well-connected employer, in the absence of leaks, might have convinced influential others to come to its aid and join the disparagement of the whistleblower Christian Smalls. Instances of blacklisting in recruitment circles are common in cases of public, external whistleblowing, par-ticularly where a whistleblower no longer works in the organization and where they have revealed serious wrongdoing.[17] This can erode the credibility of the whistleblowing speaker, paint a flawed character and deter would-be employers, all of which we saw in Dawn Wooten's case for example.

In certain situations, leaks help turn this around. The memo sent by Facebook's VP for Global Affairs to workers aiming to discredit Frances Haugen's claims was quickly shared with members of the press. At Amazon, a leak was how the world began to understand the retaliation against Christian Smalls as racially motivated, against a backdrop of mounting racial tensions in the US. While leaks have always been a feature of corporate life, today's digital methods of transmission, whether via camera phone, email or on social media, have made leaks exponentially easier and faster.

In addition, social media and online news sources helped the rapid spread of information emanating from whistleblowing disclosures in Frances's case. This was exemplified with Christian Smalls and his colleagues. Social media was, he later told me, decisive in connecting people. 'A lot of people that were speaking up at these different facilities ... We all know social media is a very big tool for organizing now. So that's what helped us connect, we all stay connected pretty much throughout the course of the pandemic, we worked together on further future demonstrations.' When Christian organized another protest for 1 May together with former colleagues at several Amazon facilities, and workers in Target, Walmart and other major companies, online videos were pivotal in planning and sharing news of the gathering.[18] The video went out on YouTube. Blogs like Tim Bray's gave protesting insiders direct access to the public, attracting comments and shows of support that escalated the sense of outrage at the firing of his whistleblowing colleagues.

Inspired by psychosocial theory, scholars have argued that, when it comes to the creation of connections and relationships, we are seeing something quite different in the circulation of certain kinds of messages online. Digital affective forces give rise to powerful fantasies of togetherness and participation – a buzz – which hide how different those involved in the sharing can actually be. The affective forces generated through rapid online sharing are more than feelings; they encompass a powerful sense of something beyond ourselves that moves us to connect with others.[19] The intensity and speed with which such sharing happens leads to a potent sense of membership, as messages instantly reverberate around the online network. Digital network technologies come with a promise of community.

In our cases, we saw how digital reverberation was rapidly shared and escalated; it enabled Christian's whistleblowing disclosure about a life-and-death crisis to become 'more than itself', and quickly, as supporters from Senators to Attorney Generals rallied to the cause: all within the space of two weeks. This amplification meant Christian and his colleagues encountered a rapidly enhanced level of connectivity, and relatedly, credibility, in this flurry of enthusiasm and support. For Frances and Dawn, social media platforms, personal websites and podcasts helped their message directly reach a potential audience, in a quick and cheap way. Online whistleblowing groups, including the Tech Workers' Collective, use such methods to bring people's messages to the public, while the many groups emerging from the global #MeToo movement exemplify this potential of online connection.[20]

It is not always clear that the mere sharing of information is enough to have people truly listen. Nor is it clear, as we saw earlier, that the kinds of relationships forming around sharing tweets and socials posts will translate into actual high-risk activism in support of whistleblowers, as will be explored later. What we can say is that the information spread far and wide, its attraction and 'stickiness' heightened by the feelings of empathy and outrage to which it gave rise.[21] Overall, whether through inadvertent internal leaks or deliberate shares with the outside world, it appears that the digital infrastructure within which all business is done today represents a step-change in what is possible.

Rethinking Aggressive Reprisal and Organizational Power

How do we make sense of these elements apparently disrupting the dominance of the retaliating organization? Perhaps we need to rethink what whistleblower reprisal actually means in terms of its capacity to shore up power. Perhaps the harm that reprisal causes, alongside the unintended materials for subversive resistance occasioned by the attacks, indicates something more than organizational domination.

Hannah Arendt was a philosopher keenly interested in organizations, institutions and the exercise of power. Among her contributions is her famous distinction between violence and power explained in *On Violence*. Authoritative institutions – she was talking about governments – rely on violence in direct proportion to the rate of decline in authority and power they are facing. Violence, Arendt notes, is always an act of desperation. When authoritarian rulers lose the support of the people they rule, their power wanes. It is then that we see the resort to violence and cruel acts of suppression, especially suppression of dissent. 'We know or should know', she reminds us, 'that every decrease in power is an open invitation to violence – if only because those who hold power and feel it slipping from their hands ... have always found it difficult to resist the temptation to substitute violence for it.' Hence, 'rule by sheer violence', according to Arendt, 'comes about when power is being lost'. The support of the masses, the acquiescence of the governed to be governed, the silent agreement of the millions one would rule, is what bestows power upon an authority. And violence signals that the deal is off. Violence, therefore, contrary to popular belief, is not akin to power: it is its opposite. Violence represents a desperate attempt to restore power as it drains away. This is the marvellous idea within Arendt's framing: she exhorts us to detach power from violence and look for situations in which the former grows as the latter is utilized as a last resort.

Arendt's depiction is an institution-level perspective of what we have already explored: the deep-seated anxieties and fears on the part of many employers and managers, when threats to their organization's boundaries emerge. One example of the violence she points to is violence channelled into reprisal against those who represent the threats. By linking this anxiety to a draining away of power, Arendt helps us to see how the situation of domination can be reversed. It can be turned around by chipping away at the smaller cracks that appear in the apparently rigid hierarchy of control.

Considering these ideas in light of our analysis of public whistle-blowing, what this suggests is that we should look a little closer at our desperate, anxious, boundary-defending employers, to see what their actions might be telling us. We should perhaps look for the moments in which power returns to centre stage via workers engaging in acts of resistance, even if these are small and local, and examine how these moments link up with others involving similar even if distant acts.

Each public whistleblower we saw here represented a whole array of others – of colleagues – sharing a subculture of dissent. These others had already been speaking up – albeit to the whistleblower and to each other rather than to management. Perhaps we can call these the 'shadow-whistleblowers' of the public whistleblower. Whether it was Seamus's on-the-ground workers coming to him with dread fear for their safety each day, or Christian Smalls' seventy-odd reports in the JFK8 ware-house expressing concern for their exposure to COVID-19, Dawn Wooten's terrified detainee patients at ICDC sharing their worries about irreversible operations on women's bodies, or colleagues critical of Facebook in Frances Haugen's Civic Integrity team, for every whistle-blower there were many others for whom they were speaking.[22]

Much attention is paid to the question of why workers do not speak up about wrongdoing, but we might rephrase the question. What do the many workers who *are* voicing concerns, but softly and quietly, and on whose behalf whistleblowers speak up, represent? When we take the dissenting subcultures of shadow-whistleblowers into consideration, it seems they comprise a form of power, a form of will. Some workers, as we know, do not agree with the decision to speak publicly, and, as we also know, whistleblower isolation occurs as a result. Even so, there exist vast numbers of discreet beneficiaries of these public disclosures. People whose muted concerns were ignored for years, but are finally given voice, form the backdrop for each case we examined here.

If we read our cases through the lens Arendt provided for us, it appears that power has already been crumbling for some time. Yet widespread damage has been kept at bay by senior figures reinforcing the boundary around the organization and maintaining the strong fantasy of control. This works through laws that silence, siloed work practices, aggressive reprisal, public smear campaigns and an overall shutting down of the capacity to take disclosures further.

Looking closely, however, it seems as though moments in the public whistleblowing scenes we witness signal a further slippage in the relationship between control and controlled: the beginning of the reversal of the apparently entrenched relations of domination. One of the most surprising aspects of these cases of public whistleblowing is just how self-defeating certain aspects of organizational domination actually are. The aggressive and defensive employer, we have seen, creates the materials enabling whistleblowers to prevail. If, as detailed in Chapter 5, information matchmaking is about finding ways to deflect public attention onto the employer enacting aggression against the whistleblower, it is important to look at the help one gets from a surprising corner: the powerful employer itself. Our analysis showed us five ways in which this works, from investment in management practices to forced errors and leaks. Being alert to the unintended consequences of reprisal is an important aspect of our concept of collective bricolage.

Whistleblower Allies

Local Troubles to Public Issues

When a public whistleblower first discloses, their concerns are typically local, specific to the setting in which they work. They relate to their own firm, their management, perhaps even their industry. If the whistleblower receives retaliation for speaking up, these new troubles are perceived as individual ones, divorced from any bigger picture, related solely to their milieux. But, on another view, the public whistleblower is often in fact speaking about a small albeit vital piece of a bigger concern, what sociologist C. Wright Mills describes as 'an issue'.

An issue, according to Mills, is a bigger deal than a person's own complaint; an issue is something that has been elevated to the status of a known, shared concern. An issue is 'a public matter', in which 'values cherished by publics are felt to be threatened'.[23] An issue is the demise of water quality in Dublin, if we take Seamus's case, and the underfunding of utilities in a privatized market with impacts for safety of workers and the public. Issues are things that happen on a wider scale, at a higher level: 'It is the very nature of an issue . . . that it cannot very well be defined in terms of the everyday environments of ordinary men', Mills explains. Powerful interest groups like to keep it this way, to retain the sense that the private and the local should remain at the level of the private and the local. The official solutions to problems typically 'slip past structure', ignoring the big picture in order to 'focus on isolated situations', giving the impression of a remedy where, in reality, no meaningful change has been achieved. Thus, problems become 'problems of individuals'.[24] Seamus's 'private trouble' was deemed as such by HR: a personal issue, something belonging to him alone. Yet his highlighting the countless everyday dangers to life he encountered was in fact a critical part of the overall picture: it helped the Environmental Protection Agency, for example, in their attempts to convince its audience that problems were occurring across the city.

The trick to counter this, Mills argues, is to make the connections between local setting and wider issue. This is because issues, at their core, are merely 'the organization of many such [local] milieux into the institutions of society as a whole'. And when we encounter serious issues, it is often because there is 'a crisis in institutional arrangements' remaining obscured, a crisis serving the interests of a group that would rather we were not aware. Linking the individual and their milieux with 'big picture' structural inequalities was the genius of the feminist movement, with activists explaining that the personal troubles experienced by women in the home do not belong behind closed doors, because they point to significant injustices in a patriarchal society.

While Mills does not expand upon whistleblowing, we see here that the whistleblower is a vital link in uncovering issues, first because they show the concrete impacts of these issues on the ground: the men in danger of explosion, the precise levels of the toxic chemicals in the canal. But also because the depth of reprisal against them indicates how entrenched the issue has become.[25]

Writing in the *Financial Times*, Harvard Professor Shoshana Zuboff explained what Facebook whistleblower Frances Haugen meant to the bigger picture. Frances was more than a whistleblower; she was a critical part of a wider landscape. Prior to her disclosures, some people had examined the dangers of big tech overreach and tried to break through the fog of obfuscation. Progress had been painfully slow, largely driven by 'a dedicated cadre of scholars and journalists relying on informants, leaked documents and painstaking research [that] has documented this web of deceit'.[26] Zuboff detailed how Frances's whistleblowing brought a vital piece to the puzzle. 'Now Frances has delivered the ledger books and personal witness that cannot be ignored. She undertook substantial risk to stir the world from slumber.' Her private milieux had been operationalized to bear witness to the impacts of this public issue that had been perceived as a potential threat but, to date, had been a threat that was both under-specified and vague. Frances's role was that of the deliverer of the information, the in-person witness: the face of a movement.

All the work that goes into discrediting the public whistleblower effectively severs these ties between whistleblower and issue. Disbelieved, their claims are not valued and hence there is no connection to any greater issue – they explain nothing. The discrediting work adds to the suffering of the whistleblower, which is seen as just that: their suffering, their local problem. Their isolated claims of bullying or harassment are not linked to anything wider: mere concerns about one-off misdemeanours rather than systemic wrongdoing. Linking the individual whistleblower with a public issue was the innovation of activist-lawyers' information matchmaking described in Chapter 5. This is its underlying ethos. The work involves figuring out how to get the public to surround the employer: to take the focus off the whistleblower and move that focus onto the issue.

Issues and Partners: The Work

For each case of a whistleblower whose individual concerns end up shedding light on a critical public issue, there were partners in the background. Throughout this book we saw whistleblowers working together with, and supported by, family members, colleagues, advocate organizations, journalists, lawyers, academics, activist groups, politicians and other whistleblowers, to secure an audience who can listen and act. It is helpful to break it down, to examine precisely what it is that partners do for the whistleblower and vice versa.

Lending Credibility to the Whistleblower: Trust is essential in whistleblowing relations. For an audience to pay attention to a new disclosure, there needs to be some level of trust in the source. But trust is a complex matter, essentially involving a bet on an unknown situation to work out a certain way.[27] 'Trust is characterized by insufficient information and emotionally-enabled leaps of faith';[28] when we trust, we essentially ignore, or at least sideline, the uncertain and the unknown that inevitably accompanies the chance we are about to take. Our investments in authoritative structures in society help us ignore the risk. Carefully chosen allies lend credibility by channelling authority, building the bridge across the unknown, helping the audience to feel they can trust the whistleblower. This is badly needed when whistleblowers are treated with suspicion. We saw how, for example, Seamus was able to channel the heft of a government inquiry committee via its stamp of approval, and the Environmental Protection Agency through its appearance on the prime-time documentary supporting his disclosures. The young graduates at Theranos were suddenly allied with the hundred-year-old institution that was the *Wall Street Journal*, while the Amazon warehouse workers had US Senators and the New York Mayor in their corner. This flow of authority from institution to source meant each whistleblower became credible. The audience believed. In some cases, the partners gained credibility too. Movements need a face – a person with whom the public can identify. As Shoshana Zuboff explained in the case of Frances Haugen, a whistleblower can play this role; their personal witness story is the missing link in making a somewhat abstract public issue come alive for the audience.[29]

Although it is rarely recognized as such, academics play a role when it comes to sharing credibility via institutions of authority. Academic experts appear near the top of the list when people are asked which professions are the most credible: ranked significantly higher than journalists, government representatives and CEOs. Working with colleagues in my area, we try where possible to share the platform the university represents, inviting whistleblowers as guest lecturers, co-authors and researchers, offering a forum to speak where possible. More needs doing, of course, but it is something. This is not to imply that any such work comes near the intensity, commitment and stress that more active alliance partnerships can involve. It is support-act work, with little of the risks others encounter, including other more activist academics.[30]

Amplifying the Disclosure: The whistleblower's message is a lot louder where public support has been mobilized via allies. This strengthens the likelihood of the whistleblower's specific demands being met: the cessation of the wrongdoing they have specifically identified.[31] Thanks to allies, Christian Smalls and his colleagues' whistleblowing disclosure rapidly spread, as supporters from Senators to Attorney Generals rallied to the cause: all within the space of two weeks. Painted as an instance of 'David versus Goliath' with lowly workers taking on the big powerful firm, but also an instance of racial discrimination tied up with the wider 'Black Lives Matter' movement, the disclosure suddenly became much more than itself, and quickly. It was expanding far beyond the local scene in which Christian and his staff suffered unchecked vulnerability to the virus, but, at the same time, this amplification ensured this scene remained a pivotal image within the overall landscape of the unfolding awareness of a public issue. And it was allies who kept it there.

Sometimes strengthening the whistleblower means persuading them to end the whistleblowing attempt. 'Not knowing when to stop' is number seven of Brian Martin's 'Seven Common Traps' for whistle-blowers. Many continue despite a futile campaign that damages both them and their family. The work of an ally can involve being the one person who will tell them to quit.[32] This differentiates the ally from other kinds of partners motivated to keep the whistleblower talking: the opportunistic journalist chasing a scoop, for example, or a lawyer working towards a payout upon a successful prosecution. From her experience of organizing and coordinating among advocacy organizations as Executive Director of Whistleblowing International Network, Anna Myers makes this clear. When whistleblowing is instrumentalized by such actors, she reflects, the discloser's well-being gets ignored. When supporting a whistleblower is merely seen as a means to prosecute wrongdoers, for example, the rights of the person at the heart of the story get overlooked; in such cases 'you have to then be really clear, this IS a free speech rights issue, this is a human rights issue, and so this isn't just about people blowing the whistle for the prosecution authorities.'[33] The difference in orientation between different kinds of whistleblower partner – and the implications of this – is critical to recognize. Dana Gold of Government Accountability Project agrees. She explained how, when speaking to public-interest stakeholders and journalists, she is at pains to highlight the importance of care for the person at the centre of the story. To bring this home, she created training sessions for the organizations that act as mediators. These stakeholders, who share a keen interest in the whistleblower's information, must understand just how complicated and risky whistleblowing is. The danger, Dana explains, is that even 'helpful' stakeholders who just focus on publicizing the information can inadvertently put a whistleblower at risk, either because they don't know enough about how to protect them, or they don't care enough to do what is needed. These experts are clear: amplifying a disclosure is not always best for the whistleblower.

Strengthening the Whistleblower: Allies are people who can offer practical support. Support can come from former colleagues helping the whistleblower to confirm that the wrongdoing they are disclosing is still happening. Work processes in large organizations can be complex involving multiple systems and actors. It is critical but not always easy to be sure of what one is witnessing. When I spoke to Erika Cheung, for example, she described how she stayed in touch with the people she had worked with at Theranos even after she moved to Hong Kong. These conversations with former colleagues were essential for reinforcing what she knew. This was technical, practical support. Allies can also help with the personal impacts of whistleblowing, including the self-doubt and stress that can accompany attacks on one's reputation as part of retaliation.[34] As we saw, this is vital for public whistleblowers because this group is particularly vulnerable.[35] Dawn Wooten reflected on the comfort and hope the *New Yorker* podcast invitation provided at a time of struggle, with other examples throughout this book.

In many cases, however, whistleblowers themselves feel they simply cannot approach would-be allies for personal support and strength, because of the risks. Erika Cheung reflects how she was careful not to involve former colleagues in her whistleblowing actions, especially when Theranos's legal team was pursuing her.[36] She did not want to implicate them, hence conversations remained at the level of practical fact-checking.

Rewriting the Subject Position: A psychosocial perspective shows how we can invest in public figures in different ways, projecting our fears and desires onto them. Whether deliberately or implicitly, the work of whistleblower allies often involved anticipating these dynamics and shaping how the projections might go. This works through enhancing and defending the subject position the whistleblower is seen to occupy, which can shift and change depending on the context. As we saw, one of the most insidious ways in which whistleblower reprisal works is by creating new, shameful, subject positions for the worker speaking out. When they go outside official channels, they are painted as 'invalid' workers breaching norms of loyalty. This can lead to extreme reprisals. In some of our cases, the stain of illegality marks their identities, where their whistleblowing contravenes non-disclosure agreements despite being in the public interest. Here the whistleblower has become an 'illegal subject', a transgressor of legal and enforceable contracts. This outsider subject position again helps justify aggressive reprisal, this time in the form of lawfare. What effective allies do is reverse all this: they rewrite the subject position and place the whistleblower in a chain of other people, all united in speaking about the same public issue.

In Chapter 3, for example, we see such a 'linked-up' subject emerge in the form of Christian Smalls. Having been excluded from Amazon through all-out dismissal, he was granted a position, by commentators and journalists, in which all kinds of fears, desires and rage could be projected onto him, with Christian appearing as the antidote. People's anger about worker inequality, the disproportionate power of big tech firms making exponential profits in the context of the pandemic and racism in US society found a focus in the whistleblower Christian, who had been fired for speaking out about the workplace injustices underlying Amazon's unprecedented gain in wealth. This bolstered the significant support he received. To back Christian was to voice anger at all these injustices. The power of a single whistleblower figure to represent so much else was also evident in the final days of Theranos CEO Elizabeth Holmes' trial. Commentators described just how pivotal the presence of the whistleblowers was: it was the treatment of Erika Cheung and other ordinary workers speaking out that showed just how organized and widespread the techniques of silencing had been. We saw a similar fantasmatic projection onto the figure of Frances Haugen in Chapter 4. She and her team worked hard to create a certain kind of subject position, one that was both in conflict with Facebook by whistleblowing with insider information but also, crucially, a friend and indeed healer of the powerful firm. This seems to have drawn unprecedented levels of credibility as she enjoyed an apparently unassailable (with a few exceptions) position.

Supporters worked to ensure the subject position of Dawn Wooten was not the focus of stories emanating from ICE in response to her disclosure. As we saw in Chapter 5, she remained more or less in the background, a professional whistleblower: a status that showed how well information matchmaking was working in her case, albeit she was suffering along with her family when blacklisted in her town because of disclosing.

Allies help shape these subject positions. They can help marshal and shepherd the fantasmatic projections of an audience onto the figure of the discloser. And the ways in which this subject position emerges in the public eye can be decisive for the whistleblower's survival. Lending credibility, amplifying, strengthening and rewriting subject positions are all important dimensions of ally work and its linking of local concerns to wider issues. As others have shown, validating the targets of attack and mobilizing support to help with this are critical counter-methods in resistance struggles against injustice.[37] Building on this, this book shines a light on whistleblower allies who do this.

Ally Partnerships outside the Formal Structures

As we develop our understanding of the practices of whistleblowers working together with allies, it is useful to take a closer look at these relationships. These partnerships are unusual. On one level, they are 'work relationships', but the connections emerge from the common desire to disrupt the status quo. This means that they, by their nature, form and grow in zones that are far outside the organizations and institutions that are in place to support other kinds of workplace bonds. There is little of the institutional infrastructure – the scaffolding – that guides more traditional kinds of work relationships. This context can pose challenges.

We know from research into various kinds of social movements that partnerships in such contexts are not easy to sustain. Social movements form when people find themselves locked out of the prescribed paths for critique and excluded from the normal systems for voicing dissent.[38] Collective resistance arrangements result from necessity, and solidarity arises between people and groups who find they must struggle together to resist.[39] Whistleblower partnerships share similarities. They are relationships that emerge and persist in stressful, conflict-ridden and fast-changing spaces: outside the official channels, and in some cases, outside the legal protections, outside the organization and often with few blueprints or prescribed paths to follow.

Without supporting structures and prescribed norms of engagement, the sense of solidarity that first brought people together around a common cause can be tricky to maintain. People have multiple, sometimes conflicting, agendas, and competing demands on their time.[40] The cause itself can change. A person's commitment to it might shift, and outside pressures can help this along. As reprisals against both the whistleblower but sometimes, also, their new-found partners intensify, the differences between people can become amplified.[41] Staying the course is challenging.

We must recall that most whistleblowers who try to disclose in public fail to gain a meaningful audience. To do so is incredibly difficult: a rare achievement.[42] Because of this, the stories presented in this book do not represent the full gamut of public whistleblowing. But they do offer exemplars of how it can work in some cases. A close examination enables a deeper dive into the dynamics at play. From what we have learned thus far, therefore, the question emerges: if whistleblower allies are vital, but partnerships come with all these challenges, what is it that holds them together?

Personal Relationships and Affective Connections

Robust whistleblower–ally partnerships seem to be based on more than just the work of bringing a local concern to the status of a public issue. Even if that work is, as we have seen, intricate and multifaceted. Where people managed to work effectively together, it was from a place of connection, a bond that took time to develop. We saw this again and again. Recall Christian's relationships developed over twelve-hour work stints and gathering 'shoulder-to-shoulder' in break rooms, and his practice of defending colleagues long before the outbreak of COVID-19, all of which gave rise to the backing that accompanied his whistleblowing moment at which we joined the case. We had Erika and Tyler's shared night shifts during which they exchanged opinions and voiced concerns about the Theranos machines, breaking the company norms of siloed work practices and developing a mutual trust.

Frances Haugen and journalist Jeff Horwitz spent significant time in conversation prior to deciding to disclose. Despite what previous research suggests, what is at stake is more than the tactical formation of strategic alliances around a common cause: alliances that help with the information exposure that would connect whistleblowing disclosure to issue. These aspects are important, but they do not represent the full picture. Relationships developed that proved essential to the ally work that was to come.

The ways in which whistleblowers recollect encounters with ally partners are notable. It is as though they have each, in different ways, been moved. Studies of other resistance struggles point to the critical role of affect. Affect is an elusive yet powerful concept, referring to the 'felt emergences and intensities that shape how we encounter the world, other people and ourselves'.[43] There is something going on when we encounter others in this way, something that is more than cognition and more elemental than emotion: affect is a felt and embodied sense of having been impacted by another.[44] To explain what affect involves within solidarity relationships working towards a common goal in stressful settings outside of the normal institutional frameworks, concepts from feminist solidarity studies are helpful.[45]

Compassion: Effective relationships encompass an element of compassion, as this kind of work is impossible without embodying the perspectives of other people. Compassion can involve the mutual recognition of a self by another. I had encountered this in other whistleblowing scenes. Former Army Captain Tom Clonan had been persecuted by senior members of the Irish Defence Forces for his research into widespread sexual violence and harassment against his female colleagues. This research was picked up by the newspapers and became a big story. Tom was singled out for a targeted smear campaign; he and his family suffered. During this time, he was contacted by John Devitt, CEO of Transparency International Ireland. John reached out to tell him that what he was experiencing was commonly known as whistleblower reprisal, something Tom, like many others in the 1990s, was not aware of. 'I cannot overestimate to you how important it was just to have somebody there who sort of went "we understand"', Tom recalled.[46] The compassion shown at that time was pivotal: 'I think my contact with [John's team] was kind of transformative on a number of levels. One: It gave me the language to describe what was happening. Two, it made me feel that I was not on my own, and three, it gave the broader public discourse, the media narrative, a kind of reference point ... whistleblower reprisal.' He continued, '... and that was a very – that was a very, very powerful thing to me. It allowed me to sort of, explain it, better.' John also connected him with support services available, but it was his compassion in voluntarily reaching out that Tom recalled; this had enabled him to continue his campaign for justice.

With a colleague, I interviewed whistleblower support professionals to learn more about this kind of work. They describe many challenges. One helpline operator spoke of how callers needing assistance can be in very stressful circumstances. Yet it is often necessary for the advocate to try to make complex legal rights comprehensible to callers who have no legal training nor knowledge of the terminology. Such tensions were common across our research findings. But we also found that, when advice-givers felt a sense of connection through some shared experience or observation, it helped generate a sense of care, even if they had never met.[47] If the content of a whistleblower's disclosure resonated with something the advice-giver had themselves experienced, for example if they or a close one had spoken out in the past, this made a big difference.

Reflecting on this, it would be disingenuous not to acknowledge the sense of connection I sometimes feel. As academics we are human (most are, anyway); we are relational, intrinsically dependent on others. We live lives touched by the serious issues whistleblowers report, and we have friends and families suffering from problems caused by the dysfunctions of large organizations. I have met whistleblowers who tell me that academic studies – the readable ones at least – help explain what is happening as they progress their disclosures, and also give a sense that others experience similar things. Contrary to appearance, organizations do not always act rationally, and the legal system can be inherently unfair. Detailed research, these whistleblowers tell me, can be useful for reminding people just how widespread irrationality is, and also how common reprisals can be. Research can also be practically useful, a source of information supporting campaigns for change. I work hard on my research, so it feels good to have this connection: this sense that it has been worthwhile. It is frustrating that more cannot be done.

Vulnerability: Research indicates solidarity relationships that thrive also comprise vulnerability, because one must give a part of oneself to even begin the work. For whistleblower support professionals, this can involve reliving a painful memory in order to empathize with another, for example.[48] In addition, committed support, as we saw with our cases, requires whistleblower allies to put themselves in the 'firing line' of likely reprisal. Employers can engage similar strategies to pressure partners as they do with disclosers. We saw how John Carreyrou endured long-standing vilification by Theranos employees and was personally pursued by its legal team. For a time, he was the only voice calling out the company. Lawyer Robert Tibbo reports ongoing harassment for his role as Edward Snowden's original legal counsel and supporter of the 'Snowden Refugees', who helped hide and support the NSA whistleblower while he was applying for asylum status in Hong Kong.[49] The lawyer acting for the White House whistleblower who brought forward information leading to Donald Trump's impeachment hearings received a death threat and was dropped by his insurance firm. For these allies, vulnerability was part of the job.

Academics working on whistleblowing can experience vulnerability – albeit on a much smaller scale. They can receive abuse on social media, although it rarely comes close to what public-facing supporters encounter. Reflecting on my work, most people don't pay any attention to anything I have written about whistleblowing. Many others are supportive, creating connections on social media, sharing useful information and generally emanating goodwill. But some social media commentators find the work objectionable. Even benign articles on the details of a new whistleblower law can yield interesting responses. One message informed me that my recent book was less useful than a sado-masochism website, to which they helpfully provided a link. It was quite difficult to figure out whether in fact this was 'trolling', because as an act of online aggression it was rather incoherent. And even on a minor scale, online escalation can feel overwhelming. When criticism is shared on social media, it can multiply exponentially – each click causing notification numbers to rise and the atmosphere to sharpen. The irony is that, as many whistleblower allies will tell you, much of this vulnerability from online abuse comes from whistle-blowers themselves, lashing out for the lack of support their campaigns are receiving. When this kind of thing happens, I tell myself trolling is part of the territory. I am quite aware of how minimal this attention is, but it offers me a small glimpse into what other whistleblowers and supporters suffer on a much larger, more organized and more painful scale.[50]

Ambivalence: Alliances are not all positive. We are not simple beings. And for every relationship there is naturally a shadow side. Ally partnerships can comprise ambivalent feelings, whether we like it or not. We grow tired, frustrated and people do not act the way we want.[51] There can be stark differences between people, which can make collaboration very difficult.[52] Difference can be basic, including structural inequalities between partners. Think of the salaried lawyer helping the precarious worker who has been blacklisted, or the staff journalist writing a story about the public whistleblower without the financial means to fight a legal battle. Our study of whistleblower advocacy groups running legal advice helplines showcased this. We encountered people with a keen desire to make a difference, pleased to be in a job that let them do so. But mundane challenges of comparing one's low-paid and stressful position to that of college classmates now earning six figures in corporate law, while a minor part of the scene, were present in the background. Such things shape the landscape when things get tough.[53] So also did differences in training and experience: the demands for simpler language to explain the intricate laws, which legally trained helpline operators found difficult. The precise nature of legislation meant it was vital to be exact about people's rights and entitlements. This often necessitated a complicated response. Helpline workers felt the frustration of the callers whose expectations of help were not being met, matching this with frustration of their own.

This is just one example of the overall scene: the challenges posed by the vulnerability and emotional energy needed for compassionate, committed engagement are not insignificant for whistleblower allies. So, there is stress on all sides, as we saw from our Government Accountability Project activist-lawyers reporting burnout as a hazard of the job. And interpersonal difficulties inevitably emerge. Ambivalent feelings towards those being helped are a natural result of this.

Ally partnerships fall apart when differences become too challenging. Meanwhile, the increasing capacity of corporate opponents to engage resources like lawfare and ever more sophisticated worker surveillance increases the obstacles. What studies of feminist solidarity movements show is how, despite what we might wish, negative aspects of these relationships can rarely be organized out nor should we try. In fact, they are an important part of the work. The challenge is to acknowledge and check them, before they can destroy relationships.[54] For Christian Smalls, understanding the limits of potential allies was critical. He quickly realized the divergent interests of journalists, stuck in a news cycle where only large protests would attract attention. Christian acted accordingly. Some commentators pointed to the 'tensions' between Frances Haugen and the journalist partners she worked with. But when it came time to engage more than one newspaper and share the story he had first broken, Jeff Horwitz seemed to anticipate and recognize this as a necessary part of her activism. Erika Cheung articulated the delicate balance between care, respect and objectivity that was required to work with the reporter on her case. In Chapter 5, Dana Gold was open about how Dawn's speaking out had jeopardized her; Dana worked with this reality to purse whatever avenues she could to support her client years after the disclosures. In each case, the tensions and ambivalences were worked with productively.

As Executive Director of Whistleblowing International Network Anna Myers notes, reflecting on the challenges of supporting whistleblowers and advocacy organizations even as the same kinds of problems emerge again and again, '[w]histleblowers will keep coming ... I guess if you're not an optimist, you wouldn't last in this job. And I see change.'[55] More than just aspects to be 'coped with', or somehow managed out, the contradictions within the jumble of personal relationships and common purpose that made up ally partnerships with whistleblowers appeared to lend vital energy to the struggles, as studies in other areas have shown.[56]

Allies that Stick: It is important to avoid the idea that any of this is easy. What looks like whistleblower allyship on the surface might not always run so deep. Recall the fervour of commentators Christian Smalls had never met, all lining up to help from their positions in the mainstream media: politicians writing letters, far-flung colleagues speaking up online. Emotions played a powerful role in this show: empathy for warehouse workers, outrage at the implied racism and the inequalities between white-collar and manual staff. Influential allies joined with the New York State Attorney General in declaring Christian's treatment 'disgraceful ... immoral and inhumane'. For sure, there was mobilization, and there was emotion. But did these emotive expressions give rise to long-term commitments and investments in the whistleblowers' projects? It is not so clear.

Supporters' connections to causes are often based on weak social ties, finding expression in one-off displays of activism. Social media in particular is a powerful enabler of these kinds of expressions. Its platforms provide instant access to information about events and causes, and rapidly channel potent feelings connecting us to distant 'friends' with similar ideas. But these weak ties do not translate easily to what sociologist Doug McAdam terms 'high-risk activism'. This kind of activism tends to require strong ties based on deeper relationships giving rise to commitment to action. Studies examine, for example, the months of collective preparatory training that took place before people physically came together to protest at segregated lunch counters during the US civil rights movement,[57] or leaving their houses to join demonstrations in East Germany prior to the fall of the Berlin Wall. It turns out people are moved to act because of relational ties to others involved in the cause. It seems that people's impulses to come together and repeatedly engage in activist protest – to commit, to organize and to risk themselves in doing so – are greatly enhanced by deeper, long-formed connections, for example where friendships have developed over time. This has significant implications for the role of social media in public whistleblower struggles: it seems to be effective for enabling apparent allies to share news, click on petitions and express outrage. But when it comes to the deeper connections required for action, it is not so useful.

This is important for our purposes. Many whistleblowers enjoy a certain amount of media spotlight when their cause is in the news. This can provide a sense that support is available from others they meet online. But when the news cycle moves on, they can find themselves alone, with just the reprisals for company. Weak-tie friends are, it would seem, relatively useless by this stage. The partnerships that last, with people willing to go down a risky road with the whistleblower, are based on relationships forged over time.

So, what does this mean in practice? We could say that elements of what psychosocial scholars call a 'holding environment' characterize these emergent relations.[58] This is a kind of social context – a zone – in which relationships are such that disturbing intrusions are reduced, and people within are given the space to make sense of their environment in safety.[59] Such spaces are able to contain difficult emotions: absorbing, filtering and managing them, in order for the emotions to be worked with. This allows interpretation, in which experiences that may not have been processed are given time for reflection so that connections, comprehension and meaning can emerge. Holding environments are not just for formal clinical settings. Groups, informal organizations and even interpersonal relationships can encompass these dynamics. In fact, several studies show how, in times of crisis when workplaces are clearly hostile places to be, those who fare best survive by finding or creating holding environments in which to contain and interpret what they go through.[60] Ally relationships allowing the time and space for holding the tensions encountered in whistleblowing struggles can help those involved and create more robust and lasting partnerships.

In understanding how ally partnerships with whistleblowers work, attentiveness to relationships tells us a lot. There is more than logic and rational calculation at play, and more even than emotional responses. Comprising compassion, vulnerability and ambivalence, relationships between partners are imbued with affect: that felt and embodied sense of having been impacted by another. These affective connections take time to form. They generate desires to work together. They stoke passion for, and commitment to, a shared cause.[61] Allies are moved to help, even where it is tough.

Collective Bricolage

This book has examined ally work and its constitutive aspects. A psychosocial lens opened up new perspectives in how we view this work, including the connections between partners involved, and also, uniquely, the point of view of retaliating managers. We focused on the specific practices of ally work: building a whistleblower's credibility by supporting them, amplifying their voice and strengthening their position. We studied the challenges that new forms of reprisal bring to this work, including the weaponizing of whistleblowing channels and legal loopholes through lawfare. We examined the surprising opportunities to which these challenges give rise: how employers make self-defeating mistakes while their aggressive tactics grow subcultures of dissent draining power from senior management. We learned that whistleblowers' former training as managers can end up strengthening their capacity to capitalize on these unintended consequences. Amid all this, we saw how relationships and affective connections with allies work both to foster the sense of solidarity and commitment required and to help support the whistleblower. These relationships are an important element of this unique kind of collaboration that typically emerges in a challenging, fast-changing environment with scant structural support for enduring partnerships.

Bringing these dimensions together gives us a sense, overall, of the organizing practices underlying successful ally partnerships in public whistleblowing cases. This is represented in Table 6.1. The table shows in turn each specific aspect: the area of focus, the analytic dimension and the learning outcome for people interested in this topic. By analysing cases in this way, we see more clearly what allies and partners can do for, and with, the whistleblower.

The result gives us a valuable perspective on this important vocation. This is summed up in the concept of collective bricolage. The work of ally partners involves disruption: interrupting the status quo in which wrongdoing continues unabated. The work involves troubling the apparently dominant positions of power of retaliatory employers and reversing the normal story of whistleblower as victim. None of this is easy. But in these chapters we have seen how ally partnerships creatively utilize the unexpected and diverse resources available to them, as new opportunities emerge, and unintended consequences of employers' actions and errors become clear. Bricolage, a social sciences term, captures this idea of ongoing experimentation as a necessary response to challenging and uncertain circumstances.[62] The "bricoleur" does not enjoy optimum tools and materials to work with. They must "make do": tinkering with available options, reflecting, revising and altering accordingly. Bricolage cannot be described as a tool for planning, something that can be fixed in advance. Rather, it is an approach to action: an orientation on how to move forward. We see whistleblower–ally partnerships engage in collective bricolage with the resources they have to hand. Disparate elements are cobbled together to create new entities, often with surprising and innovative results.

Collective bricolage represents both an extension of and a challenge to C. Fred Alford's *Broken Lives*, the title of his book that offered such depth of insight into the suffering experienced by whistleblowers and how it maps the power of organizations, but that nonetheless leaves us with a sense of futility about the possibility for change. Collective bricolage evokes the idea that the power of a retaliating employer can potentially be resisted by an alternative form of organizing, albeit with limited resources and little capacity to plan fully in advance. And it paints a broad picture of this counter-organization and its practices.

The framework of collective bricolage, and its elements described in Table 6.1, by no means represent the final word; they are a starting

Table 6.1 *The organizing practices of collective bricolage: a conceptual framework*

Aspect of ally work	Area of focus	Analytic insight	Dimensions
Challenges	Perspectives of managers engaged in reprisals	Anxiety leads to social defences	Managers' anxiety yields: • New forms of reprisal, including weaponized official whistleblowing channels • 'Secret-protecting' lawfare • Enhancing whistleblower isolation • Amplifying blacklisting
Opportunities	Experiences of public whistleblowers	Aggressive silencing practices give rise to unintended consequences	Unexpected sources of advantage: • Prior investment in management role generating skills for organizing • Whistleblowing subcultures comprising ally-colleagues • Privately dissenting colleagues lending power to discloser • Employers' mistakes and forced errors • Digital leaks, affective forces and rapid connections attracting new allies
Practices	Activities involved in ally–whistleblower work	Linking local whistleblowing concerns to bigger issues Linking whistleblowers to other concerned parties	Effective advocacy involves*: • Lending credibility to the whistleblower • Amplifying the disclosure • Strengthening the whistleblower • Rewriting the whistleblower's subject position

Table 6.1 (*cont.*)

Aspect of ally work	Area of focus	Analytic insight	Dimensions
Relationships	Interactions between allies and whistleblowers	Backdrop of unstructured, chaotic environments outside the normal law and structures Personal relationships and affective connections	Effective relationships comprise: • Compassion for the other • Willingness to be vulnerable • Ambivalence and darker feelings • Mutual commitment leading to deeper connections • Holding spaces

* Note: As is clear throughout this book, effective public whistleblower advocacy must be accompanied by appropriate legal support, and ideally psychosocial and financial support where needed.[63]

point. Nor do they signify some kind of easy solution or blueprint to follow in cases of whistleblower reprisal, this insidious and persistent phenomenon.[64] Collective bricolage is inspired by the work of activists and advocates, and their articulation of an information matchmaking philosophy and strategy as key to whistleblowing campaign success. It is enhanced by analyses of exemplar cases and extant research, yielding this novel conceptual lens. The result is something of an 'ideal type' concept, but one we can work to enhance. If nothing else, collective bricolage shines a light on the latent capability of groups of workers, and their supporters, wishing and needing to speak up, but prevented from doing so.

A collective bricolage approach is both timely and urgent. Public whistleblowing has always been challenging; information is always mediated: by the biases of the listener, the power of the group controlling the medium and, of course, the perceived credibility of the speaker. Against this backdrop, what a collective bricolage lens enables is an understanding of the new forces and dynamics emerging to shape the landscape of public whistleblowing, including the weaponization of official channels and lawfare, the unintended consequences of these new innovations in organizational control and the complex, ambivalent connections between those who work to capitalize on these unexpected fissures to force a rethinking of the status quo.

Viewing public whistleblowing as collective bricolage does not imply that someday, once and for all, extreme whistleblower reprisal will come to an end. To say this would be to give free rein to our own fantasmatic projections and desires for an ideal, neat future. This approach instead suggests that we make peace with the opposite: employing organizations will, to some degree, always engage in reprisal. But at the same time, it is the very practice of organization: the organizing of allies with whistleblowing workers that stands to counter this. There has, to date, been little if any mapping of what this organizing might look like: its vagaries, challenges and opportunities; this framing represents a first step.

Even as collective bricolage offers insights into public whistleblowing, we cannot ignore the inequalities marking the scene. The exemplars of public whistleblowing presented here help clarify how there are groups for whom it remains almost impossible. We have seen how, in some cases, the chance of success is enhanced by privileged access: to resources including finance, to social capital based on education and networks and to having the right kind of face. These things can influence who gets to be seen as a credible dissenter. On the other hand, against a background of persistent racism and misogyny, those public whistleblowers finding themselves at the intersection of social identities that are devalued and under-recognized in a given setting may struggle. If collective bricolage is the game, and it is a good game, the playing field is not level. Not all workers have the same capacity to take part. And there are not enough experienced, knowledgeable supporters to go around. In the competition for their attention, some groups struggle.

Some people are excluded from the activity of collective bricolage, or at least find it more difficult to access. That only a privileged few can engage the kinds of support enabling ethical speech is wrong. Moral injury emerges from a psychic dissonance that takes place when we are forced to do work with which we fundamentally disagree. Being required to engage in unethical acts, without the capacity to redress the situation, is a form of harm. When it comes to public whistleblowing, ally partners in collective bricolage are essential. Where oppressive structures of racism, misogyny and precarious employment conditions prevent people accessing strategies of resistance, we must work towards enabling the kinds of alliances that counter these exclusions. If we don't do this, silenced voices will remain silenced. Going forward, those engaging in this work must strive to acknowledge and address these inequalities.

Collective Bricolage: Temporary Relief in an Ongoing Crisis

Whistleblower allies are vital for helping public whistleblowers link their immediate and local disclosures to wider issues in society. Particularly in situations of oppressive silencing and active aggression against whistleblowers, this work is very difficult. We saw something of how it can proceed: the mechanisms by which partnerships succeed in elevating the local concerns and the 'personal troubles', to cite C. Wright Mills, to which whistleblower reprisal is often reduced. We saw how, paradoxically, the troubles themselves can be used to dismantle the strategies of discrediting that make reprisal so effective, such that the official narrative might be challenged – and reversed. Bringing all this together, we see a more complex picture of the relationship between whistleblower and ally, one in which compassion and the willingness to be vulnerable are important elements, along with acceptance of the darker sides, and perhaps even the capacity to work within the tensions they bring.

The changing landscape of whistleblowing will require new strategies of collective bricolage. The proliferation of ignorance and 'fake news' on the part of an employer with greater access to social media platforms than a whistleblower can amplify adverse responses and retaliation. Meanwhile, organizational secrecy is on the rise abetted by sophisticated worker surveillance systems that aim to weed out whistleblowing before it occurs.[65] On top of this, new forms of retaliatory injury are emerging for use against whistleblowers, including the weaponization of law via SLAPPs and other tools intended for silencing would-be critics by draining their resources and their will to continue. We see more and more use of pre-emptive silencing contracts – non-disclosure agreements and the growth of information deemed trade secret and classified – with the fear these evoke in workers uncertain whether to make disclosures that might illegally reveal their contents.[66] With the increasing power of lawfare to silence journalists, too, traditional avenues for transparency, including media and regulation, weaken.[67] Adding to these dangers are new and chilling kinds of reprisal against disclosers like death threats, doxxing and public harassment fuelled by disinformation and social media platforms. The challenges of whistleblowing increase accordingly, and those involved in collective bricolage will have to respond.

As yet, the forms that collective bricolage might take remain underspecified. This is understandable; the project of this book was to explore the organizing dynamics comprising public whistleblower support and survival. The aim was to outline nascent organizing dynamics and critical relationships as a basis for other work exploring the institutional arrangements and structures that might best support them. Likely such work will be needed. As philosopher Judith Butler notes, resistance to forms of oppression depends upon a certain, basic, level of infrastructure in place supporting the resister.[68] In light of our insights here, infrastructure supporting people's capacity to defend against moral injury and ensure accountability for wrongdoing through the formation of robust ally partnerships is essential.[69] Without some basis of security and safety, it is not reasonable to ask public whistleblowers to persist. The argument is, therefore, that 'infrastructures of resistance', whatever form this might take, must be in place to enable the work of collective bricolage by public whistleblowers and their allies. The aim is to make the scenes in which public whistleblowers are often forced – unwillingly – to make their disclosures 'more just, more equal and more enabling' for effective resistance to take place.[70] As part of this work, fore-grounding the role of whistleblowers' families is critical. In each case described here, people's families and loved ones were an important aspect enabling survival both personally and practically. Future research will usefully foreground these all-important allies.[71]

Of course, none of this work – to create ally partnerships in order to challenge retaliating employers – should be needed. Workers should not be the last resort when it comes to addressing wrongdoing. The entire landscape of whistleblowing – its advice-givers, ally-partners, official channels and laws – is an overall assemblage whose presence points to one undeniable public issue, to paraphrase C. Wright Mills: the crisis in institutional arrangements for accountability.[72] The lack of regulation and oversight of employers pushes all the risk of their wrongful practices onto the individual worker who feels compelled to speak up. And the evisceration of would-be sources of support – trade unions, for example – makes things yet riskier for the worker acting alone. For an entrenched, defensive and retaliatory-minded employer, the deterrents are weak. And, of course, workers read the situation for what it is. The main reason people don't speak up? Fear that nothing will be done. And if their colleagues cannot stand the pain of dissonance resulting from acquiescence, the full consequences of that risk are felt by the whistleblowers and their families.

Shifts over the past fifty years, with the rise of neoliberal logics in public, private and third-sector work, and the erosion of oversight and interference, have led to the situation we are in. Whistleblowing as a phenomenon came to the fore as a result of these changes, and it is shaped by them too. The framing developed here is a mere band-aid on a shaking, flawed situation. The same is true for the powerful work being done to reform and bolster whistleblower protection laws across the world. These activities all take place against a similar backdrop. To place the inherent risk of an unfettered state–capital relationship onto the bodies of workers and their families is an indication of the systemic injustice inherent in the manner in which things are run today. It should not be this way. While we work towards change, we have collective bricolage.

Writing about Collective Bricolage

All of these proclamations must be tempered with the context from which they emerge. My own subjectivity, experiences and biases come into play in arriving at this point. Attempts to formalize and control chaotic situations can represent defence mechanisms at play in one who tries. As the author here, I acknowledge that, having worked in this area since about 2012, I likely have fantasmatic desires for solutions. While engaging with academics, advocates, lawyers and dissenters, and simply reading news stories about the ongoing struggles of whistleblowers, the landscape can appear dismal. It seems the same tales of reprisal appear again and again. I feel frustration meeting public whistleblowers at events showcasing innovations in official channels systems or celebrating new whistleblowing law, because I know they have little use for someone in their situation.

Many whistleblowers I meet are courageous in ways I am not sure I could ever be, and they get punished for it. I owe them for what they do but I have struggled to understand how I might repay the debt. I feel somewhat sheepish recalling one particular wake-up call. I was carrying out a series of interviews ten years ago, for a research project on 'whistleblower identity'. More than once, when the tape recorder was shut off at the end of the discussion, the whistleblower I was interviewing would ask softly whether I had come across examples of others who had spoken out, lost their job and managed to create a new career. 'How had they managed it?' they wanted to know. These moments rendered my investigation into identity in a different light. Frankly, it felt a bit obtuse. This spurred colleagues and me to carry out survey research into the financial and material costs of speaking up, described in Chapter 5.[73] We get news sometimes of how the resulting report is being used. This kind of thing helps with the sense of frustration, but never fully.

It may be, therefore, that the concept of collective bricolage, and the neat(ish) table that sums it up, are defences against a wickedly persistent situation. This very model might well be my own tactical protection against disturbing thoughts and feelings emanating from my work, enabling my 'regaining a sense of safety at the cost of [my] contact with reality'.[74] On some level, all such conceptual models are exercises in this direction; the hope is that this one might be useful.

That said, when I describe tendencies or patterns, both in the experiences of whistleblowers and in the reactions and responses of employers and other actors in the landscape, it is because they spark recognition. I see them over and over again. This recognition led to a desire to present them together in this way and, to paraphrase C. Fred Alford, to listen to what they might be telling us. Perhaps the next time I meet a public whistleblower, I will have something more to say.

Notes

1. For example, authors show how, through blacklisting and stigmatizing whistleblowers, ordinary people can take on the exclusionary work of the organization, thus continuing the exile even after the whistleblower has left the organization; see, for example, Kenny (2019), Rothschild & Miethe (1999).
2. Alford (2001, p. 99).
3. Devine & Maassarani (2011, p. 15).
4. Alford (2001, pp. 4–5).
5. Martin (2012).
6. Identification with structures of authority, particularly in the context of work and organization, is a central concept in psychosocial studies; see, for example, Kenny (2010, 2012), Fotaki et al. (2012) for overviews.
7. *Wall Street Journal* podcasts (2021).
8. *Time* (2022), Linebaugh (2022).
9. Christian Smalls quoted in Press (2022).
10. For a useful discussion from a psychosocial perspective, see Gabriel (1999).
11. In his memoir, *Permanent Record*, Edward Snowden describes his need to disclose infringements of citizens' rights to know how they are being governed as similar to that experienced by Thomas Drake and Daniel Ellsberg. In turn, Drake describes how, for him, dissent was a valued thing to do: as a teenager he had watched Daniel Ellsberg's actions revealing the Pentagon Papers motivated by a sense of injustice. Ellsberg for years reached out to government and intelligence whistleblowers offering support and a sense they were not alone, as does whistleblower Jesselyn Radack today along with others. See also Mistry & Gurman (2020).
12. See Gabriel (1995, 1999).

13. Edward Snowden, for example, details having watched what happened to Thomas Drake and John Kiriakou – US government whistleblowers who used the internal channels to speak up. Both were charged under the US Espionage Act, with harsh sentencing and no ability to give a public-interest defence for the act of 'revealing secrets'. Snowden notes how, in Drake's case, documents that had not been deemed classified – that is, secret – were found in his home. These were classified post hoc supporting his prosecution (albeit that this led the case to fall apart on the eve of trial, as a plea deal was arranged). Snowden interpreted these and others' experiences to mean that, as a national security whistleblower, his own chances of exoneration would be minimal. The Trump whistleblower showed similar learning from watching other whistleblowers' experiences – writing a note instructing the recipient of his information not to classify this document after the fact, thus pre-empting what had happened to Drake and others like him.

14. For useful discussion of how the experiences of whistleblowers lead to their further politicization, see Mansbach (2011, p. 16), Uys (2000).

15. Martin & Rifkin (2004); see also Devine & Maassarani (2011, p. 50).

16. Martin (2012).

17. Kenny, Vandekerckhove & Fotaki (2019b), Kenny & Fotaki (2021).

18. Author interview.

19. Dean (2010, 2015); see also Endrissat & Islam (2022).

20. Vachhani & Pullen (2019), Kenny (2023a); see also Devine & Maassarani (2011), Munro (2017).

21. Ahmed (2004), Boler & Davis (2021).

22. This builds upon my study of whistleblowing in financial services, *Whistleblowing: Toward a New Theory* (2019). I argued that examining scenes of whistleblowing reveals how the prevailing conception that the autonomous self is the basis of ethical relations is illusory. In ways that are beyond our own control (or, indeed, conscious awareness), we are embedded with others, ek-statically so. As Butler (2004) and Butler & Athanasiou (2013) emphasize, our need for recognition means that our subjectivity is always in process, beyond itself.

23. Mills (1967, p. 396).

24. Mills (1967, p. 534).

25. See Uys (2022) for a thorough analysis of Mills' Sociological Imagination applied to whistleblowing in the context of South Africa and beyond.

26. *Financial Times* (2021). Zuboff concludes by reflecting just how powerful Haugen's disclosures will end up being: 'The question is whether lawmakers will respond with the seriousness of purpose required to restore public governance to our information and communication realm.'

27. Kenny et al. (2019c).
28. Möllering (2013, p. 291).
29. Individual whistleblower stories often spark, or at least become the symbol for, campaigns to reform whistleblowing legislation, as we saw with the Panama Papers and LuxLeaks in the EU, and Markopolos's whistleblowing on the Madoff Ponzi scheme in the US.
30. For a thoughtful account of what that position is like, it is useful to read Professor Brian Martin's blog in which he reflects on his work with whistleblowers since the 1980s. The insights are illuminating. He describes cases of Australian and US academics who went against the wishes of their institutions to call out serious wrongdoing, sometimes alongside other whistleblowers, other times acting alone. 'When you speak out and offend those with power, you're at risk of adverse actions', he wrote. 'This is true for anyone, including academics. Scholarly dissent is supposed to be protected by academic freedom, and sometimes it is, but in too many cases it is not, as shown in numerous case studies in Australia, the US and elsewhere.' Martin describes how '[a]cademics who dissent from orthodoxies or who challenge powerful groups need to be prepared for the tactics used against them'. See Martin (2017).
31. Vandekerckhove & Phillips (2019).
32. Martin (2013, p. 9).
33. Interview with research collaborator Meghan Van Portfliet.
34. Contu (2014), Kenny et al. (2019a).
35. Dworkin & Baucus (1998).
36. Interview with author, 2024. An exception was her relationship with Tyler Shultz. They shared information in the initial phases of her disclosures because they had worked together, and also because Erika felt Tyler's connections to the Theranos board might help persuade its members that something was wrong. As time went on, contact was less.
37. Martin (2012).
38. Wickstrom et al. (2021).
39. Durkheim (2013 [1902]), e.g. Barros & Michaud (2019), Zanoni & Janssens (2007).
40. Banting & Kymlicka (2017), Laitinen & Pessi (2015), Lindenberg (1998).
41. Lindenberg (2015, p. 42), Hemmings (2012), Kouri-Towe (2015), Saunders (2008).
42. 'The majority of whistleblowers suffer in obscurity, frustrated by burned career bridges and vindication they were never able to obtain' (Devine & Maassarani, 2011, p. 18). See also Jones (2013).
43. Affect is an important dimension of psychosocial approaches; different interpretations of affect exist, some drawing on psychoanalysis and

others not (Seigworth & Gregg, 2010). For a discussion and overview in the context of organization studies, see Fotaki et al. (2017); see also Van Portfliet & Kenny (2022).

44. When we describe affect as a powerful force, it is important to distinguish it from emotion. Emotion, an immediate expression of a named feeling, can be tied to affect, but the two are not the same (see Fotaki et al., 2017).

45. Why feminism? There has been nothing particularly feminist thus far about this journey we have been on. Yet, if solidarity is our interest, feminist movements are among the longest-standing and most robust sources of insight and inspiration into the nuances of solidarity relationships. Feminist solidarity research is a complex area with multiple interpretations (Littler & Rottenberg, 2021), but emphasizes how, when groups struggle to challenge an entrenched status quo, interdependency, affect and radical care among members are critical. Specifically, psychosocial feminist theory helps us to understand how attachments form and maintain between partners that work together.

46. Author interview.

47. The authors draw on insights from feminist psychosocial approaches, specifically philosopher Bracha Ettinger's ideas of matrixial trans-subjectivity. Drawing on the experience of maternity, this concept emphasizes how subjects experience both co-dependence and intersubjective difference, thus we can think about 'being together with' an other who may be very different: both unknown and unknowable.

48. Van Portfliet & Kenny (2022).

49. Munro & Kenny (2023).

50. For more on vulnerability of whistleblower researchers and academics, see Martin (2017).

51. Pullen & Vachhani (2018), Tonkiss (2018), Vachhani & Pullen (2019). For some scholars, the idea of fascinance is helpful: devised by Bracha Ettinger fascinance is inspired by the matrixial encounter between the intertwined subjects of mother and baby. It represents an affective 'impulse for mutual care' that emerges in relationships where each is fundamentally dependent on the other, and where the positions of people emerge and are shaped through the relationship itself: they become different by being in interaction, even where seemingly impossible differences emerge (Van Portfliet & Kenny, 2022).

52. Weatherall (2020). Transnational feminist movements challenging gender violence have engaged with differences across race, class, sex and nationality along these lines (Kouri-Towe, 2015, Weldon, 2006).

53. Van Portfliet & Kenny (2022), Haberman (2020); see also Munro (2018).

54. Care Collective (2020, p. 95), Weldon (2006), Smolović Jones, Winchester & Clarke (2021). A psychosocial perspective on political activism emphasizes how healthy democracy and healthy subjectivity depend on the capacity to live with the inevitable ambivalence marking psychic life in order to protect both the other and the self (Butler, 2009, p. 182).
55. Interview as part of research for Van Portfliet & Kenny (2022).
56. See Pullen & Vachhani (2018).
57. Martin & Coy (2017).
58. Petriglieri & Petriglieri (2020) for discussion in the context of organizations.
59. Petriglieri & Petriglieri (2010), Shapiro & Carr (1991).
60. Lawrence (2003).
61. Kouri-Towe (2015).
62. Originating with anthropologist Lévi-Strauss studying the creative means by which societies generate meaning from new and unexpected situations using available cultural scripts and artefacts, the concept of bricolage has been used across the social sciences including in management and organization studies (Boxenbaum & Rouleau, 2011, Perkman & Spicer, 2014, Visscher et al., 2017, Weick 1993). The bricoleur is a craftsperson who must work with limited means, often combining elements not related to the current project, the left-overs from other endeavours, which are used as a starting point, adjusted and experimented until a workable solution is found.
63. Kenny & Fotaki (2021).
64. For more practical advice, others provide invaluable analyses structured into handbooks that present guidance and steps for surviving what can be a chaotic, overwhelming experience; see Chapter 4, fn14.
65. Beyes & Pias (2018), Zuboff (2019).
66. Kenny (2023b).
67. Please refer to Appendix 2.
68. Butler (2015, p. 133).
69. This echoes feminist organizational theorist Melissa Tyler (2019), who specifies the implications of Butler's work for how organizations are conceived going forward: their part in denying workers' recognition but also the need to provide infrastructural support for marginalized groups. See also Kenny & Fotaki (2021).
70. Butler (2016, p. 19).
71. See Cole (2016) and Richardson (2023).
72. Uys (2022).
73. Kenny & Fotaki (2019, 2021).
74. Freud, 1936; and in the context of organization studies Petriglieri & Petriglieri (2010, p. 47).

Appendix 1

Ignoring Public Whistleblowers: Literature, Method and Analysis

Academic Research on Public Whistleblowing

There is a lack of scholarly attention to the role of external allies and partners in public whistleblowing struggles. The vast majority of whistleblowers – a full nine out of every ten – first speak up inside their organization.[1] But if their disclosure is ignored, and/or they experience retaliation for speaking out, some turn to parties outside their organization: journalists, supportive lawyers, activists or politicians for example. Named publicly and finding themselves the targets of reprisal, public whistleblowers must seek an external audience that will listen, assist and act.

Failed by institutional supports, securing external help is critical. But this group frequently struggles in the face of public ambivalence and a hostile, retaliatory employer.[2] Blacklisting is prevalent even though many whistleblowers had been, prior to their disclosures, high achievers known and respected for their commitment to the employer.[3] Retaliated against, with weak legal protections and vulnerable to personal and financial detriment, public whistleblowers often find themselves trying in vain to secure support for their cause from sources outside the organization. Not all public whistleblowers encounter these obstacles, but many do. Yet research is lacking. The question guiding this book is: what new theoretical perspectives can inform our understanding of public whistleblowers and the support available to them? Before beginning, it is useful to explore what we do know in this area.

Whistleblowing is not a major focus for any academic research discipline. But since the 1980s, studies have emerged and now it is a fairly well-established, if small, field of enquiry. This work is carried out by researchers in law, business ethics, organization and management studies. Topics vary widely. Legal researchers examine the interpretation and application of statutes, comparing legislation between countries, identifying strengths, flaws and omissions. Ethics scholars enjoy abstract, philosophical musings on what whistleblowing 'means'; what would Kant say about it? Was Socrates a whistleblower? And so on. Other studies are explicitly practical, coming from the perspective of the employer, and are aimed at helping the manager deal with whistleblowing. Research sets out to predict when and where whistleblowing will occur, who is most likely to do it and the best way to design official channels so as to help a manager in charge. Comprehensive reviews map the extent of this field.[4] While interesting, these approaches are of little use for our project.

Some research, including my own, examines the experience of whistleblowing from the perspective of the whistleblower herself. Here, research tends to focus on negative responses encountered, or 'whistleblower reprisal'. Reprisal actions can restrict access to organizational systems, diminishing working conditions, extreme surveillance and micro-management, to name but a few.[5] More serious retaliation can take the form of demotion, dismissal, intimidation and even prosecution for the act of speaking out.[6] If a whistleblower discloses externally while remaining employed in the wrongdoing employer, they are more likely to suffer retaliation than if they had spoken up inside the firm.[7] The likelihood and severity of retaliation increases in cases where wrongdoing is systemic: fundamental to the overall purpose or operation of the employer, as in the cases of public whistleblowing featured in this book. Whistleblower reprisal can have negative impacts for the individual of course, but also for their family. Speaking up can lead to substantial damages like income loss, and increased expenses such as legal fees and health costs. Less tangible but equally challenging impacts include mental health difficulties, relationship breakdown and social isolation.[8] Linked to all this, a sense of shame in relation to financial hardship can plague whistleblowers, with debilitating effects on their ability to seek new work, rebuild their livelihood or continue with their whistleblowing action.[9]

Parrhesia, Public Whistleblowing and a False Sense of Equality

This focus on the lived experience of whistleblowers has certainly helped us to understand more. But scholarly insight is lacking in some important respects. The first relates to a silence around public whistleblowers.

In my field, business ethics and organization studies, researchers seem reticent to focus on how workers who disclose deep-seated, structural or systemic wrongdoing are failed by the institutional speak-up avenues ostensibly open to them. Both whistleblowing laws, and organizational speak-up arrangements, offer protections to this group that, in practice, often prove weak. In some cases, these 'protective shields' are used to actively retaliate against whistleblowers. Instead of addressing this, the academic research tends to progress incrementally and conservatively, focused on tweaking and strengthening legal protections and improving internal organizational speak-up arrangements.[10] On the one hand, this is understandable. The problems of whistleblower retaliation and suffering, and the impacts of organizational wrongdoing, could – theoretically – be solved if employees were enabled to blow the whistle internally, safely and effectively and were adequately protected by the law in cases where this did not work. Yet systems can and do fail.[11] And powerful interest groups tend to want to protect themselves. In such cases, whistleblowers can find themselves exposed and vulnerable, particularly when named in public.

Some research does examine public whistleblowing, but here again there exists a persistent blind spot. Theoretical approaches to whistleblowing in organizations tend to draw on the concept of parrhesia, a recognized practice during specific periods of Ancient Greece. Ethical parrhesia is exerted by a speaker who, despite risk to themselves, freely speaks the truth as they perceive it to be, often from a position of lower status than one's intended audience.[12] Writing about parrhesia in the 1980s, French philosopher Michel Foucault brought it to the attention of a wide range of academic disciplines. Parrhesia inspired many business ethics and organization researchers examining whistleblowing as a form of resistance to power.[13] Scholars were enthused by the idea because it offers a powerful metaphor for whistleblowing, and even a useful identity for whistleblowers, including public ones. Parrhesia involves more than a one-off speech act; it represents a whole transformation of one's self and identity.[14] Through the process of engaging in this kind of risky truth-telling from one's own specific perspective, and coping with the sometimes painful consequences, one redefines who one is. You don't just 'do' parrhesia: you *become* a parrhesiastes, with a new sense of self and a new way of being. The appeal of this concept is clear. Before, when it came to theorizing about whistleblowing, there were only three types: workers who helpfully disclosed through the official channels, risking little because their disclosure was welcome. Or there were one-dimensional victims of reprisal, doomed only to suffer. Or a third category, the stereotypical hero: the infallible and extraordinarily brave whistleblowers one sees in films and on television. Against this, parrhesia helped bring to life the figure of the real worker who risks, struggles and is changed as a result of speaking out. Parrhesia gives us whistleblowing as an ethical practice of self-constitution with the goal of acting politically to challenge power, rather than a simple caricature of victim, hero or rule-following worker.[15]

Parrhesia is a very useful concept. But problems persist. Scholars drawing on it tend to assume something of a level playing field for organizational whistleblower-parrhesiastes. They all speak truth to power from below, true, but the differences in the capacities of real-life whistleblowers to do this are not accounted for. Recently, researchers have examined how power and status shape who is considered to be a valid truth-teller. Gender, race, class and the intersections of these dimensions are going to play a role in how audiences receive the statements of different whistleblower-parrhesiastes, but little research is available on how this works.[16] It seems simplistic to assume for today's whistleblowers the relative equality among truth-tellers that the Ancient Greek male citizens of the city of Athens may have enjoyed. In fact, the social norms deciding who will be considered an acceptable, 'valid', truth-teller are likely decided long before a worker even begins to decide to speak up.[17] And if a whistleblower finds they don't fit these norms because of who they are, they are likely vulnerable to harsher treatment and more intense whistleblower reprisal.[18] In short, whistleblowing as parrhesia is rarely – in practice – as equally available as implied by many theorists. Yet this aspect tends to be ignored in organizational scholarship and business ethics. Any examination of public whistleblowing would benefit from accounting for how different dimensions come into play, to shape how a given speaker is going to be received.

Public Whistleblowers and Their Allies

The third oversight relates to the first two. The role of supportive partners in whistleblowing struggles tends to be overlooked. Some limited recent work has begun to explore, for example, the importance of advocacy organizations.[19] Alliances can form between whistleblowers and activists in social movements, all concerned with a common cause: stopping identified wrongdoing.[20] A respected newspaper's framing of a whistleblowing disclosure, and of its discloser, can shape public perceptions.[21] Journalists and media outlets can help secure, or alternatively block, public support.[22] Where speaking out is perceived to be an important part of a professional's role, this can render whistleblowers more sympathetic in the eyes of would-be allies.[23] Meanwhile, whistleblowers who go outside their job description, reporting on activity in another part of the employer for example, are less favoured. Whether a whistleblowing claim fits with dominant political agendas is also important,[24] as is the perceived legitimacy and credibility of the speaker.[25]

The internet represents new opportunities for whistleblowers to persuade an audience of the importance of their disclosure, for example, through social media platforms.[26] New information and communication technologies (ICTs) enable a reshaping of the space for whistleblowing disclosures as hybrid online–offline methods of public disclosure emerge.[27] At the same time, however, new technology benefits retaliating employers who can use similar tools and technologies to respond to accusations of wrongdoing, deflecting attention away from a scandal and back upon an isolated whistleblower.[28]

With a public audience that can be ambivalent towards a previously unknown whistleblowing worker arriving on the scene, the process of disclosure can be fraught and contentious. But how it is framed can be crucial to success in reaching – and being taken seriously – by the intended listeners.[29] Questions of how disclosures are presented, and by whom, are critical, with allies playing an important role.

Academic scholarship has only begun to explore such alliances between whistleblowers and partners. But the linkage is something that experienced 'whistleblowing practitioners', including professional advocates, journalists and lawyers, have known about for some time. That email I had received from Government Accountability Project's Dana Gold made this clear.[30] To counter the vulnerability of an isolated whistleblower, connecting them with a variety of parties that can help, is a vital first step in effective advocacy when their name has been made public.[31] But sustaining these kinds of alliances can be challenging. Partners naturally have different agendas and commitments at any given time.[32] Support can be short term and partial, based on the specific aspects of a whistleblower's claim that temporarily align with the partner's interests, rather than sticking with the whistleblower for the entirety of the disclosure. Concern for the whistleblower's own well-being is not always top of the agenda.

Those who partner to support whistleblowers can themselves experience stigmatization and reputational risk.[33] And whistleblowers tend to be cautious before contacting potential helpers, particularly if there is any sense that the partner is less than wholly independent of the employer against which they struggle, or untrustworthy for another reason.[34] At the same time, however, some limited research into whistleblowers and their partners describes the power of close connections when these partnerships do emerge. Strength can be drawn from empathy, the sharing of humour and a sense of connection around common values.[35] These kinds of alliances can also help bring peace of mind and in some cases a transformative, new, political awareness for whistleblowers.[36] What we know from limited research, therefore, is that achieving an effective network of support is as critical as it is complex, but conceptual understanding of how this occurs is lacking.

Beyond fragmented studies, anecdotal commentary and observations from whistleblower advocates, evidence is all but absent on how partners allied around a common cause affect whistleblowing success.[37] Again, it is useful to examine why this scholarly blind spot persists. A tendency to overlook public whistleblowers per se naturally contributes to ignoring the alliances they form. But also, theoretically, whistleblowing scholarship typically promotes an individualist perception of the whistleblower. Research downplays the role of other people in the experience and process of speaking out, with some exceptions.[38] The whistleblower engaged in parrhesia is assumed to act alone.

This theoretical preoccupation with individuals is clearly at odds with the practice of whistleblowing, something I wrote about in 2019 in the book *Whistleblowing: Toward a New Theory*. Whistleblower advocacy organizations have long considered building solidarity with supportive others as a first step in supporting a new whistleblower in their journey to disclose. Experienced whistleblower lawyers are clear on the point: networks are critical for both the success of a disclosure and the well-being of a whistleblower who has been isolated and excluded.[39] Yet a scholarly oversight persists such that the specific dynamics of whistleblower partnerships – how they emerge and what helps them work – are rarely addressed in research. Instead, a focus on the individual whistleblower continues. Scholars have, of late, called for new perspectives.

Wim Vandekerckhove is a professor of business ethics and researches whistleblowing. In 2021, he wrote that we must 'move[s] the field of whistleblowing scholarship beyond studying the relation between whistleblower and those who retaliate against them', and particularly to examine the 'important – yet thus far scholarly neglected – role of whistleblower support groups and media to the construction of whistleblowing and the naming of whistleblowers'.[40] To date, the response from researchers has been limited and piecemeal, despite the fact that recent legislation has moved to protect whistleblowing partners from reprisal.[41] Theoretical explication, therefore, remains limited.

To ignore such calls to move the field of scholarship forward in this way is dangerous. Right now, practical supports for whistleblowers are overwhelmingly focused on the official channels. Speak-up systems, regulatory disclosure pathways and whistleblower protection laws are perceived as the best shields for enhancing the capacity of whistleblowers to raise concerns. But these only help certain kinds of whistleblowing – institutionalized disclosures: ones that are acceptable within the current status quo. The kinds of challenges they pose to the system are not fundamentally destabilizing. The dominant project within whistleblowing policy – as in whistleblowing scholarship – aims at making those shields better.

But what about the outsiders – the public whistleblowers who attract the full force of organizational retaliation for disclosing deep-seated, fundamental wrongdoing that threatens to destabilize the very structures of the organization and institution within which they speak? Where are their shields? Support is helpful, we know this, but effective support is elusive and attempts to secure it often end in failure. Awareness of these well-known difficulties deters many employees from speaking out about serious wrongdoing in the first place. This empirical fact notwithstanding, organization theory is more or less silent. And practical help is extremely limited.

Researching Public Whistleblowing: Research Approach and Methods

It is clear that we need new ways of seeing this problem. Organization scholars have developed a useful approach – interpretive theorizing – for reframing and rethinking the concepts we have to describe a particular area when these concepts clearly are not working.[42] The idea is to examine the area through a deep dive into a small number of case studies, chosen because they exemplify the topic of interest.[43] Existing research relating to the topic is also interrogated while a fresh theoretical lens is brought to bear in order to invite fresh perspectives and open up thinking. Through this, new concepts can be proposed, examined and refined alongside analyses of the cases. Departing from more positivist approaches, the aim is not to test existing hypotheses, but rather to develop new framings that can inform future research. This kind of theoretical provocation is needed to shake things up a little, when we find our existing lenses are not working and blind spots prevail.[44] In the context of this book, if we are to respond to calls for greater ambition in how we conceptualize whistleblowing in – and beyond – organizations, such an approach offers promise.

For this study, a set of five well-publicized cases were chosen to examine whistleblowing at Amazon, Facebook, Theranos, ICE and ESB. Fewer cases allow more depth and richness of insight; the aim was to paint a picture of the unfolding scenes of public whistleblowing and the challenges and opportunities encountered by those engaging in them. This approach is valuable because we rarely have access to the 'inside' of how public whistleblowing disclosures emerge.

A Psychosocial Lens

The new theoretical lens brought to bear on all of this is a psychosocial approach to studying organizations. There are two reasons for this choice. First, the concept of organization itself is often overlooked in examinations of public whistleblowing; we rarely pay attention to the organizing dynamics and activities going on outside the official channels. Second, a psychosocial lens provides valuable and unusual insights into organizations.[45] The idea is that the unconscious plays a role in how organizations work – or how they fail to work. The unconscious represents an unmanaged, unmanageable territory in which fears, desires and fantasy are active players. Attending to these, a psychosocial lens helps us understand more about how apparently irrational behaviour emerges in organizations; how we attach to our professional roles, how organizational cultures function or self-destruct and how the pleasures and struggles accompany the relationships we form at work.[46] Most of the ideas informing a psychosocial approach originated in studies of clinical psychoanalysis, but over more than forty years scholars have worked to bring key concepts to shed light on social settings, including, and especially, organizations.[47]

It may appear that the interpretive, subjective nature of psychosocial work is too loose to generate useful insight. Not so. Such work requires a level of openness about the researcher's own involvement in the setting that is inevitable but typically occluded and hidden in other kinds of empirical work that cling to fantasies of complete objectivity. An important part of psychosocial organizational research therefore is the recognition that, as researchers, any notions that we can be fully objective coming to our topics free of bias is a fantasy. The job instead is to make explicit our investments as and where they appear to us, and to recognize that, as unconscious dimensions, many do not appear to us at all.[48] Where possible, I tried to follow this here.

Careful documentation and argumentation are required within psychosocial research; the chapters in this book are based on extensive data gathering. Sources include first-person interviews with whistleblowers and experts, secondary and publicly available interviews, legal statutes, newspaper articles, books, podcasts and observations at industry events. All are referenced throughout. And while the researcher's interpretation is a central part of the analysis, this does not lessen the value of studies of this kind. As with good history, or good anthropology, for example, psychosocial research 'must make sense, pull together as much of the known data as possible, [and] provide a coherent and persuasive account'.[49] As Petriglieri notes, the aim is to be 'both compelling and convincing, precise and poetic'. While not yet in the mainstream of social science research, studies of this kind are increasing in number. And it is often from the margins that new meanings are found and new theoretical perspectives opened up.[50]

As is clear by now, we need to innovate. If we are to understand more about how disclosers reporting deep-seated, systemic problems, named publicly and subject to reprisals by their employer, can prevail, and how alliances with partners organize to enable this, we need to look beyond existing theories. A psychosocial approach to studying organizations holds potential, and this informed the analysis for this book.

(Our) Fearless Speech: Parrhesia and Allies

Having examined the scholarly lacuna surrounding public whistleblowers and the reasons for it, and outlined the research approach, we can now reflect on the outcome of a study as a whole and its implications. We can ask: 'what does collective bricolage mean for research on whistleblowing?' and specifically 'what new theoretical perspectives can inform our understanding of public whistleblowers and the support available to them?'

Collective bricolage adds to our understanding of organizational parrhesia, that appealing concept often used to describe organizational whistleblowers who, through following their own compulsion to speak the truth as they see it, can risk much and find themselves changing in the process. Recall the work that is being done by many scholars: to return parrhesia to an accepted right of citizens, particularly of workers.[51] Parrhesia often remains an abstract notion in business ethics and organization studies debates: an idealized construct about which people philosophize. Placing this notion against the lived experiences of public whistleblowers discussed here gives rise to some useful observations.

First, the concept of collective bricolage enables a deeper understanding of how public disclosures can prevail, and specifically the importance of disclosing in tandem with valuable others. Parrhesia only makes sense in the context of an engagement between the speaker and the listener who is open to hearing information, even if it is disturbing, and acting upon it.[52] Utterances die without listeners, and particularly depend upon those first listeners who agree to join the act.[53] If we assume parrhesia must have an audience, then for public whistleblowers, those most risky of all whistleblowing risk-takers, the practice of parrhesia cannot be separated from the presence of allies. As we saw with the help of C. Wright Mills, allies take disclosures – and the troubles they cause the discloser – from the local, apparently inconsequential, setting of one's immediate workplace, to the broader stage upon which public issues are debated. They help amplify, strengthen and lend credibility to the speaker and to what they are saying. Gaining support in this way is as important as it is complex and rare.

The persistent image we have, therefore, of the contemporary parrhesiastes appearing alone and acting by themselves needs to be rethought. This furthers nascent work in this area.[54] What we see here is that robust relationships between partners are vital to foster and they must be sustained. The development of strong ties seems important. Yet whistleblowing scenes, imbued with stress and conflict, create background problems. Relationships are tricky, riven with personal agendas and interests, fears and desires. Whistleblower partners can increasingly find themselves isolated and stigmatized within their own professions, when speaking out on controversial topics. In many cases they too must risk a lot because they now, in partnering with the whistleblower, engage in parrhesia themselves. Moreover, as we saw, the exercise of parrhesia alongside allies in an online world is complicated. Even as new digital landscapes appear to enable support to be extended from far-flung parties, it remains to be seen how robust this might be. The securing of effective partners is by no means straightforward.

We also see how collective bricolage challenges the assumed dominance of the 'power' involved in parrhesia's 'speaking truth to power'. The relationship between speaker and power is more intertwined and more dialectical than is often assumed in the conception of parrhesia. A focus on the organizing practices of allies via a psychosocial lens enabled us to see the dynamics and nuances therein, allowing us a much clearer view of how power is not monolithic, even in situations in which it seems to be. Power, as residing in the many, works against extreme aggression. And the unintended consequences of action and messy realities of the 'power' – in fact an anxious, panicked employer – gives rise to its own undoing in certain cases. Parrhesia remains a risky act, in public whistleblowing, but it is a risk shaped by ongoing circumstances, sometimes lessened, other times reinforced: it is not set in stone.

This all forces us to extend our understanding of the figure of the whistleblower-parrhesiastes. First, it suggests that the Ancient Greek evocation of parrhesia as mere speech act, in which a personal truth is declaimed, and left at that, is not sufficient in analyses of contemporary whistleblowing. In so doing, we must blur the boundaries between speech act, and post-speech activism, as we saw in cases like Frances's and Christian's where whistleblowing quickly morphs into direct action. Yet, we also saw with Seamus, Dawn and Erika, whose appearance in the public gaze was less willed and more reluctant, that, when public exposure occurred, there was little choice but to become somewhat activist in shaping public opinion in order to defend themselves. To be a public whistleblower requires an active (re)creation of oneself-as-parrhesiastes, in tandem with others, in an overall scene of critique. This highlights both the value of the parrhesiastic subject position and the almost coercive nature of public exposure that requires one to adopt it, if one is to survive at all.

Second, parrhesia's heritage in the classics has led to an assumption that, as an idealized abstract construct, it is more or less available to all citizens possessing the right to engage in it. While Michel Foucault's work on parrhesia – fearless speech– traced the different capacities of parrhesiastic subject positions that depended, for example, on one's status as citizen, or adviser to the ruler, or philosopher's privilege during specific eras in Ancient Greece, contemporary interpretations tend to overlook these contingencies.[55] The differential capacities of different people to even be considered potentially credible 'fearless speakers' are generally ignored.[56] If we celebrate people who challenge power but fail to acknowledge their pre-existing advantages and privileges enabling this, we have a flawed view. Not all ethical parrhesiastes begin from an equal place; job security, sexuality, race, class and gender dynamics potentially colour which whistleblowers come across as credible and which ones are not to be listened to. If we fail to point this out, studies will end up glorifying only some kinds of scenes that see workers 'speaking truth from below', blind to the fact that the speaker's (white, male, for example) privilege lends unique credibility and a prior advantage. We are no longer in Athens, a point sometimes lost on those whose sole focus is ethical frameworks in their abstract form, glorifying an ideal of parrhesia that is divorced from lived scenes of struggle. Parrhesia remains a very helpful concept but only if we understand and examine just how much pre-existing biases, and very real material capacities to resource one's speech act, shape its execution.

The persistent ignoring of the role of allies, when it comes to how whistleblowers are depicted in public commentary, but also academic scholarship, is clearly wrong-headed. To counter, our analysis expands our understanding of parrhesia, to see the overall assemblage of parrhesia as a scene of dissent involving more than one dissenter. Contemporary parrhesia in the form of public whistleblowing, therefore, is contingent on the work of allies, engaged in collective bricolage as an approach to organizing and resisting. We see how powerful employers inadvertently create the conditions of worker resistance, how cracks emerge and can be exploited by people working together. This offers an important new lens on an aspect of whistleblowing disclosure that is, in the main, avoided by researchers but that remains increasingly vital for our learning about egregious wrongdoing.

Future Research

Going forward, scholars will usefully develop the tangents explored here. The aim is to paint a clearer picture of the landscape in which the public whistleblower finds themselves, and of how to navigate it. In terms of collective bricolage specifically, questions emerge from what we have seen: what kinds of resources are required to ensure the presence and maintenance of these collectives? What new technologies for disclosure and for support might be developed? How do ally partnerships play out in different sectors, including the sectors known for prevalence of whistleblower reprisal: health, government, policing, education, financial services and NGO work? Where are effective allies more likely to be found: for example in the pro-bono-focused law schools that produced the initial activist-lawyers emerging from the US in the 1970s? What role do whistleblowers' families play? Are there ways of formally connecting the various legal, activist, media and academic supporters, but still ensuring spaces that allow these informal yet deep-seated relations to grow? What potential for exploitation by ally partners exist, amid the emergence of cash rewards for whistleblowing? What is the impact of competition between supporters? And what kinds of reprisals against partners, to add to those against whistleblowers, might we expect? Each of these dimensions will require deeper investigation.

Academics: Social science academics often downplay the impacts that they can have outside the university, but it is worth remembering that our work can, now and then, make a difference to people in difficult situations. As one example, it can help show these things in a new light. Academics are granted the time and the space (or at least some time and space) to explore a phenomenon in depth. Gathering narratives can be invaluable. Whistleblowing is lonely. From my discussions with people who have spoken out, it seems that stories of others who have been through similar situations across the world are a source of comfort. Other whistleblowers have families too, have mortgages and experience financial struggles. Others have found themselves pretty much on their own, suffering from stress. The research can offer a sense of connection and hopefully research can continue.

Academics can play a more direct role in collective bricolage, but with some exceptions their involvement rarely extends beyond writing and research. Principles of academic freedom remain in place in many countries' higher education systems. Academic freedom, as it appears in Ireland's Universities Act 1997, for example, tells us that Irish academics are safe to 'question and test received wisdom, to put forward new ideas and to state controversial or unpopular opinions', without detriment. When it comes to whistleblowers, scholars are not always as active in the questioning and testing as they are invited to be. As Brian Martin reflects, 'many academic dissidents avoid publicity, out of embarrassment, unfamiliarity with campaigning, or a trust in official channels'. He is talking about academics avoiding whistleblowing on wrongdoing in their institutions, but his sentiments can be extended to academics who might otherwise involve themselves in collective bricolage alongside dissenters. As we see clearly, in public whistleblowing disputes, the balance of power is often with large employers with deeper pockets that can outspend most challengers. The traditional sources of support for those who expose abuses of power – independent investigative journalism and well-funded unions among others – are in rapid decline. Without deluding ourselves about the extent to which academics can effect change, perhaps making it a little more difficult for employers to wield this power is a reasonable aim. While some scholars have begun this work, more research into how and where this occurs, the challenges and opportunities therein, would be welcome.[57]

Trade Unions: Collective bricolage is undertaken by alliances and partnerships that workers can form as they struggle to whistleblow in public. Clearly, trade unions play a potential role as the traditional institutional form of worker solidarity, ostensibly set up with the interests of workers, rather than employers, at the forefront of their mission and activities. Yet trade unions are often left out of discussions of whistleblowing-related legislative and policy change, or granted limited input.[58] The involvement between unions and whistleblowing workers differs across countries, depending, for example, on the labour market model in place, or the sectoral history of union activity.[59]

Challenges to union involvement in whistleblowing include, for example, potential union bias in how whistleblowers are perceived, where long-standing social partnership arrangements see unions unwilling to jeopardize employer–union collaboration. For some, such partnership arrangements mask the intrinsic pluralism and conflict embedded in the employer–worker relationship.[60] Debates are ongoing. What we can say is that, as yet, the role of trade unions, and what it could be, remains under-researched. Notable exceptions point to the potential for unions to play a larger role, having the reach and scope to work across a variety of levels and tiers inherent in whistleblowing processes.[61] Unions might become more involved in promoting speech rights on the part of workers, for example, and be at the forefront of defending other higher-level principles that matter to a demographically changing workforce. There is rich potential in exploring collective bricolage involving whistleblowers in alliance with unions; and future work will valuably examine both the opportunities and challenges therein.

Errors and Unintended Consequences: We saw throughout our cases how unintended consequences give rise to surprising outcomes. The use of management techniques by dissenters, the surprising rise of whistleblowing subcultures and workers with much less power capitalizing on errors were just some examples of these spaces in which power turns to counter aggressive acts. We saw how finding the chinks and fissures is not something easily done alone. Nor is the work of linking the individual troubles of the whistleblower to the wider public issue. Interstices and gaps emerge in the anxious backlash of the threatened employer, and it is connections between people that best enable their exploitation. When it comes to forced errors and self-inflicted wounds on the part of retaliatory employers, future research will usefully aim to spot these fractures and openings in the overall apparatus in other settings, and explore the new scenarios to which they give rise.[62] A closer examination of allies and partnerships of different kinds in this is an important direction for future research.

Planned Campaigns and Whistleblower Rewards: Planned campaigns are on the rise. As whistleblowing law grows in sophistication and reach, whistleblowing lawyers will increasingly be on hand to seek out potentially successful clients with whom to work, and with whom to win cases. This kind of ally is now incentivized well in places like the US, South Korea and other countries offering monetary sums to disclosers coming forward with information that ultimately saves the state money.[63] As this happens, we see many of the lessons learned from our exemplar cases being applied by legal advocates working with whistleblowers. And we will likely see more of this. And as popular awareness of whistleblowing – and of incentives for supporting whistleblowers – grows, more people will become involved in such work, studying the strategies of former dissenters and learning from their mistakes. These planned campaigns, and exemplar cases, are instructive for the new scenes of ally partnership they represent. It will be important to examine how this move is shaping whistleblowing: for example whether incentives change the landscape of ally partnership and in what ways.

Excluded from Collective Bricolage: Collectives help public whistleblowers disclose and survive, but they are not available to all whistleblowers to the same extent. Going forward, we must consider who gets left out of the ally partnerships engaged in bricolage: who struggles to even begin contemplating the development of relationships required. Gender, race and class seem to play a role in how public whistleblowers are perceived by would-be supporters, albeit in different ways depending on the setting. It will be important to examine the specific intersections of these dimensions in a given situation. As one example, emerging research points to the value of collective shields in the form of social movements, including online ones, that can help disclosers speak up confidentially yet effectively. With platform feminist movements based on whistleblowing disclosures such as #MeToo offering early exemplars, this mode is being repeated in other struggles, including, for example, the Tech Workers' Collective. Shields can help to counter some of the risks of public whistleblowing, albeit our understanding is as yet nascent. In practice, whistleblower anonymity and confidentiality can be difficult to maintain: colleagues often sense who spoke out, for example, or a name is released when a case passes to another party to carry out the investigation. Deeper exploration of the protections offered by these collectivities and the collective bricolage practices they engage will be useful. Likewise, attention must be paid to the advantages enjoyed by some: of privileged access to supporters, or a more open door to the audience than others might enjoy.

Notes

1. Vandekerckhove & Phillips (2019).
2. See Andrade (2015). While some view the activity as heroic (Grant, 2002), an underlying attitude that speaking out represents a traitorous violation of loyalty to one's organization can persist (Alford, 2001, Hersch, 2002). Meanwhile, almost four out of ten employees express an aversion to working with someone who has disclosed wrongdoing in the past (Transparency International Ireland, 2017).
3. Rothschild (2013, p. 653).
4. See Culiberg & Mihelič (2016), Miceli et al. (2008).
5. Alford (2001), Devine & Maassarani (2011), Rehg et al. (2008, p. 222), Rothschild & Miethe (1999).
6. Glazer & Glazer (1989), Kenny et al. (2019a), Mesmer-Magnus & Viswesvaran (2005), Stein (2021).
7. Park et al. (2020a), Smith (2014b), Van Portfliet (2020), Vandekerckhove et al. (2014).
8. Bjørkelo (2013), Kenny & Fotaki (2021), Lennane (2012).
9. Kenny (2019), Kenny & Fotaki (2021).
10. Culiberg & Mihelič (2016), Kenny et al. (2019c), Lewis & Vandekerckhove (2015).
11. IBA (2018), Lewis (2008).
12. As Foucault makes clear in his books and lectures on the subject (Foucault, 2001, 2005), parrhesia has had various meanings over time. These range from critical speech in the Agora as part of Athenian democracy to one-on-one advice-giving to monarchs in the Hellenistic age, the public challenges to those in power by philosophers including Socrates, and the visible enacted critique of the Cynics (Foucault, 1983, 2011a, 2011b). We cannot therefore directly compare with today's organizational whistleblowers (Jack, 2004), but the metaphor of a figure engaging in straightforward and critical speech despite the power differential between them and the target has been compelling. See Barratt (2008, 2019), Skinner (2011) for useful examples.
13. Jack (2004), Kenny & Bushnell (2020), Mansbach (2009), Munro (2017), Weiskopf & Willmott (2013), Vandekerckhove & Langenberg (2012).
14. Foucault (2005, pp. 318–319); in the context of whistleblowing, see Mansbach (2009).
15. Kenny, Fotaki & Vandekerckhove (2019b), Mansbach (2009), Munro (2017), Weiskopf & Willmott (2013).

16. For exceptions, see Agostinho & Thylstrup (2019), Kenny & Fanchini (2023), Maxwell (2019).
17. Kenny (2019).
18. Alford (2001), Kenny (2019), Perry (1998).
19. Van Portfliet & Kenny (2022).
20. Bushnell (2020), Munro (2017), Munro & Kenny (2023).
21. Park et al. (2020a), Perry (1998).
22. Cole (2016), Martin (1999). (Note: Updated version = Martin (2013).)
23. Mansbach (2009), Rothschild (2013), Weiskopf & Tobias-Miersch (2016).
24. Kenny & Bushnell (2020), Weiskopf & Willmott (2013).
25. Near & Miceli (1995), Vandekerckhove & Phillips (2019).
26. Lam & Harcourt (2019).
27. Munro (2017), Nayar (2010).
28. Alford (2001), Warren (2007).
29. Fanchini (2019).
30. See Prologue.
31. Devine & Maassarani (2011); see also Mueller (2019).
32. Mueller (2019, p. 63).
33. Munro (2018).
34. Miceli et al. (2008), Vandekerckhove & Phillips (2019).
35. McGlynn & Richardson (2014), Van Portfliet & Kenny (2022).
36. Kenny & Fotaki (2021), Rothschild (2013), Weiskopf & Willmott (2013).
37. Dreyfus et al. (2013), Park et al. (2020).
38. See Kenny (2019) for discussion.
39. Devine & Maassarani (2011); Interview with Tom Devine, Government Accountability Project, 2018; Interview with Mary Inman, Constantine Cannon, 2018.
40. Vandekerckhove (2021). This review of my book, alongside that of Professor Stewart Clegg, led me to want to do the research for this book. See also Vandekerckhove et al. (2014, p. 317), Martin & Rifkin (2004).
41. EC Council Directive (2019, Article 4.4).
42. Emancipatory theorizing is an approach in which a phenomenon is re-examined through alternative theoretical framings, allowing deeper investigation and alternative concepts to emerge. Case studies are used to illustrate emerging concepts. See Cornelissen et al. (2021), Husted & Just (2022), Nyberg (2021), Janssens & Zanoni (2021) for examples in organization theory development. This approach has been used in theoretical work on whistleblowing (Alford, 2001, Ceva & Bocchiola, 2019, Maxwell, 2019).

43. Flyvbjerg (2006). Case material is subject to thematic analysis, with sources including primary interviews with whistleblowers, newspaper documents, court transcripts, secondary literature, webinars, film, podcasts and radio broadcasts, alongside interviews with senior leaders at whistleblower support organizations worldwide, journalists, lawyers and other support professionals. Analysis draws on sensitizing concepts from extant literature (Alvesson & Sköldberg, 2009, Bowen, 2006). As the book proceeds, these case studies are used to illustrate theoretical points, weaving examples through discussion of specific concepts (Rhodes, 2016).

44. Cornelissen et al. (2021).

45. See in particular Fotaki et al. (2012), Kenny & Fotaki (2014), Petriglieri & Petriglieri (2020).

46. Gabriel (1995, 1999), Petriglieri & Petriglieri (2020).

47. See Kenny & Fotaki (2014).

48. Gabriel (1995), Kenny (2010).

49. Mitchell & Black (1995).

50. Parker & Fotaki (2014), Petriglieri & Petriglieri (2020).

51. Andrade (2015), Kenny et al. (2019b), Mansbach (2009), Weiskopf & Willmott (2013).

52. Andrade (2015), Catlaw, Rawlings & Callen (2014), Contu (2014).

53. Jones et al. (2005, p. 121), Vandekerckhove & Langenberg (2012).

54. Bushnell (2020), Kenny (2019), Van Portfliet & Kenny (2022), Munro (2017).

55. Discussing ethical parrhesia, Foucault recalls figures from Ancient Greece as exemplars of the practice, from Socrates to Euripides' character Ion. Yet he fails to fully account for their a priori advantages as males, and as citizens, and thus their unique access to power and status from which other potential speakers – women and slaves for example – were excluded.

56. See Agostinho & Thylstrup (2019), Kenny & Fanchini (2023), Maxwell (2018, 2019) for discussion.

57. See, for example, Professor Brian Martin's work with whistleblowers in Australia.

58. Lewis (2008), Vandekerckhove & Lewis (2012). Trade unions were, however, involved in discussions leading up to the introduction of the 2019 EU Whistleblower Directive; for details, see Vandekerckhove (2022). The EU Directive now requires member states to consult and agree with 'the social partners where provided for by national law' prior to mandating organizations to establish channels and procedures for internal reporting.

59. Skivenes & Trygstad (2010, 2017), Lewis & Vandekerckhove (2018).

60. Contu (2014), Kuldova (2023), Vandekerckhove & Rumyantseva (2014).
61. Drawing on examples from the UK, leading whistleblowing researchers David Lewis and Wim Vandekerckhove map out the landscape of potential union involvement in whistleblowing, which could, they argue, range from involvement in disclosures: inside the organization, to outside regulators and oversight bodies, and publicly (to the media for example) along with union voice. See Lewis & Vandekerckhove (2018); see also Phillips (2017).
62. Martin (2012).
63. Laws like Dodd Frank emerged from keenly felt frustration at the fact that successive financial crises from the Savings and Loan scandal to the 2008 financial crisis happened because insiders were routinely ignored. Billions of dollars were lost. The new laws appeared to provide it all: whistleblowers can come forward anonymously and join the Department of Justice in taking a case against a fraudulent organization. They can work in secret to build the evidence. They are protected against reprisals if their names do emerge. Incredibly, organizations have actually been sanctioned by the SEC for retaliating against whistleblowers. And famously some are entitled to a reward – a percentage of the monies recouped, the money going to the whistleblower and of course her legal team. And because the government is prosecuting the organization, the wrongdoing – ideally – gets stopped. These laws have proved so popular that the tax department and the transport department followed suit, while other countries are bringing similar provisions. Digging a little deeper, however, it seems problems exist. Cases that win involve significant effort and upfront investment.

    There is the temptation to only go for sure things. The government departments are limited in the resources they can give to such cases – again, only the definite wins are taken on. The result: a tiny percentage of cases are taken on.

Appendix 2

A Legal Revolution

The focus of this book is on people whom the law has failed. But valuable work is ongoing to reform whistleblowing legislation, and this is essential. Best practice guides tell us what makes a good whistleblowing law.[1] Since the 1970s, activists, lawyers and policymakers have been working hard to close legal loopholes that fail workers, to replace what people refer to as 'the cardboard shields' of existing, weak, whistleblower protections with hardy, metal shields of robust law. There have been many hard-won successes: US campaigners fought to outlaw silencing contracts in whistleblowing cases, for example. The 2019 EU Whistleblowing Directive, meanwhile, insists member states introduce penalties for people who bring vexatious proceedings against reporting persons, with countries like Ireland introducing criminal sanctions. Similar moves aim to prohibit the prosecution of whistleblowers for disclosing secrets in the public interest through SLAPP-style suits featured in Chapter 2. A simple but important ask is for an option for courts to quickly dismiss claims of this kind that are clearly not going to win, thus avoiding the time, cost and stress that gives SLAPPs their power.[2]

Most employers across Europe are now accountable for managing their whistleblowing processes in more transparent ways, with the interests of the worker disclosing at the centre, along with protection for anyone wrongfully accused.[3] Employers must have systems that support disclosing workers and are of a minimum standard, and they must make annual reports detailing these disclosures. The 2019 Directive contains some other critical innovations: requirements for regulators and governments to actively monitor employers and sanction non-compliance, for example, and reversing the burden of proof in reprisal cases, so that the employer can no longer rely as easily on its information and power advantage.

Changes also include member states being obliged to offer legal aid to protected whistleblowers requiring it, which, as we saw in

Chapter 2, can be critical. None of this is easy work. Opponents fight to challenge whistleblowing laws. Such lobby groups are strong, often carrying a pro-business message, generally along the lines of how awful it would be to burden organizations with yet more processes and policies. And every time there is a change in the law that favours whistleblowers, teams of lawyers go to work to figure out the loopholes, the exceptions and the angles that will strengthen their corporate clients' defences. Finally, the arrival of new protection laws tends to bring a parallel increase in employers enforcing secrecy agreements against whistleblowers in court.[4]

Government Accountability Project's Tom Devine feels that right now, public opinion has never been more supportive of whistleblowers. With laws changing across the world, we are, he argues, at 'a critical moment in the revolution' to install the metal shields that are essential. The campaign to reform law in favour of the whistleblowing worker goes on. Campaigning groups have taken on strong forces and won. A significant part of this is to harmonize those siloed, piecemeal laws across sectors and states we saw in Chapter 2. A further demand is to get rid of confusing and redundant pieces of law – including special clauses that are written into whistleblowing legislation, specifying sanctions for 'false or vexatious reporting'. False and defamatory claims have long been dealt with in other areas of the law, so any such special treatment just adds to the chill effects deterring workers from availing of their rights to speak up.

Harmonizing laws and making sure they are implemented with care will help bolster whistleblower protections. Without clarity, workers with disclosures to make will be put off.[5] As we saw, neither Erika Cheung nor her colleagues were aware of their rights for protection as whistleblowers, remaining vulnerable for a long time. And even after Erika apparently found a safe harbour when disclosing to the appropriate body, whether she was actually protected against prosecution remained a grey area: a fearful place to be. Law is needed that is simple, understandable by all and accessible, through for example legal aid.

Stronger legal protections must extend to public whistleblowers. Whistleblowing protection laws tend to favour people going internally and disclosing to their employer, or to a regulator, then waiting to see if something will be done. Only when a worker is sure no action is being taken can they go outside, for example to the media. But what about situations where the wrongdoing is happening right now, and there is slim to no chance that the employer will stop it? Whistleblowers who go to the media are often not protected, or very weakly protected. Yet as we saw throughout this book, public whistleblowing can be both the last resort and an essential outlet for a desperate worker with urgent information to disclose. In an ideal world, people would have the luxury of time to give the system a chance to work. Until then, whistleblower protection law should better reflect the reality of public whistleblowing.

The list of desired changes grows. Each new law, once implemented, shows the gaps and loopholes in its use in practice. Hence the work continues, and this is just a partial glimpse. Whatever the solution, what we do know is whether we focus on strengthening laws, policies, official channels or outsider alliances with whistleblower partners, the individual who discloses and the risks and vulnerabilities they encounter must be at the centre of the work.

Notes

1. See, for example, IBA (2021).
2. Rogal (2021, p. 1700).
3. Vandekerckhove (2022).
4. Dworkin & Callahan (1998).
5. Rogal (2021, p. 1699).

References

Agostinho, D., & Thylstrup, N. B. (2019). '"If Truth Was a Woman": Leaky Infrastructures and the Gender Politics of Truth-Telling'. *Ephemera*, *19*, 745–775.

Ahmed, S. (2004). 'Affective Economies'. *Social Text*, *22*, 117–139.

Alford, C. F. (2001). *Whistleblowers: Broken Lives and Organizational Power*. Ithaca, NY: Cornell University Press.

Alimahomed-Wilson, J., & Reese, E. (2021). 'Surveilling Amazon's Warehouse Workers: Racism, Retaliation, and Worker Resistance amid the Pandemic'. *Work in the Global Economy*, *1*, 55–73.

Alter, C. (2022). 'He Came Out of Nowhere and Humbled Amazon: Is Chris Smalls the Future of Labor?' Retrieved 8 December 2022 from *Time*.

Alvesson, M., & Sköldberg, K. (2009). *Reflexive Methodology*. London: Sage.

Andrade, J. A. (2015). 'Reconceptualizing Whistleblowing in a Complex World'. *Journal of Business Ethics*, *128*, 321–335.

Bain, A. (1998). 'Social Defenses against Organizational Learning'. *Human Relations*, *51*(3), 413–429.

Banting, K., & Kymlicka, W. (2017). 'Introduction: The Political Sources of Solidarity in Diverse Societies'. In K. Banting & W. Kymlicka (Eds.), *The Strains of Commitment: The Political Sources of Solidarity in Diverse Societies* (pp. 1–58). Oxford: Oxford University Press.

Barbaro, M. (2022). 'How Two Friends Beat Amazon and Built a Union' [Podcast Episode]. Retrieved 8 December 2022 from *New York Times*.

Barratt, E. (2008). 'The Later Foucault in Organization and Management Studies'. *Human Relations*, *61*, 515–537.

Barratt, E. (2019). 'Speaking Frankly – Parrhesia and Public Service'. *Management and Organizational History*, *14*, 294–310.

Barros, M., & Michaud, V. (2019). 'Worlds, Words, and Spaces of Resistance: Democracy and Social Media in Consumer Co-ops'. *Organization*. Epub ahead of print 7 March 2019. https://doi.org/10.117 7/1350508419831901.

Bauman, Z. (1989). *Modernity and the Holocaust*. Ithaca, NY: Cornell University Press.

Beyes, T., & Pias, C. (2018). 'Secrecy, Transparency and Non-knowledge'. In A. Bernard, M. Koch & M. Leeker (Eds.), *Non-knowledge and Digital Cultures* (pp. 39–52). Lüneburg: Meson Press.

Birnbaum, E. (2021). 'The Tech Billionaire Aiding the Facebook Whistleblower' [online]. POLITICO. www.politico.com/news/2021/10/2 0/tech-billionaire-aiding-facebook-whistleblower-516358.

Bjørkelo, B. (2013). 'Workplace Bullying after Whistleblowing: Future Research and Implications'. *Journal of Managerial Psychology*, 28(3), 306–323.

Blest, P. (2020). 'Leaked Amazon Memo Details Plan to Smear Fired Warehouse Organizer: "He's Not Smart or Articulate"'. Retrieved 8 December 2022 from Vice.

Boler, M., & Davis, E. (2021). *Affective Politics of Digital Media*. London: Routledge.

Bowen, G. A. (2006). 'Grounded Theory and Sensitizing Concepts'. *International Journal*, 5(3), 12–23.

Boxenbaum, E., & Rouleau, L. (2011). 'New Knowledge Products as Bricolage: Metaphors and Scripts in Organizational Theory', *Academy of Management Review, 36*, 272–296.

Braithwaite, T. (2021). 'Top Strategies for Dealing with "Disgruntled Employees" — and Why They Don't Work [online]. [Accessed 2 February 2024]. www.ft.com/content/41b5eebd-d624-4395-a061-b8e8845044da.

Bray, T. (2020). 'Bye, Amazon'. Retrieved 8 December 2022 from tbray.org.

Bushnell, A. M. (2020). 'Reframing the Whistleblower in Research: Truth-Tellers as Whistleblowers in Changing Cultural Contexts'. *Sociology Compass, 14*, 1–13.

Butler, J. (2004). *Undoing Gender*. London: Routledge.

Butler, J. (2009). *Frames of War*. London: Verso.

Butler, J. (2016). 'Rethinking Vulnerability and Resistance'. In J. Butler, Z. Gambetti & L. Sabsay (Eds.), *Vulnerability in Resistance* (pp. 12–27). Durham, NC: Duke University Press.

Butler, J., & Athanasiou, A. (2013). *Dispossession: The Performative in the Political*. Cambridge: Polity.

Care Collective (2020). *The Care Manifesto: The Politics of Interdependence*. London: Verso.

Carreyrou, J. (2016). 'Theranos Whistleblower Shook the Company – and His Family'. *Wall Street Journal*, 18 November.

Carreyrou, J. (2018). *Bad Blood: Secrets and Lies in a Silicon Valley Startup*. London: Penguin Random House.

Casey, C. (1999). '"Come, Join Our Family": Discipline and Integration in Corporate Organizational Culture'. *Human Relations, 52*(2), 155–178.

Catlaw, T. J., Rawlings, K. C., & Callen, J. C. (2014). 'The Courage to Listen'. *Administrative Theory & Praxis*, *36*, 197–218.

Ceva, E., & Bocchiola, M. (2019). *Is Whistleblowing a Duty?* Cambridge, MA: Polity.

Cherry, M. A. (2004). 'Whistling in the Dark? Corporate Fraud, Whistleblowers, and the Implications of the Sarbanes–Oxley Act for Employment Law'. *Washington Law Review*, *79*, 1029–1049.

Cheung, E., & O'Dea, A. (2019). 'Erika Cheung and Ann O'Dea Discuss Theranos and Ethics in Entrepreneurship at Inspirefest 2019'. *Silicon Republic*, 16 May. YouTube.

Cole, J. (2016). 'Staying Together'. *The Whistle, No. 87*, July. BMartin. www.bmartin.cc/dissent/contacts/au_wba/whistle201607.pdf.

Conger, K. (2020). 9 Senators Ask Amazon for Details on Firings. *New York Times*, 8 May.

Contu, A. (2014). 'Rationality and Relationality in the Process of Whistleblowing: Recasting Whistleblowing through Readings of Antigone'. *Journal of Management Inquiry*, *23*, 393–406.

Cornelissen, J., Höllerer, M. A., & Seidl, D. (2021). 'What Theory Is and Can Be: Forms of Theorizing in Organizational Scholarship'. *Organization Theory*, *2*, 1–19.

Cuffari, J., Quinn, C., Giles, T., & Paulk, D. (2020). 'Lack of Medical Care, Unsafe Work Practices, and Absence of Adequate Protection against COVID-19 for Detained Immigrants and Employees Alike at the Irwin County Detention Center'. Project South.

Culiberg, B., & Mihelič, K. K. (2016). 'The Evolution of Whistleblowing Studies: A Critical Review and Research Agenda'. *Journal of Business Ethics*, *146*, 787–803.

Da Silva, C. (2019). 'Reality Winner: Snowden Condemns Sentencing of U.S. Election Meddling Whistleblower as Family Asks How Trump-linked Criminals Get Off Easy'. Retrieved 12 December 2022 from *Newsweek*.

Dean, J. (2010). *Blog Theory: Feedback and Capture in Circuits of Drive*. Cambridge: Polity Press.

Dean, J. (2015). 'Apps and Drive'. In A. Herman, I. Hadlaw & T. Swiss (Eds.), *Theories of the Mobile Internet* (pp. 232–248). New York: Routledge.

Devine, T. (2015). 'International Best Practices for Whistleblower Statutes'. In D. Lewis & W. Vandekerckhove (Eds.), *Developments in Whistleblowing Research* (pp. 7–19). International Whistleblowing Research Network.

Devine, T., & Maassarani, T. F. (2011). *The Corporate Whistleblower's Survival Guide*. San Francisco, CA: Berrett-Koehler.

Devine, T., & Thomas, J. (2014). 'Wall Street's New Enforcers Aim to Muzzle Whistle-Blowers'. DealBook. [Accessed 2 February 2024].

Dickerson, C., Wessler, S. F., & Jordan, M. (2020). 'Immigrants Say They Were Pressured into Unneeded Surgeries'. *New York Times*, 29 September.

Digital Insider (2022). 'Frances Haugen: Surveillance Capitalism's Whistleblower'. Spotify [Accessed 2 February 2024].

Döveling, K., Harju, A. A., & Sommer, D. (2018). 'From Mediatized Emotion to Digital Affect Cultures: New Technologies and Global Flows of Emotion'. *Social Media+ Society*, *4*, 1–11.

Dreyfus, S., Lederman, R., Brown, A. J. et al. (2013). 'Human Sources: "The Journalist and the Whistleblower in the Digital Era"'. In S. Tanner & N. Richardson (Eds.), *Journalism Research and Investigation in a Digital World* (pp. 48–61, e-book). Melbourne: Oxford University Press Australia & New Zealand.

du Plessis, E. M. (2022). 'Speaking Truth Through Power: Conceptualizing Internal Whistleblowing Hotlines with Foucault's Dispositive'. *Organization*, *29*(4), 544–576.

Dunn, T., Thompson, V., & Jarvis, R. (2019). 'Episode 4: The Whistleblower'. The Drop-Out Podcast, ABC News.

Durkheim, É. (2013 [1902]). *The Division of Labour in Society*. Basingstoke: Palgrave Macmillan.

Dworkin, T. M., & Baucus, M. S. (1998). 'Internal vs. External Whistleblowers: A Comparison of Whistleblowing Processes'. *Journal of Business Ethics*, *17*, 1281–1298.

Dworkin, T. M., & Callahan, E. S. (1998). 'Buying Silence'. *American Business Law Journal*, *36*, 151–191.

EC Council Directive (2019/1937/EC) of 23 October 2019 on the Protection of Persons Who Report Breaches of Union law [online]. [Accessed 25 January 2020]. EC Council Directive.

Ekman, S. (2012). 'Fantasies about Work as Limitless Potential – How Managers and Employees Seduce Each Other through Dynamics of Mutual Recognition'. *Human Relations*, *66*(9), 1159–1181.

Ekman, S. (2013). 'Fantasies about Work as Limitless Potential: How Managers and Employees Seduce Each Other through Dynamics of Mutual Recognition'. *Human Relations*, *66*(9), 1159–1181.

Endrissat, N., & Islam, G. (2022). 'Hackathons as Affective Circuits: Technology, Organizationality and Affect'. *Organization Studies*, *43*(7), 1019–1047.

European Parliament. (2017). 'Resolution of 24 October 2017 on Legitimate Measures to Protect Whistle-Blowers Acting in the Public Interest When Disclosing the Confidential Information of Companies and Public Bodies (2016/2224(INI))'. Accessed 8 December 2022.

Evelyn, K. (2020). 'Amazon Fires New York Worker Who Led Strike over Coronavirus Concerns'. Retrieved 12 December 2022 from the *Guardian.*

Fanchini, M. (2019). 'Those Who Listen: On the Role of External Recipients in Whistleblowing Cases'. *Ephemera, 19*(4), 697–720.

Financial Times (2021). 'The FT's 25 Most Influential Women of 2021'. *FT.*

Fineman, S., & Gabriel, Y. (1996). *Experiencing Organizations.* London: Sage.

Flyvbjerg, B. (2006). 'Five Misunderstandings about Case-Study Research'. *Qualitative Inquiry, 12,* 219–245.

Fotaki, M., Long, S., & Schwartz, H. S. (2012). 'What Can Psychoanalysis Offer Organization Studies Today? Taking Stock of Current Developments and Thinking about Future Directions'. *Organization Studies, 33*(9), 1105–1120.

Fotaki, M., Kenny, K., & Vachhani, S. J. (2017). 'Thinking Critically about Affect in Organization Studies: Why It Matters'. *Organization, 24,* 3–17.

Foucault, M. (1983). 'Discourse and Truth: The Problematization of Parrhesia: Six Lectures Given by Michel Foucault'. Berkeley, CA: University of California.

Foucault, M. (2001). *Fearless Speech.* Los Angeles, CA: Semiotext(e).

Foucault, M. (2005). *The Hermeneutics of the Subject: Lectures at the Collège de France, 1981–1982.* London: Palgrave Macmillan.

Foucault, M. (2010). *The Government of Self and Others: Lectures at the Collège de France 1982–83.* London: Palgrave Macmillan.

Foucault, M. (2011a). *The Courage of Truth.* Basingstoke: Palgrave Macmillan.

Foucault, M. (2011b). *The Government of Self and Others.* Basingstoke: Palgrave Macmillan.

Freud, A. (1936). *The Ego and the Mechanisms of Defence.* New York: Routledge.

Gabriel, Y. (1995). 'The Unmanaged Organization: Stories, Fantasies and Subjectivity'. *Organization Studies, 16*(3), 477–501.

Gabriel, Y. (1997). 'Meeting God: When Organizational Members Come Face to Face with the Supreme Leader'. *Human Relations, 50*(4), 315–342.

Gabriel, Y. (1999). *Organizations in Depth.* London: Sage.

Gelles, D. (2020). 'Corporate America Has Failed Black America'. *New York Times,* 6 June. Retrieved 12 December 2022.

Glazer, M., & Glazer, P. (1989). *The Whistleblowers: Exposing Corruption in Government and Industry.* New York: Basic Books.

Glynos, J., West, K., Hagger, B., & Shaw, R. (2014). 'Narrative, Fantasy, and Mourning: A Critical Exploration of Life & Loss in Assisted Living Environment'. In K. Kenny, & M. Fotaki (Eds.), *The Psychosocial and*

Organization Studies: Affect at Work (pp. 185–214). Basingstoke: Palgrave.

Gold, D. L. (2013). 'Introduction: Speaking Up for Justice, Suffering Injustice: Whistleblower Protection and the Need for Reform'. *Seattle Journal for Social Justice*, *11*(2), Article 5. https://digitalcommons.law.se attleu.edu/sjsj/vol11/iss2/5.

Grant, C. (2002). 'Whistleblowers: Saints of Secular Culture'. *Journal of Business Ethics*, *39*, 391–399.

Greenwald, G. (2021). 'Democrats and Media Do Not Want to Weaken Facebook, Just Commandeer Its Power to Censor' [online]. Glenn Greenwald. Accessed 2 February 2024.

Haberman, M. (2020). 'Insurer Drops Whistle-Blower Lawyer, Citing High-Profile Work'. *New York Times*, 24 August.

Heater, B. (2020). 'Nine Senators – Including Warren and Sanders – Pen Open Letter to Amazon about Worker Firings'. Retrieved 17 June 2023 from *Tech Crunch*.

Hemmings, C. (2012). 'Affective Solidarity: Feminist Reflexivity and Political Transformation'. *Feminist Theory*, *13*, 147–161.

Herrera, S. (2021). 'Amazon's Profit Run Continues, Bolstered by Sustained Demand; E-commerce Giant's First-Quarter Sales Hit $108 Billion, up 44% from Year-Ago Period'. Retrieved 8 December 2022 from *Wall Street Journal*.

Hersch, M. A. (2002). 'Whistleblowers – Heroes or Traitors? Individual and Collective Responsibility for Ethical Behaviour'. *Annual Reviews in Control*, *26*(2), 243–262.

Husted, E., & Just, S. N. (2022). 'The Politics of Trust: How Trust Reconciles Autonomy and Solidarity in Alternative Organizations'. *Organization Theory*, *3*. Retrieved 12 December 2022.

IBA (2018). *Whistleblowing: A Guide*. Report from International Bar Association. Retrieved 23 January 2020.

IBA (2021). 'Are Whistleblowing Laws Working? A Global Study of Whistleblower Protection Litigation'. International Bar Association. [Accessed 6 June 2021].

ICNL (2020). 'Webinar – SLAPPs as a Global Phenomenon' [online]. Accessed 2 February 2024.

Immerman, R. (2020). 'From the Mundane to the Absurd: The Advent and Evolution of Prepublication Review'. In K. Mistry & H. Gurman (Eds.), *Whistleblowing Nation* (pp. 187–212). New York: Columbia University Press.

Irish Independent (2007). 'Army Knew of Sex Abuse for Years'. 2 September.

Isaac, M., Mac, R., & Frenkel, S. (2021). 'After Whistle-Blower Goes Public, Facebook Tries Calming Employees'. *New York Times* [online].

10 October. www.nytimes.com/2021/10/10/technology/facebook-whistle blower-employees.html.

Jack, G. (2004). 'On Speech, Critique and Protection'. *Ephemera*, *4*, 121–134.

Jackall, R. (2010). *Moral Mazes: The World of Corporate Managers*. Oxford: Oxford University Press.

Janssens, M., & Zanoni, P. (2021). 'Making Diversity Research Matter for Social Change: New Conversations beyond the Firm'. *Organization Theory*, *2*. Retrieved 12 December 2022 from *Organization Theory* website: https://doi.org/10.1177/26317877211004603.

Jaques, E. (1995). 'Why the Psychoanalytical Approach to Understanding Organizations Is Dysfunctional'. *Human Relations*, *48*(4), 343–349.

Johnson, J. (2020). 'New York AG Denounces "Immoral and Inhumane" Firing of Amazon Worker Who Led Protest over Lack of Coronavirus Protections'. Retrieved 8 December 2022 from Common Dreams website: www.commondreams.org/news/2020/03/31/new-york-ag-denounces-imm oral-and-inhumane-firing-amazon-worker-who-led-protest-over.

Jones, B. (2013). 'A Whistleblower's Guide to Journalists'. *The Whistle*, #76, October. www.bmartin.cc/dissent/documents/Jones13.pdf.

Jones, C., Parker, M., & Ten Bos, R. (2005). *For Business Ethics: A Critical Text: A Critical Approach*. London: Routledge.

Kenny, K. M. (2010). 'Beyond Ourselves: Passion and the Dark Side of Identification in an Ethical Organization'. *Human Relations*, *63*(6), 857–873.

Kenny, K. (2018). 'Censored: Whistleblowers and Impossible Speech'. *Human Relations*, *71*(8), 1025–1048.

Kenny, K. (2019). *Whistleblowing: Toward a New Theory*. Cambridge, MA: Harvard University Press.

Kenny, K. (2023a). 'Feminist Social Movements and Whistleblowing Disclosures: Ireland's Women of Honour'. *Gender, Work & Organization*, *31*(3), 961–982.

Kenny, K. (2023b). 'Constructing Unknowers, Destroying Whistleblowers'. *Ephemera*, *23*(1). https://ephemerajournal.org/sites/default/files/2023-04/23%281%29Kenny.pdf.

Kenny, K., & Bushnell, A. (2020). 'How to Whistle-Blow: Dissensus and Demand'. *Journal of Business Ethics*, *164*, 643–656.

Kenny, K., & Fanchini, M. (2023). 'Women Whistleblowers: Examining Parrhesia, Power and Gender with Sophocles' Antigone'. *Organization Studies*, *45*(2), 275–296. https://doi.org/10.1177/01708406231187073.

Kenny, K., & Fotaki, M. (2014). *The Psychosocial and Organization Studies: Affect at Work*. Basingstoke: Palgrave.

Kenny, K., & Fotaki, M. (2021). 'The Costs and Labour of Whistleblowing: Bodily Vulnerability and Post-disclosure Survival'. *Journal of Business Ethics*, *182*, 341–364. https://doi.org/10.1007/s10551-021-05012-x.

Kenny, K., Fotaki, M., & Scriver, S. (2019a). 'Mental Health as a Weapon: Whistleblower Retaliation and Normative Violence'. *Journal of Business Ethics, 160,* 801–805.

Kenny, K., Fotaki, M., & Vandekerckhove, W. (2019b). 'Whistleblower Subjectivities: Organization and Passionate Attachment'. *Organization Studies, 41*(3), 323–343. https://doi.org/10.1177/0170840618814558.

Kenny, K., Fotaki, M. & Vandekerckhove, W. (2019c). *The Whistleblowing Guide: Speak-up Arrangements, Challenges and Best Practices.* Chichester: Wiley.

Kenny, K., Fotaki, M., & Vandekerckhove, W. (2020). 'Whistleblowing, Organization and Passionate Attachment'. *Organization Studies, 41,* 323–343.

Kenny, K., Vandekerckhove, W., & Irfan, M. (2020). 'Whistleblowing as Escalating Voice'. In A. Wilkinson, J. Donaghey, T. Dundon & R. B. Freeman (Eds.), *Handbook of Research on Employee Voice,* 2nd ed. (pp. 437–454). Cheltenham: Edward Elgar.

Kets de Vries, M. F. (1979). 'Managers Can Drive Their Subordinates Mad'. *Harvard Business Review, 57*(4), 125–127.

Kets de Vries, M. F. (1988). 'Prisoners of Leadership'. *Human Relations, 41*(3), 261–280.

Kets de Vries, M. F., & Engellau, E. (2010). 'A Clinical Approach to the Dynamics of Leadership and Executive Transformation'. In N. Nohria & R. Khurana (Eds.), *Handbook of Leadership Theory and Practice* (pp. 183–222). Boston, MA: Harvard Business Press.

Kets de Vries, M. F., & Miller, D. (1984). *The Neurotic Organization: Diagnosing and Changing Counterproductive Styles of Management.* San Francisco, CA: Jossey-Bass.

Kierans, L. (2023). 'Whistleblowing Litigation and Legislation in Ireland: Are There Lessons to Be Learned?' *Industrial Law Journal.* https://doi.org/10.1093/indlaw/dwad009.

Kouri-Towe, N. (2015). 'Textured Activism: Affect Theory and Transformational Politics in Transnational Queer Palestine-Solidarity Activism'. *Atlantis: Critical Studies in Gender, Culture & Social Justice, 37*(1), 23–34.

Kriegstein, B., & McShane, L. (2020). 'Leaked Amazon Memo Proposes Smear Campaign of Worker Leading Coronavirus Protests at Staten Island Facility: Report'. *Daily News (New York),* 3 April, p. 14.

Kuldova, T. Ø., & Nordrik, B. (2023). 'Workplace Investigations, the Epistemic Power of Managerialism and the Hollowing Out of the Norwegian Model of Co-determination'. *Capital & Class.* https://doi.org/10.1177/03098168231179971.

Laitinen, A., & Pessi, A. B. (2015) 'Solidarity: Theory and Practice: An Introduction'. In A. Laitinen & A. B. Pessi (Eds.), *Solidarity: Theory and Practice* (pp. 1–29). Lanham, MD: Lexington Books.

Lam, H., & Harcourt, M. (2019). 'Whistle-Blowing in the Digital Era: Motives, Issues and Recommendations'. *New Technology, Work and Employment, 34*, 174–190.

Lennane, J. (1993). '"Whistleblowing": A Health Issue'. *British Medical Journal, 307*, 667–670.

Lennane, J. (2012). 'What Happens to Whistleblowers, and Why?' *Social Medicine, 6*(4), 249–258.

Lewis, D. (2008). 'Ten Years of Public Interest Disclosure Legislation in the UK: Are Whistleblowers Adequately Protected?' *Journal of Business Ethics, 82*, 497–507.

Lewis, D., & Vandekerckhove, W. (2015a). 'Does Following a Whistleblowing Procedure Make a Difference? The Evidence from the Research Conducted for the Francis Inquiry.' In D. Lewis & W. Vandekerckhove (Eds.), *Developments in Whistleblowing Research* (pp. 85–105). London: International Whistleblowing Research Network.

Lewis, D., & Vandekerckhove, W. (2015b). 'Introduction'. In D. Lewis & W. Vandekerckhove (Eds.), *Developments in Whistleblowing Research* (pp. 3–6). London: International Whistleblowing Research Network.

Lewis, D., & Vandekerckhove, W. (2018). 'Trade Unions and the Whistleblowing Process in the UK: An Opportunity for Strategic Expansion?' *J Bus Ethics, 148*, 835–845. https://doi.org/10.1007/s10551-016-3015-z.

Lindenberg, S. (1998) 'Solidarity: Its Microfoundations and Macrodependence. A Framing Approach in the Problem of Solidarity'. In T. J. Fararo & P. Doreian (Eds.), *Theories and Models* (pp. 61–112). The Netherlands: Gordon and Breach.

Lindenberg, S. (2015). 'Solidarity: Unpacking the Social Brain'. In A. Laitinen & A. B. Pessi (Eds.), *Solidarity: Theory and Practice* (pp. 30–54). Lanham, MD: Lexington Books.

Linebaugh, K. (2022). 'We Just Took Down Amazon:' Activist on Amazon's First U.S. Union [Podcast Episode]. Retrieved 8 December 2022 from *Wall Street Journal* website.

Listen Notes. (2021a). 'Facebook Files Reporter Jeff Horwitz on his Source Relationship with Whistleblower Frances Haugen – and Why he Felt "properly paranoid"' [online]. [Accessed 2 February 2024]. https://www.listennotes.com/podcasts/reliable-sources/facebook-files-reporter-jeff-LAUT2nmZeuD/.

Listen Notes. (2021b). 'UNLOCKED: How WSJ Reporter Jeff Horwitz Got the Facebook Whistleblower to Talk' [online]. [Accessed 2 February 2024].

www.listennotes.com/podcasts/the-new-abnormal/unlocked-how-wsj-repo rter-03yQswBnMhq/.

Littler, J., & Rottenberg, C. (2021). 'Feminist Solidarities: Theoretical and Practical Complexities'. *Gender, Work & Organization, 28,* 864–877.

Mac, R., & Kang, C. (2021). 'Whistle-Blower Says Facebook "Chooses Profits over Safety".' *New York Times.*

Mansbach, A. (2009). 'Keeping Democracy Vibrant: Whistleblowing as Truth-Telling in the Workplace'. *Constellations: An International Journal of Critical and Democratic Theory, 16,* 363–376.

Mansbach, A. (2011). 'Whistleblowing as Fearless Speech: The Radical Democratic Effects of Late Modern Parrhesia'. In D. Lewis & W. Vandekerckhove (Eds.), *Whistleblowing and Democratic Values* (pp. 12–27). London: The International Whistleblowing Research Network.

Martin, B. (1999). *The Whistleblower's Handbook: How to Be an Effective Resister.* Charlbury: Jon Carpenter. (Note: Updated version = Martin (2013).)

Martin, B. (2012). *Backfire Manual: Tactics against Injustice.* Sparsnäs, Sweden: Irene.

Martin, B. (2013). *Whistleblowing: A Practical Guide.* Sparsnäs, Sweden: Irene.

Martin, B. (2017). 'Academic Dissidents'. https://comments.bmartin.cc/201 7/10/16/academic-dissidents-be-prepared-for-reprisals-and-more/.

Martin, B. (2020). *Official Channels.* Sparsnäs Sweden: Irene.

Martin, B., & Coy, P. (2017). 'Skills, Training and Activism'. *Reflective Practice, 18*(4), 515–525. https://doi.org/10.1080/14623943.2017.1323730.

Martin, B., & Rifkin, W. (2004). 'The Dynamics of Employee Dissent: Whistleblowers and Organizational Jiu-Jitsu'. *Public Organization Review: A Global Journal, 4,* 221–238.

Maxwell, L. (2018). 'The Politics and Gender of Truth-Telling in Foucault's Lectures on Parrhesia'. *Contemporary Political Theory, 18,* 22–42. https:// doi.org/10.1057/s41296-018-0224-5.

Maxwell, L. (2019). *Insurgent Truth: Chelsea Manning and the Politics of Outsider Truth-Telling.* Oxford: Oxford University Press.

Maxwell, L. (2020). 'Celebrity Hero: Daniel Ellsberg and the Forging of Whistleblower Masculinity'. In H. Gurman & K. Mistry (Eds.), *Whistleblowing Nation: The History of National Security Disclosures and the Cult of State Secrecy* (pp. 95–123). New York: Columbia University Press.

McGlynn, J. III, & Richardson, B. K. (2014). 'Private Support, Public Alienation: Whistle-Blowers and the Paradox of Social Support'. *Western Journal of Communication, 78*(2), 213–237.

Mesmer-Magnus, J. R., & Viswesvaran, C. (2005). 'Whistleblowing in Organizations: An Examination of Correlates of Whistleblowing

Intentions, Actions, and Retaliation'. *Journal of Business Ethics*, 62(3), 277–297.

Miceli, M. P., & Near, J. P. (1985). 'Characteristics of Organizational Climate and Perceived Wrongdoing Associated with Whistle-Blowing Decisions'. *Personnel Psychology*, 38(3), 525–544.

Miceli, M. P., Near, J. P., & Dworkin, T. M. (2008). *Whistleblowing in Organizations*. New York: Routledge.

Miceli, M. P., Rehg, M., Near, J. P., & Ryan, K. (1999). 'Can Laws Protect Whistle-Blowers? Results of a Naturally Occurring Field Experiment'. *Work and Occupations*, 26(1), 129–151. https://doi.org/10.1177/0730888499026001007.

Miller, E. J. (1999). 'Dependency, Alienation or Partnership? The Changing Relatedness of the Individual to the Enterprise'. In R. French & R. Vince (Eds.), *Group Relations, Management, and Organization* (pp. 98–111). Oxford: Oxford University Press.

Mills, C. W. (1963, 1967). *Power, Politics and People: The Collected Essays of C. Wright Mills*. Edited by Irving H. Horowitz. New York: Oxford University Press.

Milmo, D. (2021). 'How Losing a Friend to Misinformation Drove Facebook Whistleblower'. The *Guardian* [online]. www.theguardian.com/technology/2021/oct/04/how-friend-lost-to-misinformation-drove-facebook-whistleblower-frances-haugen.

Mistry, K., & Gurman, H. (Eds.). (2020). *Whistleblowing Nation*. New York: Columbia University Press.

Mitchell, S. A., & Black, M. J. (1995). *Freud and Beyond: A History of Modern Psychoanalytic Thought*. New York: Basic Books.

Möllering, G. (2013). 'Process Views of Trusting and Crises'. In R. Bachmann & A. Zaheer (Eds.), *Handbook of Advances in Trust Research* (pp. 285–305). Cheltenham: Edward Elgar.

Monk, H., Knights, D., & Page, M. (2015). 'Whistleblowing Paradoxes: Legislative Protection and Corporate Counter-Resistance'. In A. Pullen & C. Rhodes (Eds.), *The Routledge Companion to Ethics, Politics and Organizations* (pp. 300–317). London: Routledge.

Mueller, T. (2019). *Crisis of Conscience*. New York: Penguin.

Munro, I. (2017). 'Whistle-Blowing and the Politics of Truth: Mobilizing "Truth Games" in the WikiLeaks Case'. *Human Relations*, 70, 519–543.

Munro, I. (2018). 'An Interview with Snowden's Lawyer: Robert Tibbo on Whistleblowing, Mass Surveillance and Human Rights Activism'. *Organization*, 25(1), 106–122. https://doi.org/10.1177/1350508417726548.

Munro, I., & Kenny, K. (2023a). 'Whistleblower as Activist and Exile: The Case of Edward Snowden'. *Organization*. https://doi.org/10.1177/13505084231194824.

Munro, I., & Kenny, K. (2023b). 'Networked Whistleblowing, Counter-Hegemony and the Challenge to Systemic Corruption'. *Research in the Sociology of Organizations*, 85, 121–140.

Nast, C. (2021). 'Unfriended: Frances Haugen on Her Facebook Testimony and What Comes Next' [online]. *Vogue*. www.vogue.com/article/facebook-whistleblower-frances-haugen-interview.

Nayar, P. K. (2010). 'WikiLeaks, the New Information Cultures and Digital Parrhesia'. *Economic and Political Weekly*, 45, 27–30.

Near, J. P., & Jensen, T. C. (1983). 'The Whistleblowing Process: Retaliation and Perceived Effectiveness'. *Work and Occupations*, 10, 3–28.

Near, J. P., & Miceli, M. P. (1985). 'Organizational Dissidence: The Case of Whistle-Blowing'. *Journal of Business Ethics*, 4, 1–16.

Near, J. P., & Miceli, M. P. (1995). 'Effective-Whistle Blowing'. *Academy of Management Review*, 20(3), 679–708.

Near, J., Rehg, M., Van Scotter, J., & Miceli, M. (2004). 'Does Type of Wrongdoing Affect the Whistle-Blowing Process?' *Business Ethics Quarterly*, 14(2), 219–242. https://doi.org/10.5840/beq200414210.

New Yorker. (2022). 'The Trials of a Whistle-Blower' [online]. The *New Yorker*. www.newyorker.com/podcast/the-new-yorker-radio-hour/the-trials-of-a-whistle-blower [Accessed 2 February 2024].

Nyberg, D. (2021). 'Corporations, Politics, and Democracy: Corporate Political Activities as Political Corruption'. *Organization Theory*, 2(1). Retrieved 12 December 2022 from *Organization Theory* website.

O'Toole, M. (2020). '19 Women Allege Medical Abuse in Georgia Immigration Detention' [online]. *Los Angeles Times*. www.latimes.com/politics/story/2020-10-22/women-allege-medical-abuse-georgia-immigration-detention.

OECD. (2019). 'ANNEX: G20 Compendium of Best Practices and Guiding Principles for Legislation on the Protection of Whistleblowers' in *G20 Anti-Corruption Action Plan Protection of Whistleblowers*. Retrieved 1 December, 2022 from OECD website: www.oecd.org/g20/topics/anti-corruption/48972967.pdf.

Ouriemmi, O. (2023). 'The Legalistic Organizational Response to Whistleblowers' Disclosures in a Scandal: Law without Justice?' *Journal of Business Ethics*, 188, 17–35.

Palmer, A. (2020a). 'Amazon Lawyer Calls Fired Strike Organizer "not smart or articulate" in Meeting with Top Execs'. Retrieved 12 December 2022 from *CNBC* website: www.cnbc.com/2020/04/02/amazon-lawyer-calls-fired-warehouse-worker-not-smart-or-articulate.html.

Palmer, A. (2020b). 'Amazon Fires Three Employees who Were Outspoken Critics of its Labor Practices'. Retrieved 17 June 2023 from *CNBC* website: www.cnbc.com/2020/04/14/amazon-fires-two-employees-who-were-critics-of-its-labor-practices.html.

Papacharissi, Z. (2016). 'Affective Publics and Structures of Storytelling: Sentiment, Events and Mediality'. *Information, Communication & Society*, *19*, 307–324.

Park, H., Bjørkelo, B., & Blenkinsopp, J. (2020a). 'External Whistleblowers' Experiences of Workplace Bullying by Superiors and Colleagues'. *Journal of Business Ethics*, *161*, 591–601.

Park, H., Vandekerckhove, W., Lee, J., & Joowon, J. (2020b). 'Laddered Motivations of External Whistleblowers: The Truth about Attributes, Consequences, and Values'. *Journal of Business Ethics*, *165*, 565–578.

Parker, I., & Fotaki, M. (2014). 'Prologue: Ian Parker on the Psychosocial, Psychoanalysis and Critical Psychology, in Conversation with Marianna Fotaki'. In K. Kenny & M. Fotaki (Eds.), *The Psychosocial and Organization Studies: Affect at Work* (pp. 1–17). Basingstoke: Palgrave.

Pauksztat, B., Steglich, C., & Wittek, R. (2011). 'Who Speaks up to Whom? A Relational Approach to Employee Voice'. *Social Networks*, *33*, 303–316.

Paul, K. (2020). 'Amazon Fires Two Employees who Condemned Treatment of Warehouse Workers'. Retrieved 12 December 2022 from *CNBC* website: www.theguardian.com/technology/2020/apr/14/amazon-work ers-fired-coronavirus-emily-cunningham-maren-costa.

Paul, K. (2021). 'TechScape: Netflix and the Future of Tech Employee Activism' [online]. www.theguardian.com/technology/2021/dec/01/tech scape-netflix-dave-chappelle-protests-twitter.

Perkmann, M., & Spicer, A. (2014). 'How (2014): Emerging Organizations Take Form'. *Organization Science*, *25*(6), 1785–1806.

Perrigo, B. (2021). 'How Frances Haugen's Team Forced a Facebook Reckoning' [online]. *Time*. https://time.com/6104899/facebook-reckon ing-frances-haugen/.

Perry, N. (1998). 'Indecent Exposure: Theorizing Whistleblowing'. *Organization Studies*, *19*, 235–257.

Petriglieri, G., & Petriglieri, J. L. (2010). 'Identity Workspaces: The Case of Business Schools'. *Academy of Management Learning & Education*, *9*(1), 44–60.

Petriglieri, G., & Petriglieri, J. L. (2020). 'The Return of the Oppressed: A Systems Psychodynamic Approach to Organization Studies'. *The Academy of Management Annals*, *14*(1), 411–449.

Petriglieri, G., & Stein, M. (2012). 'The Unwanted Self: Projective Identification in Leaders' Identity Work'. *Organization Studies*, *33*(9), 1217–1235.

Phillips, A. (2017). 'How Might Trade Unions Use their Voice to Engage in the Whistleblowing Process?' In D. Lewis & W. Vandekerckhove (Eds.),

Selected Papers from the International Whistleblowing Research Network Conference, Oslo June. International Whistleblowing Research Network (pp. 91–104). ISBN 9780957138421.

Picard, H., & Islam, G. (2020). '"Free to Do What I Want"? Exploring the Ambivalent Effects of Liberating Leadership'. *Organization Studies*, *41*(3), 393–414.

Pivot (2022). 'Frances Haugen at Code 2022' [online]. https://open.spotify.com/episode/6gM7tD2xOG1KcQ3W7iODHC?si=5b18b9e3fd3c4baa&nd=1&dlsi=5b64f8c8fb7c49a1. Accessed 2 February 2024.

POLITICO (2021). 'The World's Most Professional Whistleblower' [online]. www.politico.eu/article/frances-haugen-facebook-the-worlds-most-professional-whistleblower/. Accessed 2 February 2024.

Press, A. (2022). 'A Stunning New Chapter Begins for Amazon Warehouse Workers'. *Jacobin*. https://jacobin.com/2022/04/amazon-labor-union-victory-jfk8-staten-island-bessemer.

Pullen, A., & Vachhani, S. J. (2018). 'Examining the Politics of Gendered Difference in Feminine Leadership: The Absence of "Female Masculinity"'. In S. Adapa & Sheridan A. (Eds.), *Inclusive Leadership: Palgrave Studies in Leadership and Followership* (pp. 125–149). Cham: Palgrave Macmillan. https://doi.org/10.1007/978-3-319-60666-8.

PWC. (2021). 'Global Top 100 Companies by Market Capitalisation'. www.pwc.com/gx/en/audit-services/publications/assets/pwc-global-top-100-companies-2021.pdf.

Rehg, M. T., Miceli, M. P., Near, J. P., & Van Scotter, J. R. (2008). 'Antecedents and Outcomes of Retaliation against Whistleblowers: Gender Differences and Power Relations'. *Organization Science*, *19*(2), 221–240.

Rhodes, C. (2016). 'Democratic Business Ethics: Volkswagen's Emissions Scandal and the Disruption of Corporate Sovereignty'. *Organization Studies*, *37*, 1501–1518.

Richardson, B. K. (2023). '"Death Threats Don't Just Affect You, They Affect Your Family": Investigating the Impact of Whistleblowing on Family Identity'. *Management Communication Quarterly*, *37*(2), 310–339. https://doi.org/10.1177/08933189221108349.

Rogal, L. (2021). 'Secrets, Lies, and Lessons from the Theranos Scandal'. *Hastings Law Journal*, *72*(6), 1663–1702.

Rothschild, J. (2013). 'The Fate of Whistleblowers in Nonprofit Organizations'. *Nonprofit and Voluntary Sector Quarterly*, *42*, 886–901.

Rothschild, J., & Miethe, T. D. (1999). 'Whistle-Blower Disclosures and Management Retaliation: The Battle to Control Information about Organization Corruption'. *Work and Occupations*, *26*, 107–128.

RTÉ Investigates (2020). 'Whistleblowers: Fighting to be Heard'. RTÉ One, 21 September.

RWDSU. (2020). 'America's Top Unions Demand Amazon Do Better'. Retrieved 17 June 2023 from Retail, Wholesale and Department Store Union website: www.rwdsu.info/america_s_top_unions_demand_amazon_do_better.

Sadowski, J. (2021). 'Facebook is a Harmful Presence in our Lives. It's Not Too Late to Pull the Plug on it'. The *Guardian*. www.theguardian.com/commentisfree/2021/oct/06/facebook-scandals-social-media.

Saunders, C. (2008). 'Double-Edged Swords? Collective Identity and Solidarity in the Environment Movement'. *British Journal of Sociology*, *59*(2), 227–253.

Schwartz, H. S. (1991). 'Narcissism Project and Corporate Decay: The Case of General Motors'. *Business Ethics Quarterly*, *1*(3), 249–268.

Scutari, M. (2022). 'How is "Omidyarism" Faring in an Age of Splashy Tech Giving?' [online]. *Inside Philanthropy*. www.insidephilanthropy.com/home/2022/1/28/how-is-omidyarism-faring-in-an-age-of-splashy-tech-giving. Accessed 2 February 2024.

Seigworth, G., & Gregg, M. (2010). 'An Inventory of Shimmers'. In M. Gregg & G. J. Seigworth (Eds.), *The Affect Theory Reader* (pp. 1–28). London: Duke University Press.

Shapiro, E. R., & Carr, A. W. (1991). *Lost in Familiar Places: Creating New Connections between the Individual and Society*. New Haven, CT: Yale University Press.

Skinner, D. (2011). 'Fearless Speech: Practising Parrhesia in a Self-managing Community'. *Ephemera: Theory & Politics in Organization*, *11*, 157–175.

Skivenes, M., & Trygstad, S. C. (2010). 'When Whistle-Blowing Works: The Norwegian Case'. *Human Relations*, *63*, 1071–1097.

Skivenes, M., & Trygstad, S. (2017). 'Explaining Whistle Blowing Processes in the Norwegian Labour Market: Between Individual Power Resources and Institutional Arrangements'. *Economic and Industrial Democracy*, *38*(1), 119–143.

Smith, A. (2014a). '"There were Hundreds of us Crying Out for Help": The Afterlife of the Whistleblower'. The *Guardian*, 22 November. Retrieved 19 March 2020 from www.theguardian.com/society/2014/nov/22/there-were-hundreds-of-us-crying-out-for-help-afterlife-of-whistleblower.

Smith, R. (2014b). 'Whistleblowing and Suffering'. In A. J. Brown, D. Lewis, R. Moberly & W. Vandekerckhove (Eds.), *International Handbook on Whistleblowing Research* (pp. 230–249). Cheltenham: Edward Elgar.

Smith, B. (2021). 'Inside the Big Facebook Leak'. *New York Times* [online]. 25 October. www.nytimes.com/2021/10/24/business/media/facebook-leak-frances-haugen.html.

Smith, R., & Brown, A. J. (2008). 'The Good, the Bad and the Ugly: Whistleblowing Outcomes'. In A. J. Brown (Ed.), *Whistleblowing in the*

Australian Public Sector: Enhancing the Theory and Practice of Internal Witness Management in Public Sector Organisations (pp. 109–136). Canberra: ANU E Press.

Smolović Jones, S., Winchester, N., & Clarke, C. (2021). 'Feminist Solidarity Building as Embodied Agonism: An Ethnographic Account of a Protest Movement'. *Gender, Work & Organization, 28,* 917–934.

Somerville, H. (2021). 'In Elizabeth Holmes Trial, Ex-Theranos Employees Cite Culture of Fear and Isolation'. *Wall Street Journal* [online]. 13 November. www.wsj.com/articles/in-elizabeth-holmes-trial-ex-thera nos-employees-cite-culture-of-fear-and-isolation-11636812000.

Spocchia, G. (2020). 'AOC Blasts Amazon as "racist" after Leaked Notes Say Senior Execs Planned to Publicly Shame Black Worker in Meeting with Jeff Bezos'. *The Independent,* 3 April.

Stacey, K., & Bradshaw, T. (2021). 'Facebook Chose to Maximise Engagement at Users' Expense, Whistleblower Says'. *Financial Times* [online]. 5 October. www.ft.com/content/41b657c8-d716-436b-a06d-19859f0f6ce4.

Stavrakakis, Y. (2008). 'Subjectivity and the Organized Other: Between Symbolic Authority and Fantasmatic Enjoyment'. *Organization Studies, 29*(7), 1037–1059.

Stein, M. (2021). 'The Lost Good Self: Why the Whistleblower Is Hated and Stigmatized'. *Organization Studies, 42*(7), 1167–1186. https://doi.org/10 .1177/0170840619880565.

Stubben, S., & Welch, K. (2020). 'Evidence on the Use and Efficacy of Internal Whistleblowing Systems'. *Journal of Accounting Research, 58*(2), 473–518.

Swisher, K. (2021). 'Beyond Zuckerberg'. *New York Times* [online]. 26 October. www.nytimes.com/2021/10/26/opinion/zuckerberg-face book-ceo.html. Accessed 2 February 2024.

Tavares, G. M., Lima, F. V., & Michener, G. (2021). 'To Blow the Whistle in Brazil: The Impact of Gender and Public Service Motivation'. *Regulation & Governance, 18*(1), 226–244. https://doi.org/10.1111/rego.12418.

The *Guardian.* (2021). 'Amazon Fired him – Now he's Trying to Unionize 5,000 Workers in New York' [online]. www.theguardian.com/technol ogy/2021/jun/04/amazon-workers-staten-island-christian-smalls.

The Real Facebook Oversight Board. (2021). 'Whistleblowing Women: How Female Tech Workers are Taking on Big Tech' [online]. www.youtube.c om/watch?v=FGtyCAGvsHU [Accessed 2 February 2024].

Transparency International Ireland. (2017). *Transparency International Ireland: Speak Up Report 2017.* www.transparency.ie/sites/default/files/1 8.01_speak_up_2017_final.pdf [Accessed 7 June 2021].

Tonkiss, K. (2021). '"A Baby Is a Baby": The Asha Protests and the Sociology of Affective Post-Nationalism'. *Sociology, 55*(1), 146–162.

Tsahuridu, E. E., & Vandekerckhove, W. (2008). 'Organisational Whistleblowing Policies: Making Employees Responsible or Liable?' *Journal of Business Ethics, 82,* 107–118.

Tugend, A. (2019). '"It Kept Failing": Whistleblower Erika Cheung on Working at Theranos'. California: UC Berkeley Ca Alumni Association. 16 March. https://alumni.berkeley.edu/california-magazine/online/whistle blower-erika-cheung-on-working-at-theranos/.

Tyler, M. (2019). *Judith Butler and Organization Theory.* New York: Routledge.

Uys, T. (2000). 'The Politicisation of Whistleblowers: A Case Study'. *Business Ethics: A European Review, 9*(4), 259–267.

Uys, T. (2022). *Whistleblowing and the Sociological Imagination.* New York: Palgrave Macmillan.

Uys, T., & Smit, R. (2016). 'Resilience and Whistleblowers: Coping with the Consequences'. *South African Review of Sociology, 47*(4), 60–79.

Vachhani, S. J., & Pullen, A. (2019). 'Ethics, Politics and Feminist Organizing: Writing Feminist Infrapolitics and Affective Solidarity into Everyday Sexism'. *Human Relations, 72,* 23–47.

Van Portfliet, M. (2020). 'Resistance will be Futile? The Stigmatization (or Not) of Whistleblowers'. *Journal of Business Ethics.* Epub ahead of print 11 November. https://doi.org/ 10.1007/s10551-020-04673-4.

Van Portfliet, M., & Kenny, K. (2018). 'A Cold Winter for Corporate Whistleblowers'. The *Irish Times,* 30 November. www.irishtimes.com/b usiness/work/a-cold-winter-for-corporate-whistleblowers-1.3713558.

Van Portfliet, M., & Kenny, K. (2022). 'Whistleblowing Advocacy: Solidarity and Fascinance'. *Organization, 29*(2), 345–366.

Van Portfliet, M., Irfan, M., & Kenny, K. (2022). 'When Employees Speak Up: Human Resources Management Aspects of Whistleblowing'. In P. Holland, T. Bartram, T. Garavan & K. Grant (Eds.), *The Emerald Handbook of Work, Workplaces and Disruptive Issues in HRM* (pp. 533–547). Bingley: Emerald.

Vandekerckhove, W. (2010). 'European Whistleblowing Protection: Tiers or Tears?' In D. Lewis (Ed.), *A Global Approach to Public Interest Disclosure* (pp. 15–35). Cheltenham: Edward Elgar.

Vandekerckhove, W. (2021). 'Kenny's Whistleblowing and Stanger's Whistleblowers'. *Philosophy of Management, 20,* 93–98. https://doi.org/ 10.1007/s40926-020-00144-y.

Vandekerckhove, W. (2022). 'Is It Freedom? The Coming About of the EU Directive on Whistleblower Protection'. *J Bus Ethics, 179,* 1–11.

Vandekerckhove, W., & Langenberg, S. (2012). 'Can We. Organize Courage? Implications of Foucault's Parrhesia'. *Electronic Journal of Business Ethics and Organization Studies, 17*(2), 35–44.

Vandekerckhove, W., & Phillips, A. (2019). 'Whistleblowing as a Protracted Process: A Study of UK Whistleblower Journeys'. *Journal of Business Ethics*, *159*(1), 201–219.

Vandekerckhove, W., & Rumyantseva, N. (2014). *Freedom to Speak Up – Qualitative Research*. London: University of Greenwich.

Vandekerckhove, W., & Tsahuridu, E. (2010). 'Risky Rescues and the Duty to Blow the Whistle'. *Journal of Business Ethics*, *97*(3), 365–380.

Vandekerckhove, W., Brown, A. J., & Tsahuridu, E. E. (2014). 'Managerial Responses to Whistleblowing'. In A. J. Brown, D. Lewis, R. Moberly & W. Vandekerckhove (Eds.), *International Handbook on Whistleblowing Research* (pp. 298–327). Cheltenham: Edward Elgar.

Vasquez, T. (2022). 'Senate Investigation of Medical Abuse at Georgia ICE Facility Confirms Women's Stories'. https://prismreports.org/2022/12/08/senate-investigation-georgia-ice-facility/.

Visscher, K., Heusinkveld, S., & O'Mahoney, J. (2017). 'Bricolage and Identity Work'. *British Journal of Management*, *29*(2), 356–372.

Voronov, M., & Vince, R. (2012). 'Integrating Emotions into the Analysis of Institutional Work'. *Academy of Management Review*, *37*(1), 58–81.

Wall Street Journal podcasts. (2021). 'The Facebook Files, Part 6: The Whistleblower – The Journal'. *WSJ Podcasts* [online]. www.wsj.com/podcasts/the-journal/the-facebook-files-part-6-the-whistleblower/b311b3d8-b50a-425f-9eb7-12a9c4278acd.

Warren, D. (2007). 'Corporate Scandals and Spoiled Identities: How Organizations Shift Stigma to Employees'. *Business Ethics Quarterly*, *17*(3), 477–496. https://doi.org/10.5840/beq200717347.

Waters, R., & Murphy, H. (2021). 'Who is Facebook Whistleblower Frances Haugen?' *Financial Times* [online]. 8 October. www.ft.com/content/63d6d60c-d1c8-4098-bdba-115a3ad43b79.

Weatherall, R. (2020). 'Even When Those Struggles Are Not Our Own: Storytelling and Solidarity in a Feminist Social Justice Organization'. *Gender Work and Organization*, *27*, 471–486.

Weick, K. E. (1993). 'Organizational Redesign as Improvization'. In G. P. Huber & W. H. Glick (Eds.), *Organizational Change and Redesign: Ideas and Insights for Improving Performance* (pp. 346–379). New York, NY: Oxford University Press.

Weise, K. (2021). 'New York Sues Amazon, Saying It Inadequately Protected Workers From Covid-19'. Retrieved 12 December 2022 from *New York Times* website: www.nytimes.com/2021/02/16/technology/amazon-new-york-lawsuit-covid.html.

Weiskopf, R., & Tobias-Miersch, Y. (2016). 'Whistleblowing, Parrhesia and the Contestation of Truth in the Workplace'. *Organization Studies*, *37*(11), 1621–1640.

Weiskopf, R., & Willmott, H. (2013). 'Ethics as Critical Practice: The "Pentagon Papers", Deciding Responsibly, Truth-Telling, and the Unsettling of Organizational Morality'. *Organization Studies, 34*, 469–493.

Weldon, S. L. (2006). 'Inclusion, Solidarity and Social Movements: The Global Movement against Gender Violence'. *Perspectives on Politics, 4*(1), 55–74.

Wickström, A., Lund, R. W. B., Meriläinen, S., et al. (2021). 'Feminist Solidarity: Practices, Politics and Possibilities'. *Gender, Work and Organization, 28*(3), 857–63. https://doi.org/10.1111/gwao.12689.

Wong, J. (2020). 'Amazon Execs Labelled Fired Worker "not smart or articulate" in Leaked PR Notes'. Retrieved 8 December 2022 from The *Guardian* website: www.theguardian.com/technology/2020/apr/02/amazon-chris-smalls-smart-articulate-leaked-memo.

Zanoni, P., & Janssens, M. (2007). 'Minority Employees Engaging with (Diversity) Management: An Analysis of Control, Agency, and Micro-Emancipation'. *Journal of Management Studies, 44*(8), 1371–1397.

Zaveri, M. (2020). 'An Amazon Vice President Quit over Firings of Employees Who Protested'. Retrieved 12 December 2022 from *New York Times* website: www.nytimes.com/2020/05/04/business/amazon-tim-bray-resigns.html.

Zuboff, S. (2019). *The Age of Surveillance Capitalism*. London: Profile Books.

Zuboff, S. (2022). 'Surveillance Capitalism or Democracy? The Death Match of Institutional Orders and the Politics of Knowledge in Our Information Civilization'. *Organization Theory, 3*(3). https://doi.org/10.1177/26317877221129290.

Index

Printed in the United States
by Baker & Taylor Publisher Services